A Day Apart
Shabbat at Home

A Step-by-Step Guidebook with Blessings and Songs, Rituals and Reflections

by Noam Sachs Zion
author of *A Different Night: The Family Participation Haggadah*
and *A Different Light: The Hanukkah Celebration*
and Shawn Fields-Meyer
Designed by Joe Buchwald Gelles

To set apart one day a week for freedom, a day on which we would not use the instruments which have been so easily turned into weapons of destruction, a day for being with ourselves, a day of detachment from the vulgar, of independence of external obligations, a day on which we stop worshipping the idols of technical civilization, a day on which we use no money, a day of armistice in the economic struggle with our fellow men and the forces of nature — is there any institution that holds out a greater hope for human progress than the Sabbath?

— Abraham Joshua Heschel

Call the Shabbat a delight.

— Isaiah 58:13

Shalom Hartman Institute in Jerusalem, Israel — Rosh HaShanah 5766 • 2004

Dedications שָׁמוֹר וְזָכוֹר

. . . וּבַיּוֹם הַשְּׁבִיעִי שָׁבַת וַיִּנָּפַשׁ.

. . . On the seventh day God ceased from work and was refreshed.

— *Exodus 31:17*

A Day Apart
is dedicated in loving memory of our parents
Hannah and William Kriger
Frieda and Julius Herskowitz
by Jake and Linda Kriger

A Day Apart is also dedicated to my family Shabbat companions in Jerusalem — to my wife Marcelle who holds the family together, to our creative children — Yedidya, Eden, Heftziba, Mishael and his kallah Elana, and Tanya, to the most beloved and regular "guest" at our table, Opa Moshe, my father, and finally to the memory of my mother, Oma Rachel, the tireless embroiderer of Hallah covers. Together my family creates a home-made Shabbat with hand-made Hallah, Hallah cover, ceramic Kiddush cup and hand washing cup, with artfully-folded napkins and ingenious name cards, with very spirited singing and sometimes a Dvar Torah.

by Noam Zion

for Tom
כְּתַפּוּחַ בַּעֲצֵי הַיַּעַר כֵּן דּוֹדִי בֵּין הַבָּנִים
(שִׁיר הַשִּׁירִים ב:ג)
by Shawn Fields-Meyer

for Mia, who makes Shabbat a delight for everyone she touches, and whose love made it possible for me to be part of this project
by Joe Buchwald Gelles

The seventh day is a palace in time which we build. It is made of soul, of joy and reticence.

— *Abraham Joshua Heschel*

Reaching Out for Shabbat.
(Los Angeles, 1985) Photo by Bill Aron.

Table of contents: the choreography of Shabbat at Home

Introductions

Enhancing Home-made Judaism: A Manifesto 7
by Noam Zion

Essays by David Wolpe, David Hartman, and Mordechai Gafni

לִקְרַאת שַׁבָּת

Likrat Shabbat — Setting the Shabbat Mood 12

Baking Bread, Eating Cake, Collecting Tzedakah, and Meditating

נֵרוֹת

Nerot — Lighting Shabbat Candles 24

and Tekhinot — Personal Prayers

שָׁלוֹם עֲלֵיכֶם

Shalom Aleichem — Welcoming the Angels of Peace 36

and Enhancing Shalom Bayit, Domestic Tranquility

בִּרְכַּת בָּנִים

Birkat Banim — Blessing our Children and One Another .. 46

אֵשֶׁת חַיִל and/or שִׁיר הַשִּׁירִים

Shir HaShirim — Song of Songs: Renewing our Love 56

Eishet Hayil — Praising a Strong Woman 60

קִדּוּשׁ

Kiddush — Sanctifying the Day of Shabbat over Wine 68

חַלָּה

Hallah 80

נְטִילַת יָדַיִם Netillat Yadayim — Washing our Hands and הַמּוֹצִיא HaMotzi — Sharing our Bread

דְּבַר תּוֹרָה

D'var Torah — Shabbat Table Talk 94

זְמִירוֹת

Zemirot — Soul Singing at the Table 98

בִּרְכַּת הַמָּזוֹן

Birkat HaMazon — Gratitude for Nourishment 114

Blessings before and after Eating

עֹנֶג שַׁבָּת

Oneg Shabbat — A Day of Delights 134

Recommendations for a Day and Night of Pleasures

קִדּוּשׁ רַבָּא

Kiddush Rabbah — the Shabbat Morning Meal 142

and Seudah Shlishit, the Afternoon Third Meal 144

הַבְדָּלָה

Havdalah — Separating the Holy and the Ordinary 148

תּוֹדָה

Todah: In Appreciation — Thanks, Credits, Endnotes 166

Better is one hand full of quiet
than two hands full of toil
and a striving after wind.

— *Ecclesiastes 4:6*

Be content with what you have;
Rejoice in the way things are.
When you realize there is nothing lacking,
The whole world belongs to you.

— *Lao-Tzu*

It is one thing to race
or be driven by
the vicissitudes
that menace life,
and another
thing to stand
still and to
embrace the
presence of an
eternal moment.

— *Abraham Joshua Heschel*

David Sharir, The Sabbath Queen, 1969

Reflections כַּוָּנוֹת

before the Shabbat journey

Be not lax in celebrating.
Be not lazy in the festive service of God.
Be ablaze with enthusiasm . . . .

— Hildegard, the Benedictine abbess

Shabbat is a day known by many names. It is a *Rest Day* and the *Day of Peace*, a taste of the messianic world-to-come. But it is also a *Coronation Day* for our spiritual Queen — in fact it is a day in which we are all royalty and we all don crowns of added spirit. It is simultaneously a wedding day, a day of love for our Bride, Shabbat, and its metaphoric wedding ring is a band that ties us to God and to eternity. The actions we make during the week should be guided by our lives on Shabbat.

— Abram Sterne, clinical psychologist

Shabbat is different from all the other days of the week. It has no routine activities, no work commitments, no interference on the part of the authorities, no evil temptations. For one day a week, man is totally free.

The commandment to sanctify Shabbat was the first call to humanity at large for real equality. And the first summons for freeing man from the bondage of man, for freeing man from himself, from the routine of work. This was the first significant taste of freedom and equality. And this taste has never faded since.

— Shimon Peres, Prime Minister of Israel, Nobel Prize for Peace winner

That world of matter has six dimensions — all measurable, weighable. East, West, South, North, up, down. But Shabbat adds a spiritual seventh dimension — *k'dushah*, sanctity.

— Rabbi Judah Loew, Maharal of Prague

A Jew who feels a real tie with the life of his people throughout the generations will find it utterly impossible to think of the existence of Israel without Shabbat. One can say without exaggeration that more than Israel has kept Shabbat, Shabbat has kept Israel.

— Ahad Ha-Am, Zionist thinker

caricatures by Michel Kichka

One who wants to enter the holiness of the day must first lay down the profanity of clattering commerce, of being yoked to toil. He must go away from the screech of dissonant days, from the nervousness and fury of acquisitiveness and the betrayal in embezzling his own life. He must say farewell to manual work and learn to understand that the world has already been created and will survive without the help of man.

— *Abraham Joshua Heschel, The Sabbath*

Show me a person who is not a slave?!

One is enslaved to passions, a second to profit, a third to status, and everyone to fear.

— *Seneca (Roman philosopher, 1st century)*

Invitation and introduction

Invitation to a Journey

Is this book for you? Within each household there is often one person who takes the initiative to bring people together, to plan birthdays and outings, to enhance the quality time spent together. This person facilitates the transformation of normal hours into "sacred," time (some people might just call it "fun," or "meaningful"). This book is the resource for one who takes such an initiative. It provides a chance to learn, to grow spiritually, and to share, explain and experiment with others around the table. The goal is not to make the household more religious in belief or observant in practice. Rather, ***A Day Apart*** helps people celebrate a special weekly moment — Shabbat, especially Friday night dinner and Saturday night Havdalah, its bookends. This book — for weekly use for every home ritual of Shabbat — offers a flexible order of ritual involving old and new customs from which you select; you are the orchestra conductor of your household. In contemporary western society individuals are opening themselves anew to **journeys of spiritual discovery** involving rituals and structure. But these journeys need not be ascetic or exotic — all or nothing. In the Jewish spiritual journey, we have traveling companions, excitement, expectation and just the right amount of movement. Surrounded by our significant others, we transform our homes weekly for just a few hours. We make this a celebration — complete with fine wine, great cooking, sweet melodies and stimulating conversation. Let this Shabbat journey be a growing experience involving ongoing learning, a playful spirit of experimentation and the angelic touch of sanctity.

"Time to Connect"

The very essence of modern society is that it progressively releases the individual from the vice-like control of strong limits, and the coercion of the bonded group. But instead of being released to freedom, the individual is drawn into . . . **potential isolation**, where we cannot depend on each other, and have little faith in ultimate truth . . . It is total unconnectedness to any social fabric, which is to say, meaninglessness . . . .

To moderns, then, Shabbat is an opportunity for meaning, a moment in time to forge connections and to belong. If Jews will not keep Shabbat on the grounds that they are commanded to do so, . . . perhaps they will do so because keeping Shabbat will provide their otherwise disconnected lives with meaning.

— *Lawrence A. Hoffman*

Enhancing Home-Made Judaism

Judaism is made at home as is the core identity of the individual and the community.

Intuitively we know that the Pesach Seder is usually more central to being Jewish than Rosh Hashanah services. Often lighting candles — or making latkes — leaves a greater mark on personal identity than learning about the great historical events of the Maccabees, the Warsaw Ghetto or the Six Day War. Certainly the Shema's advice to *"teach your children when you sit at home"* has an effectiveness unmatched by Hebrew school classes with trained educators. The Synagogue's most effective rituals are often tied to personal, life-cycle events. If Judaism is to have a renaissance, it will have to be celebrated vibrantly in the home.

However, it is not just the Jewish people and its way of life that requires a renewed concern about enhancing home Judaism. Those weekly and annual rituals have much to contribute to our needs for personal and communal identity in general. In this era of radical individualism, our sense of isolation and deep existential loneliness, threatens our basic well-being. As God declared when first viewing the human being Adam, *"it is not good for the human to be alone" (Genesis 2:18)*. Human life needs — for pragmatic, for emotional and for spiritual reasons — someone to love and by whom to be loved. Relatedness, a covenant with God, with all Creation and with another human being, is what gives life meaning. Interdependence, not the "self-made man," is a vision worth pursuing. God is a matchmaker for "significant others" and for significant purposes to share with family, friends and community.

Many of us have succeeded professionally, allowing us to contribute to the betterment of the world and to earn a respectable name for ourselves. The "six days of labor" are ever-growing as we conquer new realms. However, our leisure time, which in fact has increased in days and hours relative to our ancestors, requires more "work." Paradoxically we need to invest in our day of rest and do "hard labor" to transform our home hours into quality time — sacred, nourishing, and replenishing.

"Holidays" have largely stopped being holy-days celebrating common values and all-important relationships. They have often become mere "vacations" — empty time free for planning diversionary activities. However we need not only "getaway" vacations to leave life behind, to get away from everyone and everybody, but also holy days to renew our connectedness to our inner soul, to loved ones, to our community, its history and its hopes, and to God and the beauties of God's Creation.

Shaping those home celebrations — in particular Shabbat — requires work in preparation just as it requires a structure and routines created by each household. Meaning is not a gift of Divine grace but a reward for an investment of self — of time and energy, of aesthetics, delicious tastes, fragrances and sounds. We literally "make" our own Judaism and the more we "make Shabbat," the more it means to us. Kiddush is an active verb meaning "to dedicate," to make sacred the time of the seventh day. We, with human intentionality and creativity, have the power to evoke Divine blessing on a weekly basis. What we do in celebrating God's creation is the re-creation of the soul, a recreation both playful and serious. That is why we produced our holiday series ***A Different Night**: The Family Participation Haggadah* and then ***A Different Light**: A Hanukkah Candle Lighting Celebration.* Now ***A Day Apart*** invites you to relax for a day of "different delights."

— *Noam Zion*

Breathers

The Torah reports that even God needs "breathers," such moments of "respiration" and "in-spiration," as it says, "On the seventh day God rested and was refreshed" — *Va-yinafash* (*Exodus 31:17*).

"Club Med's marketing department understands the dynamics of *Va-Yinafash*; they know the difference between 'leisure' and 'recreation.' Leisure is just 'time available;' recreation is a process through which one's essence (the original creation) is 're-newed.' The word *Va-Yinafash* is rooted in the Hebrew word *nefesh* which means 'soul.' A Club Med vacation is marketed as an opportunity to restore oneself to one's essence. **Shabbat was created as a tool for perpetual self-renewal.** The next time you wonder about the value of Shabbat, remember the beach in the Club Med ad."

— *Joel Lurie Grishaver*

Eternity Utters A Day

by David Wolpe

> This is the task of men: to conquer space and sanctify time.
>
> — *Abraham Joshua Heschel, The Sabbath*

Friday Night arrives. I know what my task is at this moment: I am to stop affecting the world and live in harmony with it. Even though I am a tangle of yearnings, on this day everything is to be perfect. I am to be satisfied with the many blessings that I have in my life. For once, I am to be at peace with the universe. My friends have no time. Their lives are crowded. They do not see their friends, play with their overscheduled children, put their feet up and stare out the window. They cannot; they must drive somewhere, check their email, return phone calls — in other words, conquer space.

But even if we correspond at the touch of a button with others around the world, technology does not sanctify time. We do. God's greatest gift is to endow human beings with the capacity to perceive — and to create — holiness. Jews have not, through their wanderings, had the leisure or the need to build grand cathedrals. Yet we have celebrated the Sabbath, a cathedral in time. It can be celebrated in a ramshackle hut, in a cave, in a barren field. The sanctity of time requires not technology but devotion of soul.

So on Friday night I stop. Before the candles and the wine we sing, and my wife and I bless our beautiful little girl. She is not yet four years old. She has not yet heard of Heschel, but she understands him. It takes only three things, wrote this sage, to create a sense of significant being: God, a soul and a moment. And the three, he said, are always present.

Spiritual Timing: Learning the Shabbat Rhythm

BY DAVID HARTMAN

What is the meaning of that simple yet elusive Biblical refrain, *"In six days God made the heaven and the earth and God rested on the seventh day"*? Biblical scholars commonly observe that the Creation story of Genesis fixes the week as the basic unit of time. A day is a natural unit of time determined by the revolution of the earth on its axis, but **a week is an artificial construction**. Why do we measure time in weeks? Because *"God worked six days and rested on the seventh."* *(GENESIS 2:1).*

The metaphor of God creating and resting indicates something important about the relationship between work and freedom. Shabbat symbolizes God's freedom and independence from the universe. A free and spontaneous Creator, God can stand back from the products of Divine creativity without being enslaved by them. Six days of creation, of bringing something new into existence, of shaping reality, therefore, are followed by a day of cessation from creative effort, a day of rest.

The central rhythm of Jewish living mirrors the Divine rhythm of the first chapter of Genesis, the rhythm of kodesh and chol (sacred and profane), of menucha and melacha (rest and work), of six days of doing and one day of Shabbat. The Jewish week begins with a burst of creative energy released by a dream of great achievement. For six days Jews work with the sense of time scarcity: "The day is short, the work is great, the workers are lazy, the reward is great, and the landlord is knocking on the door." *(PIRKEI AVOT 2:15)*

"Rabbi Eliezer taught: Great is work. For just as Israel was commanded to observe Shabbat so was she commanded to work. As it is written, *'Six days shall you labor and do all your work.'"* *(EXODUS 20, QUOTED IN* AVOT D'RABBI NATAN [B] *CHAPTER 21)*

And then, their work still uncompleted, suddenly and decisively they cease from their labors, and enter a seventh day of rest. How can one find spiritual peace while one feels the weight of unfinished work hanging over? How can one break one's obsession with building a career, overcome the psychological pressures entailed by the struggle for success and status in the world?

What then is the experience of menucha on Shabbat? One can get a hint of this experience by considering the central features of the Sabbath day. Shabbat is a time for family meals and studying Torah; it is a house lit up with candles at night, a meal adorned with wine and two loaves of Hallah, and singing Shabbat songs around the table.

Abraham Joshua Heschel, one of the important Jewish philosophers of our generation, expressed his understanding of Shabbat *menucha* as follows:

"Labor is a craft, but perfect rest is an art. It is the result of an accord of body, mind and imagination. To attain a degree of excellence in art, one must accept its discipline, one must adjure slothfulness. The seventh day is a palace in time which we build. It is made of soul, of joy and reticence." *(ABRAHAM JOSHUA HESCHEL,* THE SABBATH*)*

And on the seventh day, one does not relate to the world or to other people in terms of power and exploitation:

"Six days a week we wrestle with the world, wringing profit from the earth; on the Sabbath we especially care for the seed of eternity planted in the soul. The world has our hands, but our soul belongs to Someone Else. Six days a week we seek to dominate the world; on the seventh day we try to dominate the self." *(ABRAHAM JOSHUA HESCHEL,* THE SABBATH*)*

By helping people to subdue their need to relate to the world in utilitarian terms, the *menucha* experience opens them to the possibility of love. In the context of menucha they can perceive the other not as an object of their control but as an equal. On Shabbat, power relationships cease. There are no masters, no slaves — only creatures standing as equals before the Creator.

A person who can live life within rhythms of *melacha-menucha*, can work but also rest, a person who can struggle for mastery but live without total mastery — such a person can open up to a love relationship with another. Only after one has accepted the limitations of being a creature can one enter into an enduring relationship of mutuality with another person, in short, a covenant.

Time is like a wasteland. It has grandeur but no beauty. Its strange, frightful power is always feared but rarely cheered.

Then we arrive at the seventh day, and Shabbat is endowed with a felicity which enraptures the soul, which glides into our thoughts with a healing sympathy. It is a day on which hours do not oust one another. It is a day that can soothe all sadness away.

— Abraham Joshua Heschel

Do your work, then step back, that is the only path to serenity. One who clings to his work will create nothing that endures. Just do your job, then let go.

— Tao Te Ching

The Mystical Shabbat: Living Face to Face

May God's face smile upon you.

— Numbers 6:26

What lies behind us and what lies before us are tiny matters compared to what lies within us.

— Ralph Waldo Emerson

The Spell of Spelling — *Panim* and Sacred Puns

by Mordechai Gafni

Shabbat is often termed by the Kabbalists as *Panim*, "the Face."

Traditionally, the Jewish wedding ceremony is followed by a glorious week of celebration with seven festive meals. At each meal the wedding is re-enacted by the repetition of the seven blessings *(Sheva Brachot)* which were recited at the wedding. However the blessings may only be re-cited if there is at least one new face present. Those new guests are called *Panim Chadashot* (New Faces). Yet there is one day when a new face is not required to recite the blessing. That day is Shabbat, for Shabbat herself is considered the new face which is the source of all re-newal. In the presence of Shabbat we move from the surface to the infinite depth of the inner face.

In the Hebrew mystical tradition, language is not the mere random designation of sounds and letters in a particular pattern. For the mystic, words are vital portals to meaning. Language is the spiritual DNA of reality. Thus when one root word is used for seemingly disparate ideas you can rest assured that these different ideas are in fact integrally related. So let's watch for a moment as the magic of language dances before us. Let us follow the multi-face-ted word *Panim* = Face.

The Hebrew term for the Holy of Holies is *L'P'nei u L'Panim,* literally meaning "the inside of the inside." That however is but the en-trance to the magic of the words. Hold on, for the mystical magic of language, the spell of spelling — has just begun. The Hebrew word for "inside," *P'nim,* has two other meanings as well. The first, not surprisingly, is face. Face is the place where my insides are revealed.

There are 45 muscles in the face, most of them unnecessary for the biological functioning of the face Their major purpose, it would seem, is to express emotional depth and nuance. They are the muscles of the soul. Every muscle of the face reflects another nuance of depth and interiority. When I say, "I need to speak face to face," I am in need of an inside conversation. At this point all of the cell phones and sophisticated internet hook-ups won't give me what I need, for while amazingly efficient and effective, they are not adequate to the face-to-face dimension of true love conversations.

The ultimate face-to-face encounter is with the Shekhina, the feminine Divine Presence. The Shekhina abided in the Temple, God's home, in the empty space between the two cherubs statues which crowned the Holy of Holies. The cherubs in the magical mystery of Temple myth were not stationary fixtures. No, these statues were expressive, emotive. They moved. When integrity and goodness ruled the land the cherubs were face-to-face. In these times the focal point of *Shekhina* energy rested erotically, ecstatically, between the embracing cherubs. When discord and evil held sway in the kingdom, the cherubs turned from each other, appearing back to back instead of face to face. Back to back, the world was amiss, alienated, ruptured. Face-to-face, the world was harmonized, hopeful, embraced. Thus, face-to-face in biblical text is the most highly desirable state.

Face-to-face means first and foremost, being on the inside. This inner state is aroused whenever we move so deeply into what we do, who we are with, or where we are, that its interiority stirs our heart and imagination. For the Temple mystics, exile is when one's inside and outside are not connected in the day to day of living. This exile is analogous to the six days of the week. In contrast, Shabbat models interior living. Redeemed consciousness is the sweetness tasted when the distinction between Shabbat and the six days collapse into the greater oneness mentioned in the Shabbat prayer: "May we inherit the day(s) which is (are) all Shabbat." When I am not living from the inside, I am not living naturally. I am not in the flow of my own life. Love is to be in the flow of the fountain, what the Zohar calls in one of its evocative mantras, "The River of Light that flows from Eden."

The Temple and Shabbat share the core idea of the *Bayit*, Home. The Temple in Hebrew is called *Beit HaMikdash*, the Holy Home, the Home of the *Shekhina*. On Shabbat, our homes are made sacred when we welcome the *Shekhina*, the Shabbat Queen, and we welcome our own soul back home. Every person can access the Shekhina experience. Every human being needs to move beyond the imposter into his or her own deepest place of oneness; oneness with oneself, one's relationships, and one's reality. The Zohar refers to the exile from one's deepest self as *alma depiruda*, the world of separation. The most tragic separation is not from mother, not from community, but from self. The journey of a lifetime is to move from *alma depiruda* to *alma deyichuda*, from separation to oneness — At-one-ment. Love is the path back home. We are not talking about superficial love, not merely sexual love, but *Shekhina* love.

Leviticus tells of the Temple's high priest who only on the biblical Yom Kippur, the Day of At-one-ment, enters the Holy of Holies *L'Pnai Hashem*, "before God's face." Every person has a Holy of Holies which, in those most intimate of times, we let another enter as the priest to worship at our altar. And in the gorgeous paradox of the spirit, by letting a lover enter, we ourselves are let in as well. For when the Temple door is open and the lover enters, we ourselves trail behind. We gain uncommon access to our inner selves, a place which we alone are often unable to reach. The true lover always takes you home. Love lets us realize the Eden we are dwelling in every day. That is what it means to feel at home in your life, the greatest feeling in the world. It is in this sense that the Kabbalists consistently refer to Shabbat as the Garden of Eden.

The Sanctity of a Moment

It takes three things to attain a sense of significance:
God
A Soul
And a Moment.
These three things are always here.
Just to be is a blessing.
Just to live is holy.

—Abraham Joshua Heschel

Now let's add one last linguistic twist: the Holy of Holies, the innermost depth of the Temple, is the place where the cherubs embrace lovingly face to face. The Hebrew word for Temple is *Beit HaMikdash* — literally translated as Home of Holiness. Shabbat as well is termed *Shabbat Kodesh*, the Holy Day. In our homes, on Shabbat, when we face God, ourselves and our loved ones face-to-face, then we make our time and our space sacred. We have here a definition of holiness. To be holy is to be on the inside. The opposite of the holy is the superficial. Eros is about depth. Depth is an inside experience. It has its own unique nuance, texture and richness. The superficial is bland and common. **The invitation to Shabbat is thus an invitation to depth, to the interior castle, to come home and to greet the shining face of the *Shekhina* in all of those around us.**

As we keep or break
the Sabbath day,
we nobly save
or meanly lose
the last and best
hope by which
man arises.

— President Abraham Lincoln, November 13, 1862

All life should be a
pilgrimage to the
seventh day.

— Rabbi Abraham Joshua Heschel

Checking One's Time Piece
by Moritz Daniel Oppenheim
(Germany, c. 1866)

Setting the Shabbat mood

לִקְרַאת שַׁבָּת

baking bread, eating cake, collecting tzedakah, meditating

Clearing Off Our Desk Before the Shabbat Vacation

Before leaving on a vacation people usually are consumed with myriad minor tasks, all the little accumulated chores that now clutter the desktop.

. . . Each uncompleted task has its own claim on our freedom. And finishing them liberates us to begin our vacation. Indeed, finishing the last one may actually commence the vacation whether or not we ever leave home.

. . . Now obviously no one can ever complete all the little tasks. Sooner or later, as the vacation departure clock ticks down, we decree arbitrarily that whether or not they are done, we are done . . . We renounce their claims on us. To do so requires great spiritual self-control.

Well, it is like that with the Day of Being too. Every seventh day we clear off our desks. Of course we are not finished. And from the looks of our world, hopefully God isn't finished either.

— Lawrence Kushner,
The Book of Words: Talking Spiritual Life, Living Spiritual Talk, *Jewish Lights*

Pleasurable Preparations

Celebrating Shabbat begins not with sundown but with the hours — and even days — preceding it, transformed into the pleasures of preparing for a beloved and honored guest and friend. Here is a brief checklist for honoring this royal guest and getting your home, yourself and your household members into the right mood. Do some, not necessarily all — and certainly, do them in the proper spirit:

- ☐ **mark your calendar** and plan for Shabbat
- ☐ bake or buy a **special treat** — and at least two Hallahs and a good wine
- ☐ **straighten up** — put aside mentally and clear away physically the workday items *(muktzeh)* from the table and out of the dining room
- ☐ **take a hot bath** or shower
- ☐ put out and wear **special clothing**
- ☐ **set the table** with your most beautiful service items
- ☐ **arrange lighting and fragrance** — flowers, perfume or incense, and Shabbat candles
- ☐ **enjoy music** — sung or played
- ☐ **relax**, take a deep breath, meditate — take in the sanctity of the moment
- ☐ contact those far away whom you love and **hug, kiss and bless** those close to you in your household
- ☐ feed your children or your whole family a **pre-Shabbat snack** so that they will not be ravenous and impatient during the Friday night ceremonies before dinner.

The Children of Israel's first experience with Shabbat began on *Erev Shabbat* — the "eve" of Shabbat which means not Friday evening but Friday morning. Recall that Jewish days begin in the evening so the "eve of Shabbat" is the morning and afternoon before sunset of the incoming Shabbat. The first commandment was not to refrain from work but to do double work — to collect a double portion of manna from Heaven which fell in double the usual amount on the day before Shabbat. The two Hallahs on the Shabbat table signify the double portion of Divine generosity as well as the extra work put in every Friday to enable us to eat well (while still refraining from further gathering and baking of bread on Shabbat). Even in the desert era of miraculous manna, Shabbat meals required human effort and pre-planning. The Rabbis applied the motto — "Whoever does not prepare on the eve of Shabbat will not eat on Shabbat" *(Ecclesiates Rabbah 1:36)* — as general advice for all aspects of life.

Home-made Judaism

In getting ready for Shabbat, the physical activities prepare our soul for the temporal passage from the weekday into sacred time. It may be compared to the spatial pilgrimage, the climbing of a holy mountain, in which getting to the top involves a spiritual transition: the more effort, the harder the climb, the higher the level of sanctity is reached. The Rabbis' motto was *lfum tzara agra*, "the reward is equal to the effort expended." Or, in mundane terms, the harder one works at an achievement, the more it means. This is the key principle of "home-made Judaism": human meaning is derived not necessarily from an external aura, a Divine emanation, but rather from our sanctification of time and space. The investment of the self in something makes it sacred, and it invites God to dwell, also, within that space and time. That is why Maimonides requires everyone to participate in the physical preparations for Shabbat even when there is nothing to prepare:

"Even if one is a person of high rank and does not as a rule attend to the shopping or other household chores, one should nevertheless perform one of these tasks in preparation *(Kibbud)* — for Shabbat, for that is the way to honor it. There were great Talmudic scholars who used to split firewood for cooking, cook or salt meat, plait wicks, light lamps or go to the market to buy food and drink for Shabbat. In fact, none of them customarily performed such tasks on weekdays. However the more one does in the way of preparation for Shabbat, the more commendable." *(MAIMONIDES, MISHNE TORAH, SHABBAT LAWS 30:5)*

The farther in advance we prepare, the more the whole week is unified into a project aimed toward its culmination in Shabbat.

In a sense we can look upon the whole of Creation by God as six days of preparation for Shabbat. God's six days of labor are analogous to "someone who sets about to build a palace. First that person beautifies it and then lays it out, hangs its walls with embroideries and afterwards sweeps the house and adorns it with tapestries and woodcarvings." *(GENESIS RABBAH ON GENESIS 1)*

Polishing Silver Candle Sticks for Shabbat. By Faige Beer, 1980. (Beit Hatefutsot Archive)

'This is for Shabbat'

On every day of his life Shammai ate in honor of Shabbat. How? When he chanced upon a nice piece of meat [in the market, he would purchase it and] declare, "This is for Shabbat." If, on the following day, he found an even more desirable piece of meat, he would set the second piece side [for Shabbat] and eat the first [during the week] . . . From the first day of the week direct your efforts towards Shabbat. *(TALMUD BEITZA 16A)*

"An Extra Effort"

Wendy Mogel, consultant on raising children, comments that we need to put extra effort into the Shabbat meal beyond what is minimally necessary. "Even a trifle prepared in honor of Shabbat is called Oneg Shabbat, a Shabbat delight." *(TALMUD SHABBAT 118A)*

"Jewish mysticism teaches us that food starts out full of holy sparks and that we have the opportunity to transform it and elevate it further. How? By applying our humanness to it — by preparing it with care and arranging it attractively.

"When you work hard at something it means more to you. Convenience foods, although useful and practical, may undermine your family's efforts to make your table an altar. Children learn best from hands-on activities that involve many senses, so cooking and setting the table are excellent ways to transmit values. Since we have to eat anyway, cooking together, even infrequently, covers two bases: quality time and getting a necessary job done.

"Judaism commands us to perform ***hiddur miztvot***, to beautify the commandments, to go the extra mile. By preparing special foods and setting the table with special care for Shabbat dinner, the mystics say that we get a taste of the world to come.

"At our house, everybody gets involved in the Shabbat dinner preparations. My husband does the cooking. I cut the flowers from the garden and the children arrange them and set the table with the ritual objects: kiddush cup, candles, and Hallah. We don't have exciting deserts during the week but for Shabbat dinner I take down an etched glass cake stand with a pedestal and put on a paper doily. It's my younger daughter's job to arrange the bakery cookies or rugalach or fruit tart on the stand. Shabbat dinner is a big production that I would never consider doing on a daily basis. But it caps our week, slows us down, and draws us together in a powerful way." *(Wendy Mogel, The Blessing of a Skinned Knee)*

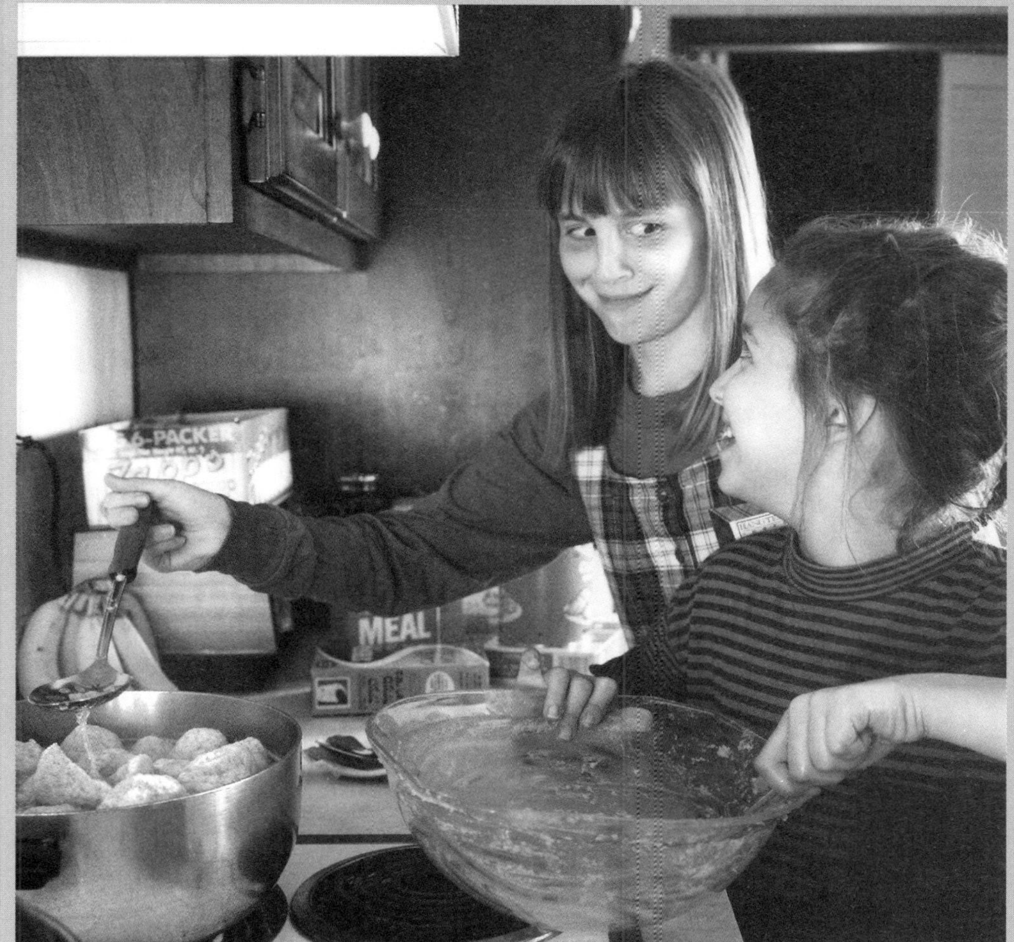

The Next Generation's Matza Ball Soup (Dorfman kitchen, Long Beach, Mississippi). Photo by Bill Aron.

The Spiritual Hot Tub

Preparing one's home and one's table to greet the Divine presence is inadequate without preparing one's own body and mind.

"Every eve of Shabbat, Rabbi Judah ben Ilai asked that a tub filled with warm water be brought to him. In it he would wash his face, his hands and his feet. Then as he sat wrapped in his linen robes with the *tzizit* fringes, he seemed like an angel of God's heavenly armies." *(Talmud Nedarim 49b)*

"The Kabbalists — Jewish mystics — viewed the hot bath as a mikveh for spiritual purification and rebirth.

"In order to receive the holiness [of Shabbat] that flows into our world, we must prepare and perfect the body, for the body is the throne for the spiritual . . . Like the house, the body must be restored." *(Moshe Cordovero, Tefilla le-Moshe 10:2)*

After the body is refreshed, it is time for a weekly meditative moment using the the special mood, melodies and lyrics of Kabbalat Shabbat. At home, that can be achieved with the proper music (perhaps played or hummed or sung) and various *kavanot* — inspirational words that focus our attention. This moment is the turning point of Shabbat as we move sharply from the activity of "making *Shabbes*" to the receptivity of welcoming the sacred *Shekhina*.

Holiness in the kitchen — spirituality and hallah baking

Taking Hallah

After kneading, recite this blessing and remove some dough to be baked separately.

BLESSED ARE YOU, Adonai	בָּרוּךְ אַתָּה יְיָ	Ba-rukh ata Adonai,
our God, Ruler of the Universe,	אֱלֹהֵינוּ מֶלֶךְ הָעוֹלָם,	Elo-hei-nu me-lekh ha-olam,
who has sanctified us with mitzvot	אֲשֶׁר קִדְּשָׁנוּ בְּמִצְוֹתָיו	asher ki-d'shanu b'mitz-votav
and commanded us to separate out	וְצִוָּנוּ, לְהַפְרִישׁ	v'tzi-vanu, l'haf-rish
a portion of dough [in your honor].	חַלָּה מִן הָעִסָּה.	Hallah min ha-isa.

And then the baker sets aside that dough and declares:

THIS IS THE HALLAH!	הֲרֵי זוּ חַלָּה!	Harei zu Hallah!

Tekhina/Meditation

Lord of all the worlds, all blessing is in your hands. I come now to honor your holiness, and pray you to give your blessing on what I bake. Send an angel to guard the baking, so that everything will be well baked, will rise nicely, and will not burn. May this baking, over which we make the holy blessing, honor your holy Shabbat, which you have chosen that your people Israel may rest thereon. God, listen to my voice, for you are the one who hears those who call upon you with the whole heart. May you be praised to eternity.

— Seyder Tkhines, 1650, 1752

God

Recipe to You
Two Parts Challenge, One Part Awe
Slowly Rising Dough.

— Jeni Friedman

In Praise of Not So Simple Hallah

Listen to this beautiful meditation on human interdependence and the human chain of food production:

"When Ben Zoma would survey with his eyes a massive crowd gathered on the Temple Mount, he would bless them: *Baruch Hakham Razim*/Blessed is the Possessor of the Wisdom of the Secrets (referring to the fact that none of the people there had identical minds, faces or talents). Thank God that you created all of them to serve my needs. Think how many exertions Adam had to invest before he could produce bread to eat. He had to plow, plant, harvest, sheave, trample, winnow, sort, grind, sift, knead, bake and only then finally eat. But I, by contrast, wake up early and find everything already prepared and set forth for me . . . In fact, all the nations of the world energetically come to my door to provide me these goods and I just wake up and find them all before me."

— Talmud Berachot 58a

The Original Baker's Gift of Hallah

Some scholars suggest that the word "Hallah" derives from the ancient Babylonian (Akkadian) for "pure." Technically, the word Hallah does not refer to the "egg twist bread" that was typical among Eastern European Jewry, but rather to a sacred gift to God (*Numbers 15:18-20*): *"When you enter the land to which I am taking you and you eat of the bread of the land, you shall set aside the first yield of your baking as a gift [terumah] to God."* This is one of 24 gifts that the Cohen received for his labors as our representative to God in the Temple.

"Hallah" is the portion of every bread baked by a Jew that was once given to the Temple and today is removed from the dough and burned. Although originally the Hallah offering was made only in the land of Israel in special appreciation of the fertility of the land that God granted to us, the Rabbis extended its obligation to include everywhere in the world. When baking bread (made from wheat, barley, spelt, rye or oat flour) the dough is subject to the laws of Hallah (*Mishnah Hallah 1: 1*) for any volume over 2½ lbs. or 1250 grams). One takes a symbolic amount (generally an ounce or about 25 grams) while saying the blessing and declaring this piece of dough to be dedicated: "This is the Hallah!" The dough that is set aside is baked but not eaten. Some people place it on a windowsill for the birds.

Because on Shabbat one is particularly careful to remove the "Hallah," the offering, the loaves themselves also came to be known as Hallah, literally, bread from which an offering has been removed.

On Shabbat, the two *Hallahs* are eaten whole and unsliced, recalling the Divine abundance, reflected in the gift of the double portion of manna from heaven that the people of Israel received while in the desert (*Exodus 16:22*).

Since it was usually the woman who baked in the home, the laws of Hallah have fallen particularly upon her and women have written and recited beautiful *tekhinot*, personal prayers to accompany their breadbaking for the household.

Benta and Marcelle's Jerusalem Hallah Recipe

Take a wide bowl:

⅔ cup (150 ml) vegetable oil

1 cup regular sugar (or less, according to your family's taste)

3 teaspoons salt

2 cups (500 ml) warm water

Then stir once and add 3 tablespoons (50 grams) dry yeast, stirring briefly.

Let this mixture settle for about 5-8 minutes until the yeast starts to bubble.

Add 2 lb. (1 kilo) flour (You may substitute whole wheat, but use less than 2 lb.) You can add seeds or raisins to the dough.

Mix well using a wooden spoon or by hand. While kneading, add more flour until the mixture becomes smooth and elastic.

Place the mixture in a large bowl, cover it with towel. In my home I place the bowl on top of a hot water bottle under a blanket, so it stays warm and the yeast can do its job. Other bakers place the mixture near a source of heat (low oven, outside in the sun). After about an hour the mixture should have doubled in size and you can proceed.

Baking Hallah in Hot Springs, Arkansas. Detail from photo by Bill Aron.

At this point you take off a small portion from the dough, say the *bracha*/blessing over the separation of Hallah (*see page 16*).

Prepare baking pans with baking paper. Pour some flour on a smooth surface and braid the Hallah. This amount of dough yields 4 big Hallahs or 6 medium size or about 16 small rolls. Before putting the Hallah into the oven, beat an egg into a small bowl and baste the Hallah. Then you may add sesame seeds on top.

Preheat oven to 350°F (180°C), bake for 15-18 minutes for regular size Hallah, less for rolls.

For special events (*b'nai mitzvah*, birthdays, weddings) my family shapes the dough to form letters of a name or numbers of a birthday.

Make sure to take a photograph of your letter-Hallah decoration!

Recipe for Liberation

First make the vision and allow it to simmer until all the right relationships are made. Gently combine outspokenness and righteousness with care and joy. Stirring constantly, add decisive leadership. Knead love and closeness until smooth. Roll out support on a foundation of trust. Cut the drama and bring the rough edges together in a well-organized plan with a heaping tablespoon of boldness. A pinch of chutzpah will ensure a tight seal, but leave a small gap of flexibility in the center to allow steam to escape. Brush with a topping of humanity and bake until firm.

— Beth Grossman, American artist

Last minute: preparations, pressures

In the hours — and then the last minutes — before the candles are lit and Shabbat begins, the Jewish home sees a flurry of activity. The transition when coming home from work and school, preparing details for a sit-down meal, urging everyone to be ready on time, anticipating the arrival of guests — all this may create stress. The last-minute bustle of activity is essential to help make Shabbat more beautiful, but this time period may also be laced with emotional dangers: family conflict, dueling priorities, and parents nudging children. Yet by the time the candles are lit, an atmosphere of tranquil sanctity can illuminate the home. The following traditional customs and reminders may help create that atmosphere.

A Mystical Warning: Beware! A Time of Marital Conflict

As Shabbat draws closer and closer, household preparations sometimes put pressure on spouses and children trying to work effectively under time constraints. Kabbalistic masters understood these pressures and referred to the pre-Shabbat hour as the "**time of temptation by the Other Side**." The danger, is that Satan — by inciting quarrels during that hour — will undermine peace in the home and defile Shabbat's holiness.

Alphonse Levy (France, 19th century)

"The afternoon before Shabbat is a time of danger that generates marital conflicts. The diabolical "Other Side"/*Sitra Akhra* — Satan — exerts himself to incite fights. So a cautious person will control the inclination to get angry and to start a fight. Instead one should pursue peace. Of course people who argue with their spouse and children certainly think themselves to be in the right. But the truth is, for anyone with a brain in his head, that whatever went wrong [for which they are blaming their spouse] is really no one's fault. It is a provocation created by Satan to promote strife. So anyone who is intelligent . . . will not argue with or berate the other members of the household for things that have gone wrong." *(Ben Ish Chai, Iraq, 19th century)*

PreShabbat Coffee and Cake: The Bo'i Kallah/ "Come, My Bride" Reception

Some families taste all their Shabbat cooking on late Friday afternoon to make sure it is all ready. That creates a flavorful anticipation. In Morocco and Tunisia it was customary for Jews to set a table of sweets and to drink coffee or alcoholic beverages in order to relax after all the Shabbat preparations had been made. That pre-Shabbat "coffee break" was called the meal of *Bo'i Kallah* — the "Come, my Bride" reception. If we reinstitute this custom, then it may calm the nerves as well as whet the palates of children and adults alike. It also makes it easier to sing and to do all the blessings on Friday night prior to dinner, when one has already eaten something earlier.

Tzedakah צְדָקָה

1. Before lighting the Shabbat candles, **COLLECT ALL YOUR LOOSE CHANGE** (with the help of your children) and put it in a Tzedakah box which has a special place near the Shabbat candelabrum.
2. You may wish to recite this **MEDITATION**: Here I am ready to give some Tzedakah to fulfill the mitzvah of "Love your neighbor as you love yourself, I am God." (LEVITICUS 19:18)

וְאָהַבְתָּ לְרֵעֲךָ כָּמוֹךָ, אֲנִי יהוה.

Even the poor who are supported by Tzedakah must give from what they receive.

— RABBI YOSEF KARO, SHULCHAN ARUCH, *YOREH DEAH* 248:1

Hillel used to say:
If I am not for myself, who is for me?
If I care only for myself, what am I?
If not now, when?

— PIRKEI AVOT 1:14

The main point of God's instructing us to give Tzedakah is so that brothers will help one another and so that all of us know that we are children of the same human being, born of one spark, one limb with a connection to the heavens above. So if one is suffering and depressed in pain of poverty, others must support him/her with Tzedakah. So too God must support us for we are part of the heavenly God.

— RABBI BINYAMIN BEN MATTAYA, THE KABBALIST

Teaching Our Children

Weekly Shabbat giving at candle lighting works most effectively when the teaching and practice of giving money or possessions away to those who need them is consistent. As an influential sixteenth-century work of Jewish ethics teaches, "A person who gives a thousand gold pieces to a worthy person is not as generous as one who gives a thousand gold pieces on a thousand different occasions, each to a worthy cause." *(ORCHOT TZADDIKIM)*

One technique, used by some parents to train their children to give, is to keep a Tzedakah (charity) box — known in Yiddish as a *pushke* — in the house, and insert coins in it just before lighting the Shabbat candles. Since Jewish tradition prohibits the use of money on the Sabbath, it is a powerful lesson to children that one's last use of funds before the holy day is for charity. *(JOSEPH TELUSHKIN)*

J.N.F Blue and White Box: Pulling Ourselves Up by Our Bootstraps

As you or your parents may remember, the blue and white box for contributions to the Jewish National Fund, *Keren Kayemet L'Yisrael*, were in every Hebrew school and on many mantles next to the Shabbat candles. Herzl envisioned a national effort to redeem the Jewish people that would not rely on the rich philanthropists but on simple Jews of very modest means contributing a coin at a time to creating the capital for reclaiming our homeland. While people refer to those contributions as Tzedakah or as charitable gifts, they are in fact something very different in intent. They were meant not to relieve the immediate needs of the poor but to help a poor nation, small, persecuted, and exiled, to regain its own dignity and redeem its endangered life and establish its political and economic independence.

On the earliest boxes which displayed a map

of Israel they also had the verse: "You shall redeem the land" which the early Zionists took as a mitzvah to pull themselves up by the bootstraps by investing in our own empowerment, rather than complaining about being victimized and demanding that others give us our rights. That "fund" was used for buying land from absentee landlords and giving it to workers, reclaiming malaria-infested swamps, and resettling refugees. Now the JNF works on reforesting the ecologically ravaged "land of milk and honey," and managing our limited water resources.

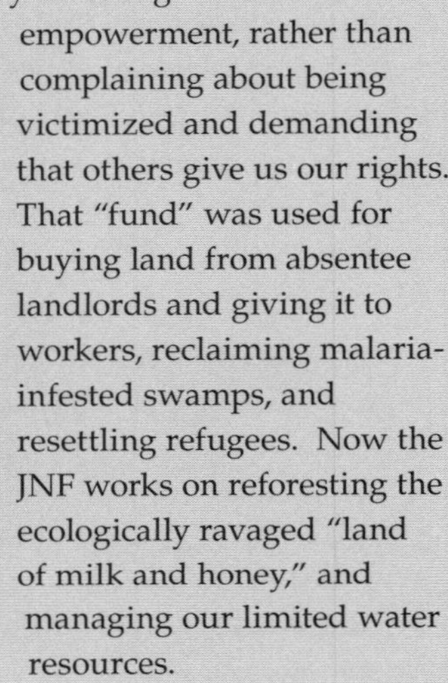

Clearly this is not an act of Christian charity but the highest form of Tzedakah, for it transforms dependence into independence by giving a people employment and the dignity accompanying it. Israel — the people and the land — still needs those investments in our own "venture capital" fund, for it grants us the opportunity to survive, to flourish, and to continue the Jewish collective adventure.

Do You Have Sick Relative? A Friend in Need of a Good Word?

Just before Shabbat do a mental check — any sick or sad relatives or friends? Perhaps give them a call and wish them a tranquil Shabbat. Do you still have time to drop off cake or Shabbat candles at their home?

Reflections on Tzedakah

"Magic Money" — The First Rule of Tzedakah

Money — miraculous, wondrous, awesome. I know $100 that bought a deaf woman a weekend at a convention of fellow Jews that brought her warmth, friends and the end of loneliness. I know $3 that bought a tree that comforted parents on the death of a child and another $3 that bought another tree that elated other parents on the birth of a child.

The first rule of Tzedakah work is never to lose our sense of wonder and of awe . . . then money becomes magic. It goes through metamorphosis, becoming now food packages for Passover, a hat that brings dignity to one who needs just that — a new hat. It buys gasoline to transport the old when they have become too old to drive. It buys sewing machines for retraining mental patients. It buys spoons for those who must be spoon-fed . . . and pays salaries for spoon-feeders to do the work.

By a regular and recurring awareness of the power and possibilities of Tzedakah, each Jew can become more aggressive and creative in his or her own giving.

— Daniel Siegel

You Are God's Hands

The Leover Hassidic Rebbe taught:

"If people come to you for assistance and you tell them, 'God will surely help you,' then you are acting disloyally to God. For you should understand that God has sent you to help the needy, not to refer the poor back to God."

The True Believer

Belief in Judaism is related to self-transcendence. It involves not only dogma and doctrine but also the psychological ability to acknowledge and respond to that which is other than oneself. A person who is imprisoned within his private needs and interests may be characterized as a non-believer insofar as his life lacks the dimension of self-transcendence. A person may utter the words "I believe," yet if he is unresponsive to others and generally unmoved by the world beyond his private domain, he fails to demonstrate belief in a transcendent God.

— David Hartman and Tzvi Marx

The Mystical and the Practical Love of One's Neighbor

The Kabbalist master, HaAri of Safed, used to begin each day of prayer "by accepting upon himself the mitzvah: 'love your neighbor as yourself'" *(Leviticus 19: 18).* In reciting a prayer of request, if your friend is in trouble, then everyone must partake in the friend's pain and add his/her prayers to your own."

Some rabbis extend this love and the prohibition to saying anything negative about a fellow human and even about an animal. HaAri recommended that each day end by proclaiming forgiveness to anyone who has insulted him that day.

Tales of giving

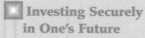

A Story: Fundraising as Consciousness Raising

During the freezing Lithuanian winters, Rabbi Yisrael Salanter, head of the Mussar Movement for increasing ethical senstivity in the Orthodox world, needed to collect contributons to buy fuel for the yeshivah where his students studied in the numbing cold.

Early one morning dressed in a warm fur coat, Reb Yisrael went to the home of a wealthy, but not very philanthropic man. The wealthy man, still dressed in his nightgown, opened the door and invited the rabbi in. But Reb Yisrael remained in the doorway and began a long presentation seemingly unaware that his host was shivering with cold. The host's teeth were chattering and before long his lips turned blue, but the rabbi continued.

Thinking he was about to faint, the host finally interrupted the rabbi and persuaded him, with difficulty, to come in. As they warmed themselves by the fire, Reb Yisrael explained, "I am sure you are wondering about my strange conduct. Why didn't I accept your first invitation to come in from the cold? Well, my students are freezing and we need money for fuel. If I had asked you to help while you were warm and comfortable, you would not have begun to understand what it means to study in an unheated room in subzero weather. Now that you feel what they feel, I am sure that you will help me." Indeed, the wealthy man provided the fuel for the house of study as long as he lived.

Investing Securely in One's Future

During years of scarcity King Monobaz spent all of his own treasures and the treasures of his ancestors on Tzedakah. His brothers and the other members of his family joined together in reproaching him: "Your ancestors stored away treasures adding to the treasures of their ancestors, and you squander them!" He replied, "My ancestors stored away in a place where the hand of others can prevail, while I have stored away in a place where the hand of others cannot prevail. My ancestors stored away something that produces no fruit, while I have stored away something that does produce fruit. My ancestors stored away treasures of money, while I have stored away treasures of souls. My ancestors stored away for others, while I have stored away for myself. My ancestors stored away for this world, while I have stored away for the world-to-come." *(Talmud Baba Batra 11b)*

Look Through the Glass

Once a Hassidic rebbe went to collect Tzedakah to the house of an infamously wealthy but selfish and lonely person. "Will you give something for the poor?" asked the rebbe. "For the poor? Why doesn't anyone ever think of me? All anyone wants is my money! But I worked hard for it and I am keeping it for myself."

The rebbe said: "Go to the glass window and tell me what you see." The rich person desribed the people in the street. Then the rebbe picked up a looking glass and held it up to his face. "Now what do you see?" The man answered: "Why, I see only myself."

The rebbe replied: "That is your lesson for today. Look at the silver [which is used to seal the back of a mirror] and you see only yourself. Take away the silver and you can see through the glass to the rest of the community. Perhaps then they will see you and care about you as well."

'G' Is for Giving — Tzedaka Box, by Beth Grossman, www.bethgrossman.com

While teaching my two year old son, Avi, to share his toys, I was surprised to find that being generous doesn't come naturally. Generosity, the capacity for giving unreservedly and without expectation of reward, is one of the defining qualities of Judaism. One of the challenges in creating a Jewish home for my family is making abstract ideas concrete in our rituals and practice. As a Jewish mother, it is my privilege to teach my son the skills he will need to help his generation continue the work of healing the world. This tzedakah box of children's wooden blocks is about building the foundation for giving and sharing abundance.

Logo at left: Ten Fingers by Dan Reisinger (Folk Art Gallery, 1974)

Meditations כַּוָּנוֹת

Setting a mood of sanctity

Menucha Shlemah/ A Perfect Rest

True rest doesn't affect us only when we are resting. It spills over into our weeks, our years, our very lives. The days preceding the day of rest become days of excitement and expectation. Even the most harried workdays become tolerable when you know a day of holy peace is shortly arriving. The days succeeding the day of rest become days of light, too. They shimmer with the afterglow of a revived spirit.

True rest gives us a completely different perspective on all of life's difficulties. It allows us to heal, to reflect, to give thanks, and to face whatever lies ahead with a renewed sense of calm.

— Naomi Levy

Breathing Meditation

Breathe slowly and deeply, in and out.
Let the clouds of your breath carry your
  daily thoughts away,
Until your mind begins to calm.
Breathe slowly and deeply,
  in and out, in and out.
Be here. See here. Feel here.
  Smell here. Be now.
Be here. See here. Feel here.
  Smell here. Be now.
Let Shalom be your core.

— Ron Rosenblatt

Kavanah

I love to change the world,
  but I rarely appreciate things as they are.
I know how to give,
  but I don't always know how to receive.
I know how to keep busy,
  but I don't know how to be still.
I talk, but I don't often listen.
I look, but I don't often see.
I yearn to succeed,
  but I often forget what is truly
  important.
Teach me, God, to slow down.
May my resting revive me.
May it lead me to wisdom, to holiness,
  to peace and to You.

— Naomi Levy, from To Begin Again

The Deep Breaths of All of You

To put ourselves in a proper mood for optimistic thought, we need a new evaluation. Take a deep breath, please, and hold tight, for I am taking you on a tour of the universe, on a quick trip to the corners of the world, on an exploration of unusual perspectives — all in the interest of a discussion of the one world of humankind. We shall talk of simple things starting with that deep breath, which you may now distribute into surrounding space.

That breath, which you found so necessary and natural, unites you quietly with the rest of us all over the earth. It was a volume of the moving air of your immediate locality, and most of it has now gone forth to join again the winds of the planet, to join the international stock of terrestrial atmosphere.

A year from now I shall breathe in and out a good many thousands of the nitrogen molecules which a minute ago were in the Deep Breaths of all of you. Wherever you are, you too, will be re-breathing some of the Deep Breath of a minute ago. I shall unknowingly have intimate association with you and, of course, you with me.

— Harlow Shapely, astronomer

Breathing is God's Name

"God passed [by Elijah's cave at Mount Sinai] and there was a great and mighty wind, splitting mountains and shattering rocks, before Adonai. But Adonai was not in the wind.

"After the wind, came an earthquake. But Adonai was not in the earthquake.

"Tfila," from "Judaism Is In Your Hands" by Larry Bush, babush@ulster.net. At right, "Shalom Bayit," and upper right, "Jewish Unity." © 2001

"After the earthquake, came the fire.
But Adonai was not in the fire.
"Then after the fire, there was a voice —
a still small voice, [the softly barely
audible sound of almost breathing]."
(I Kings 19:11-12)

The letters of the name of God in Hebrew are *yod, hay, vav,* and *hay.* They are frequently mispronounced *Yahveh.* But in truth they are unutterable. Not because of the holiness they evoke, but because they are all vowels and you cannot pronounce all the vowels at once without risking respiratory injury.

The word is the sound of breathing. The holiest Name in the world, the Name of the Creator, is the sound of your own breathing. That these letters are unpronounceable is no accident. Just as it is no accident that they are also the root letters of the Hebrew verb "to be." Scholars have suggested that a reasonable translation of the four-letter Name of God might be: The One Who Brings Into Being All That Is. So God's Name is the Name of Being itself. And, since God is holy, then so is all creation.

At the burning bush Moses asks God for God's Name, but God only replies with *Ehyeh-asher-ehyeh,* often incorrectly rendered by the static English, "I am who I am." But in truth the Hebrew future is unequivocal: "I will be who I will be." Here is a Name (and a God) who is neither completed nor finished. This God is literally *not yet.*

If God's Name is the Name of Being, then perhaps breathing itself is the sound of the unpronounceable Name. Find a place and a time that are quiet enough to hear the sound of your own breathing. Simply listen to that barely audible noise and intend that with each inhalation and exhalation you sound the Name of Being. It may be no accident that this exercise is universally acknowledged as an easy and effective method for focusing and relaxation.

— Lawrence Kushner

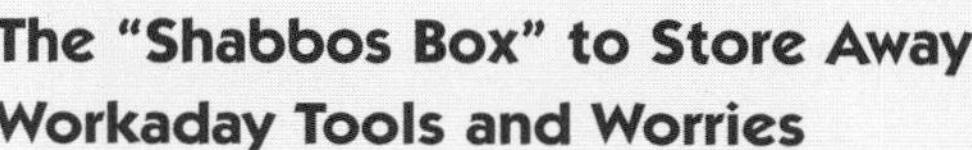

The "Shabbos Box" to Store Away Workaday Tools and Worries

Just before Shabbat some traditional Jews take care to empty their pockets of anything work-related. That is called *muktzeh.* Wayne Muller, a Protestant minister fascinated by the practice of Shabbat, reports his visit to the rabbi, Zalman Schachter-Shalomi, and his wife:

"They told me that in some families it is customary to make a Shabbos box to hold all the equipment you do not need on the Sabbath: pens, car keys, wallets, etc. On Friday someone stands at the door with the Shabbos box and as people enter the house for the evening meal, they put in anything they know should not be taken into sacred space. Then, stripped of all our tools and machines, we truly pray, God, there is nothing I can do about these concerns, so I know it is in your hands . . . ."

Then Wayne Muller suggests to his Christian audience that they adopt this custom as well.

"Make a Sabbath box. When you set aside time for Sabbath, whether it is one hour, a morning, or a day put in the box those things you do not want to use [such as a palm pilot or, to symbolize the computer, a diskette].

"You can also use the Shabbos box to hold all the things you feel you have left undone. Perhaps write down on a small piece of paper a word or phrase that signifies a particular worry or concern you would like to leave behind for the time being . . . For whatever remains to be done, for now, let it be. It will not get done tonight . . . Let it be. Then at the end of your Sabbath time, be aware of how you open the box, and how you respond to what you receive back into your life."

— Wayne Muller, Sabbath: Restoring the Sacred Rhythm of Rest

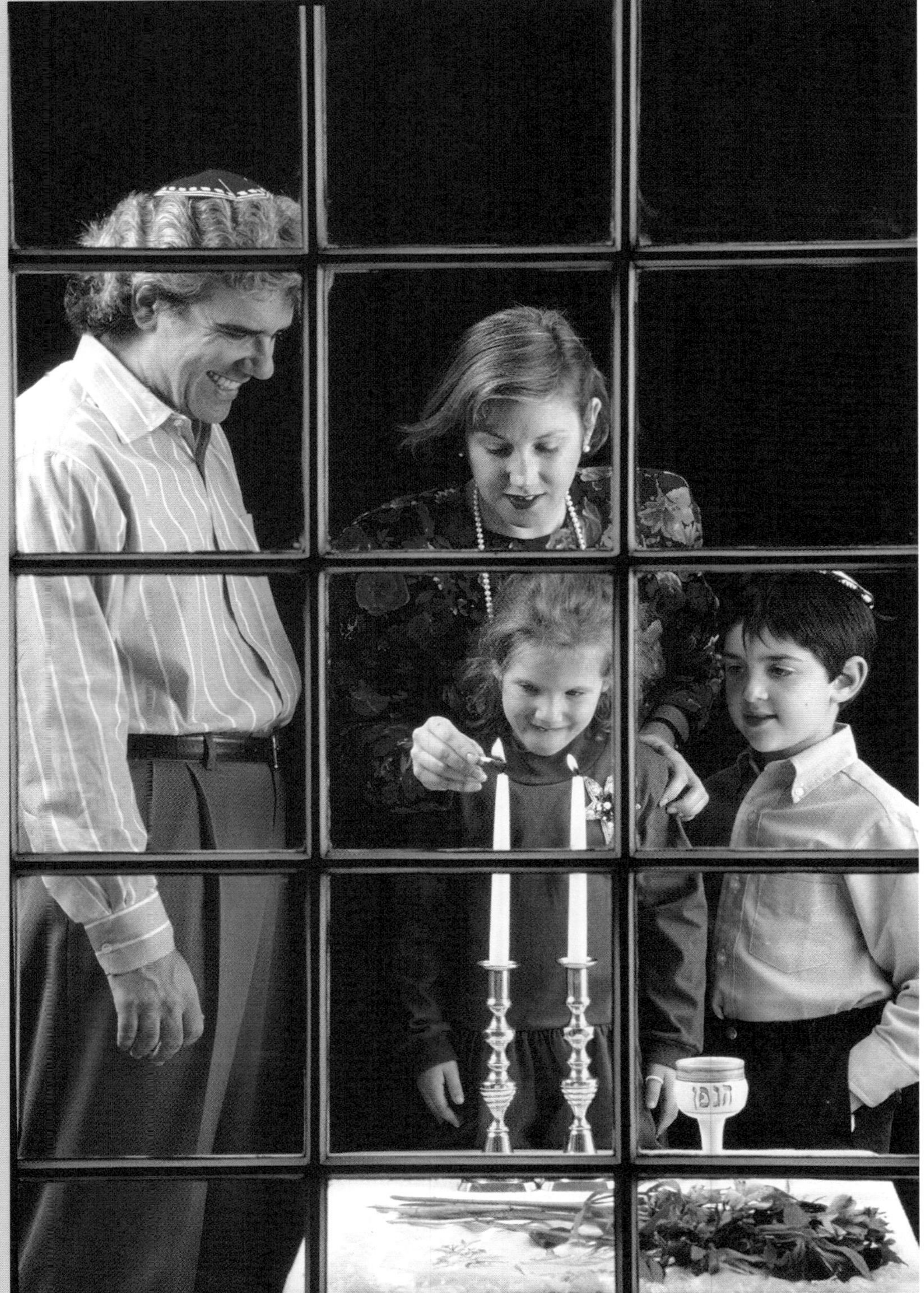

Through Our Neighbor's Window.
(Los Angeles, c. 1990)
Photo by Bill Aron.

Recollections

Rekindle an old flame.

— Reminder to light Shabbat candles, Newspaper Advertisement placed by Habad, 1996

Do you know what it meant to
me when I was called to
the [Shabbat] candles last
Friday? . . .
To this day . . . I feel
again my mother's hands
on my smooth cheeks.

— Basha, the Aliyah Senior Citizens Center in Venice, California

Nerot נֵרוֹת
lighting Shabbat candles

Candle Lighting

1. **LIGHT** the candles.
2. **COVER** your eyes.
3. **BLESS** the candle lighting.
4. **MAKE A PRAYER** for your family and friends.
5. **GREET** all with the words, "Shabbat Shalom," and with the affection conveyed by a smile, a handshake, a hug or a kiss.

BLESSED ARE YOU, Adonai	**בָּרוּךְ** אַתָּה יְיָ	Ba-rukh ata Adonai,
our God, Ruler of the Universe,	אֱלֹהֵינוּ מֶלֶךְ הָעוֹלָם,	Elo-hei-nu me-lekh ha-olam,
who has sanctified us by commanding us	אֲשֶׁר קִדְּשָׁנוּ בְּמִצְוֹתָיו וְצִוָּנוּ,	asher ki-d'shanu b'mitz-votav v'tzi-vanu,
to light the Shabbat candles.	לְהַדְלִיק נֵר שֶׁל שַׁבָּת.	l'ha-d'lik ner shel Shabbat.

OR, when it is both Shabbat and Yom Tov (Festival):

בָּרוּךְ אַתָּה יְיָ אֱלֹהֵינוּ מֶלֶךְ הָעוֹלָם, אֲשֶׁר קִדְּשָׁנוּ בְּמִצְוֹתָיו וְצִוָּנוּ, לְהַדְלִיק נֵר שֶׁל שַׁבָּת וְשֶׁל יוֹם טוֹב.

Ba-rukh ata Adonai, Elo-hei-nu me-lekh ha-olam, asher ki-d'shanu b'mitz-votav v'tzi-vanu, l'had-lik ner shel Shabbat v'shel Yom Tov.

Tekhinot — Making a Personal Prayer — תְּחִינוֹת

Loving Divine Parent

Loving Parent, please draw down your kindness upon me and upon those close to me, those I love.

Bring peace, light and joy into our home, for your people are a source of life.

By your light do we see light. Amen.

— Traditional, British prayerbook

When Children Are Far Away

I have added another brief ritual to my candle lighting, a very private one . . . I decided that at candle lighting each Friday night, I would let my thoughts dwell for a moment on each child, picture their faces and think about their lives. I once mentioned it to them, and now they all light candles on Friday night and think for a few moments about us.

— Blu Greenberg

A Handful of Light

Many people have the custom of holding out their hands and then drawing them in to cover their eyes. Some repeat the gesture of "drawing in" a number of times. Shabbat begins in darkness — a world without light, but then we open our eyes to its light. Anytime we make a rapid transition from darkness to light our eyes are dazzled by the light. We symbolically create Shabbat's brilliant radiance by moving from darkness to light. We follow this with an open-armed gesture of welcome as we draw into ourselves the light and warmth of Shabbat.

— Michael Strassfeld

Isidor Kaufmann (Galicia, 19th century)

Back to the First Light

When all work is brought to a standstill, the candles are lit.
Just as creation began with the word, "Let there be light!"
— so does the celebration of creation begin with the kindling of lights.

— *Abraham Joshua Heschel, The Sabbath*

Mark Chagall, 1946 Copyright © ADAGP Paris 2004

Welcome to Shabbat candle lighting.

Lighting a candle in the darkness is the most elemental human symbol of hope. When you light these candles, you reenact God's opening act of creation — "Let there be light." You also provide warmth — emotional as well as physical — for your home. Candle lighting sets this day apart; it creates sanctity and invites the Shekhina, God's maternal presence, to be your honored guest and sit at your table. For women, it reinforces a bond of memory between mother and daughter going back hundreds of generations. May this be a peaceful and loving Shabbat, for you and all who share your home.

Inner Light

Everyone must know and understand that within burns a candle and no one's candle is identical with the candle of another and there is no human being without a candle. So everyone must know and understand that one is obligated to work hard to reveal the light of one's candle in the public realm for the benefit of the many. One needs to ignite one's candle and make of it a great torch to enlighten the whole world.

— Rabbi Abraham Isaac HaCohen Kook

It is our light, not our darkness, that most frightens us. We ask ourselves — Who am I to be brilliant, gorgeous, talented and fabulous? Actually who are you not to be? You are a child of God. Your playing small does not serve the world. There is nothing enlightened about shrinking so that other people won't feel insecure around you. We were born to manifest the glory of God within us. It is not just in some; it is in everyone. And as we let our light shine, we consciously give other people permission to do the same. As we are liberated from our fear, our presence automatically liberates others.

— Nelson Mandela, Inauguration speech as President of South Africa, 1994, quoting from Maya Angelou

Guidelines
from tradition

1. Lighting the candles traditionally marks the beginning of Shabbat as well as the end of the sometimes frantic rush of preparation to make everything finished on time. At the moment of candle lighting, a transformation takes place: the ordinary weekday home becomes a place of great potential joy, respect, holiness and peace.

2. Before sunset it is traditional to light at least **two candles** placed on or near the dinner table to give light for the meal. Some households light one candle for each member; others prepare two candles for each woman, though men too are commanded to light the candles.

3. Candle lighting time varies according to the sunset; the exact time can be found in Jewish calendars or websites (or just check the local newspaper for the time of sunset and subtract 18 minutes). In winter, traditional candle lighting, which precedes sunset, might be as early as 4 P.M. and in the summer as late as 9 P.M. in North America. In the summer, some families bring in Shabbat earlier by lighting candles (up to approximately one hour) before sunset. Alternatively, some people eat dinner early and then, just before sunset, light candles and only then make *Kiddush* over the wine and recite *HaMotzi* over the Hallah.

4. Choose candles of a length that can burn for at least 3 hours, for the length of your dinner, so they will provide light and spread joy and peace at the table. Try to place them where the wind will not blow them out or cause them to burn too fast. However if they blow out, you are not obligated to relight them since you have already fulfilled the commandment. Let them burn themselves out rather than extinguishing them — unless of course there is a danger to life.

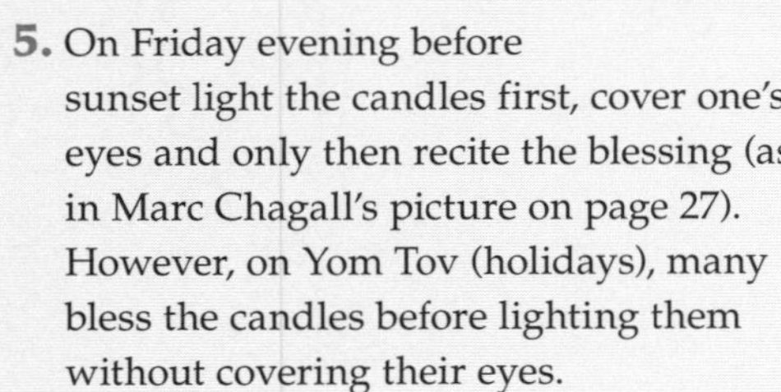

Shabbat Pendant, The Gross Family Collection, Tel Aviv

5. On Friday evening before sunset light the candles first, cover one's eyes and only then recite the blessing (as in Marc Chagall's picture on page 27). However, on Yom Tov (holidays), many bless the candles before lighting them without covering their eyes.

6. Some women cover their hair before candle lighting. Then after lighting, they motion with their hands — often three times — as if gathering in the spirit of Shabbat, before making the blessing. Neither of these customs are required, but they may have deep personal meaning.

For example, Vanessa Ochs, who has written widely on the role of blessings in everyday life, reports: "I don't usually cover my head when I light Shabbat candles at home. However when I am visiting my mother, I am happy to watch my mother light candles wearing my grandmother's shawl, and to allow her to place the shawl over my head as I light. With that cloth over our heads, I feel very close to the memory of my grandmother and I experience being 'under the wings of the Divine Presence.'"

7. When one is not living at home, but rather at college or on a trip, **portable candle sticks** can turn a temporary domicile into a home away from home.

A Woman's Mitzvah?

One's house should be illuminated on Shabbat by whoever takes care of holiday preparations. Maimonides noted that in his era, women were generally responsible for the household, so the mitzvah was incumbent primarily on them. But in families in which men perform household tasks equally (or primarily), the mitzvah is equally incumbent on them. In your home, who should be lighting candles? Of course, men living alone, or single fathers, should light candles for themselves and their households.

Guidelines

getting started

How shall I make candle lighting my weekly custom?

Recall: Begin by remembering candle lighting ceremonies which have left an impression on you — from childhood or from friends. **Your goal will be to introduce an element of sanctity into your weekly life.**

How: You may wish to share Shabbat with a more experienced friend or family member. Then begin to develop and adapt your own traditions. Experiment, and don't worry about making mistakes but about making Shabbat a time of holiness.

With Whom: Candle lighting has usually been performed by the woman of the house, often with her daughters. This contributes to female bonding for mothers, sisters, and daughters. However, men are equally obligated to light Shabbat candles in their home. Some people involve both men and women, both sons and daughters as well. Many try to gather all the household members to join together in the ceremony. However, lighting by oneself can be an opportunity for personal meditation and "centering one's self" before Shabbat. When electric lights are extinguished, the soft candle light fills the room with a warmth and sanctity.

When: For traditional candle lighting, 18 minutes before sunset is the latest time to light candles. Other households begin dinner with candle lighting at the table, even after sunset, when all are gathered after work.

With What: Any candle — oil or wax — and any candleholder will do as long as light is provided. However the more one personalizes the mitzvah the more it adds sanctity. Some households have a decorative matchbox and candelabrum to personalize and beautify this mitzvah *(Hidur Mitzvah)*. Someone may take on the weekly pre-Shabbat assignment of preparing the candles, finding the matches and taking out the book with the blessings as well as a box for Tzedakah. Collect small change from everyone's pocket or purse and, before candle lighting, deposit some coins.

Consider using non-standard candles — perhaps floating in a bowl of water or even lighting many candles and not using electric lights. Incense burning was typical in the ancient world and may be a popular addition to candle lighting in some circles.

A Family Photograph and a Personal Prayer: Since candle lighting is a time to think of family and close friends, you may wish to put up a photograph of loved ones next to the candelabrum. As you close your eyes to light the candles you can think of those intimates in your life and when you open your eyes you can use the candle light to look at their faces. Add a personal prayer *(see* Tekhinot, *page 25, 34-35)* or a reading *(see* Kavanot, *page 32-33)*.

After candle lighting: You may wish to try my wife's family custom. She serves cake, cookies or strawberries with whipped cream as a Shabbat treat that sweetens the candle lighting ceremony. *(SEE "PRE-SHABBAT COFFEE AND CAKE," PAGE 18).*

What if you are going out on Friday night? For example, you are driving to the synagogue and still want to light candles before Shabbat. You may light the candles early and yet not officially start Shabbat, as long as you have that in mind as you recite the blessing. People concerned about fire may not wish to light candles before they go out. They might light the candles at the home where they are invited. Or light the candles at home and then extinguish them before going out, or leave them burning in the sink.

A Tired Housewife's Shabbat in Warsaw, 1928.
YIVO Institute, courtesy of USHMM Photo Archive

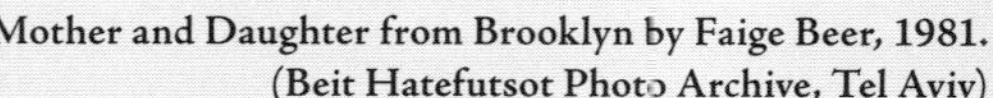

Mother and Daughter from Brooklyn by Faige Beer, 1981.
(Beit Hatefutsot Photo Archive, Tel Aviv)

Guidelines

parent-child corner

Sharing candle lighting with children has proven through the generations to imprint a powerful memory trace. Younger children in particular often desire to imitate their parents, as well as to know everything that the parents did when they were children. Candle lighting is a precious opportunity for sharing those memories and for creating new memories in a one-on-one moment of intimacy. Take out your family albums to peruse after candle lighting.

Give your children their own set of candlesticks (or have them make their own), and perhaps allow them to light the candles themselves if possible. The attraction of fire and the chance to light matches themselves — under parental supervision — is an important privilege for young children. Young children may also play pretend and imitate an imaginary candle lighting, while their parent lights the actual candles. Make the children responsible for preparing the candlesticks in advance, cleaning them perhaps, arranging the candles, providing the matchbox (which may be specially decorated), or putting out a beautiful tray or special placemat on which the candles stand.

Reaching Out for Shabbat.
(Los Angeles, 1985) Photo by Bill Aron.

Ask one child to collect all the loose change from each member of the household and deposit it in the Tzedakah box before candle lighting. A cute counting game involves the child collecting 36 cents (twice the numerical value of *Chai* = 18) — a quarter, a dime, and a penny or a quarter, two nickels and a penny. For children who cannot read, draw the shape of the coins on a paper and then they can match the coin to the size of each circle.

If you choose to recite a personalized prayer for your family *(see* Tekhinot, *page 34-35)*, then invite the children to add their own prayers in their own words — praying for the health or happiness of those close to them and expressing their thanks for that last week and their hopes for the future. The children may also pick their own melody to greet the Shabbat, giving them a chance to sing Shabbat songs learned in school. They can put on a Shabbat recording for background music. If there is time, a parent or older sibling may wish to read Bible stories with the children as they wait for dinner to begin.

A Shabbat Box, a Shabbat Shelf and an Oneg Shabbat Pleasure Basket

- Prepare a **Shabbat Box** (or labelled cabinet) containing the list of Shabbat items, so that Shabbat is easy to assemble and the children can bear some responsibility.

Checklist:

- ☐ Candles
- ☐ candle sticks
- ☐ matches – in decorative box
- ☐ coins ready for Tzedakah
- ☐ Tzedakah box
- ☐ tray or placemat
- ☐ Kiddush cup
- ☐ Hallah cover
- ☐ salt shaker (for the Hallah)
- ☐ bread knife and bread board
- ☐ book of blessings

- Designate a **Shabbat Shelf** with the title *L'kh-vod Shabbat* — "In honor of Shabbat" (as was once a custom of Jews from Afghanistan). Over two thousand years ago Shamai, the Torah scholar, used to search all week long for treats to purchase and save for Shabbat. A special fruit, say a mango or persimmon, or a special candy bar, can be put away on the Shabbat Shelf, in clear view of the family during the week. Then before candle lighting put out the treats — perhaps hiding them under the Hallah cover as a surprise.
- Prepare an **Oneg Shabbat Basket**. Oneg Shabbat means the pleasures enjoyed on Shabbat, so it might contain the games, toys, cards, musical recordings

and books that the children love to play with their parents and siblings. (Biblical charades can be played to guess Biblical characters.) Put the basket out in the living room for family time after dinner — instead of TV.

Through a Child's Eyes

We have been taught to see Shabbat in metaphors as a bride or a queen. But we can invent new images as well, especially with the help of our children's free imagination. They can help us see Shabbat in non-traditional ways.

For example, I have asked my daughter to look deeply into the candle's flames and then questioned her: What do you see emerging from the flames? More broadly speaking, what does Shabbat look like? What does Shabbat smell like? Feel like? Perhaps it is like an island separate from the rest of the week, or like a snowfall, clean and white like the tablecloth. It may smell like Bubie's brisket or her flowers.

No children at your table? Step out of the box and free associate. Remember you were once a child.

— *Phyllis Cincinatus*

A Candle for Me

One custom is to light an additional candle for each child in the family. For example, every Friday evening my mother lit four candles, the two required by law, one for my sister, Shalva, and one for me. The message this extra candle sends to each child is a powerful one. As Rabbi Abraham Twerski, a psychiatrist, puts it, "How edifying it was for me to know that our home was brighter on Friday nights because I was in existence!"

— *Joseph Telushkin*

From Birth and Beyond Death: A Poignant Family Tradition

One family buys a set of candle sticks for their children at birth. One candle stick is put away to be given to the child when they reach bar/bat mitzvah age. The other is lit by the parent and later the children as soon as they can light for themselves. When their first child, Ari, died at age two, they agonized – should we continue to light his candle every Shabbat? They decided that his spirit was still among them. When the next three children grew up, then they took turns lighting Ari's candle. When guests came, they were told that the four candles were their four children, for on Shabbat the whole family — including Ari — was together.

Candle Lighting

How Many Candles?

The blessing for lighting candles says only "to light the Shabbat candle" — in Hebrew, Ner — an oil lamp or candle. Yet many Jews light more than one candle. Here is an intriguing review of the many customs and their rationale.

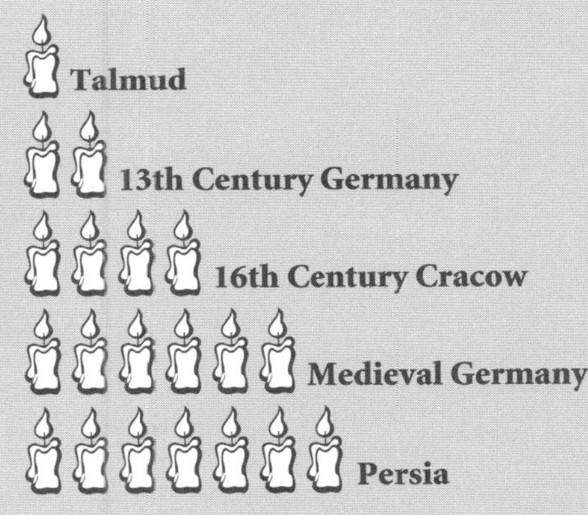

- **One Candle — JUST ENOUGH LIGHT** The Talmud established the lighting of one Shabbat candle (originally oil, not wax) in order to provide light at the Shabbat table. During the week, most people ate before sunset, for they could not afford expensive fuels for light. Yet, on Shabbat the meal follows sunset; therefore, a candle was required to illuminate one's home both for *Oneg Shabbat* (the pleasure of eating food whose aesthetics we can also see) and for *Shalom Bayit* (domestic tranquility). Social interaction at the table is enhanced by seeing another's facial expressions and hand gestures, an essential part of human communication.
- **Two Candles — MORE MEANING** Shabbat candles also have a symbolic value representing Kibbud Shabbat, Honoring Shabbat. The medieval European Ashkenazim explained that the two candles represent the two parallel formulations of the 4th commandment given at Mount Sinai — *Zachor*/Remember (Ex 20:8) and *Shamor*/Observe the Shabbat (Deuteronomy 5:12). The two candles also symbolize the male and female aspects of the Divine, united on Shabbat (or husband and wife).
- **Seven Candles — SEPHARDIC-STYLE** According to Sephardic custom, 7 candles are lit corresponding to the 7 days of the week.
- **Many Candles —** Some families light one candle for every child in the family or for every member of the household.

Reflections כַּוָּנוֹת

Setting a mood of sanctity

Expelling Sadness from our Homes

We want the *Sukkah* of Shalom to be spread over us, so the Rabbis established the Shabbat candle lighting to expel from our homes all the evil, the sadness, and the worry of the six days of the week. The gentle light of the candles illuminates our homes with the light of joy, gladness, peace and tranquillity and declares a cease-fire to the flames of argument and disagreement. Igniting the fire of the candles consumes the fire of the evil inclination and anger. Then when we enter the house we can greet the Shabbat and our families with wishes for peace — *Shabbat Shalom Um'vorakh and Shalom Aleichem.*

— From the Siddur of Rabbi Chaim Tchernovitz

Austro-Hungarian soldiers in Italy, World War I. Oesterreichische Nationale Bibliothek Bildarchiv, Vienna, Austria.

Shabbat Surrender: To Live as if Everything were Done

The Torah says: "Six days shall you labor and do all your work." (*Exodus 20:9*)

"But [the Rabbis challenged:] Is it possible for a human beings to do all their work in six days? No, rather the Torah means act as if all your work were finished. Alternatively, perhaps the Torah meant that after six days you must rest from 'all your work' — even the thought of your work." (*Mechilta 20:9*)

There is astounding wisdom in the traditional Jewish Sabbath, in that it begins precisely at sundown, whether that comes at a wintry 4:30 or late on a summer evening. Sabbath is not dependent upon our readiness to stop. We do not stop when we are finished. We do not stop when we complete our phone calls, finish our project, get through this stack of messages, or finish our report that is due tomorrow. We stop because it is time to stop.

Sabbath requires surrender. If we only stop when we are finished with all our work, we will never stop, because our work is never completely done. With every accomplishment there arises a new responsibility. Every swept floor invites another sweeping, every child bathed invites another bathing. When all life moves in such cycles, what is ever finished? The sun goes round, the moon goes round, the ties and seasons go round, people are born and die, and when are we finished? If we refuse rest until we are finished, we will never rest until we die. Sabbath dissolved the artificial urgency of our days, because it liberates us from the need to be finished.

When we breathe, we do not stop inhaling because we have taken in all the oxygen we will ever need, but because we have all the oxygen we need for this breath. Then we exhale, release carbon dioxide, and make room for more oxygen. Sabbath, like the breath, allows us to imagine we have done enough work for this day . . . Let the work of this day be sufficient.

— Wayne Muller

A Lonely Shabbat in the Peace Corps

An American Peace Corps volunteer from Brooklyn recalls that he often lit Shabbat candles alone in Guatemala. Even all by himself, the candle lighting still ushered in a sense of home and of sanctity. He recalled the Rabbinic midrash that says that while all the animals were created two by two, both Shabbat and the Jewish people were first created in isolation without a life partner though they were meant for one another. With Shabbat the Peace Corps volunteer was never without a loving partner. In fact in Guatemala he came to really appreciate the powerful role of the candles, since the village where he worked had no electricity of its own.

Shabbat is Walden Pond: Extra Time on Earth

There were times when I could not afford to sacrifice the bloom of the present moment to any work, whether of head or hands. Sometimes, in a summer morning, having taken my accustomed bath, I stay in my sunny doorway from sunrise till noon, rapt in a reverie, amidst the pines and hickories and sumachs, in undisturbed solitude and stillness, while the birds stand around. I grew in those seasons like corn in the night, and they were far better than any work of the hands would have been. They were not time subtracted from my life, but so much over and above my usual allowance.

— Henry David Thoreau

"How Beautiful the World Could Be!" — The Hope of Sunset

One evening, when we were already resting on the floor of our hut, dead tired, soup bowls in hand, a fellow prisoner rushed in and asked us to run out to the assembly grounds and see the wonderful sunset. Standing outside we saw sinister clouds glowing in the west and the whole sky alive with clouds of ever-changing shapes and colors, from steel blue to blood red. The desolate gray mud huts provided a sharp contrast, while the puddles on the muddy ground reflected the glowing sky. Then, after minutes of moving silence, one prisoner said to another, "how beautiful the world could be!"

— Victor Frankl,
psychologist and Holocaust survivor

The Limits of Sunset

The setting of the sun ushers in a unit of time where the flowers of the field stand over and against man as equal members of the universe. I am forbidden to pluck the flower or to do with it as I please; at sunset the flower becomes a "thou" to me with a right to existence regardless of its value for me. I stand silently before nature as before a fellow creature of God and not as a potential object of my control, and I must face the fact that I am a man and not God. The Sabbath aims at healing the human grandiosity of technological society.

— David Hartman, *Joy and Responsibility*

Light a Candle

Light a candle.
Drink wine.
Softly the Shabbat has plucked
the sinking sun.
Slowly the Shabbat descends,
the rose of heaven in her hand.
How can the Shabbat
plant a huge and shining flower
in a blind and narrow heart?

How can the Shabbat
plant the bud of angels
in a heart of raving flesh?
Can the rose of immortality grow
in an age enslaved
to destruction,
an age enslaved
to death?
Light a candle!

Drink wine!
Slowly the Shabbat descends
and in her hand
the flower, and in her hand the sinking sun . . .

— Zelda, Israeli poet (copyright reserved for ACUM and author)

Dreams of Eternity

Refreshed and renewed,
attired in festive garments,
with candles nodding dreamily to
unutterable expectations,
to intuitions of eternity,
some of us are overcome with a feeling
as if almost all they would say
would be like a veil.
There is not enough grandeur in our souls
to be able to unravel in words
the knot of time and eternity.
One should like to sing for all men,
for all generations . . .
There is a song in the wind
and joy in the trees.
The Sabbath arrives in the world,
scattering a song in the silence of the night;
eternity utters a day. Where are the words
that could compete with such might?

— Abraham Joshua Heschel, *The Sabbath*

Tekhinot תְּחִנּוֹת

personal prayers at candle lighting

Introduction

Immediately after candle lighting many women add a personal prayer while their eyes are still closed. It is an intimate moment in which one privately reconnects with family members and prays for their well-being. To help women express their feelings and wishes, people (both women and men) began to compose *Tekhinot* — supplications, meditations and prayers — for women in the Ashkenazi European community (17th-19th centuries). These collections of prayers enjoyed immense popularity as both an outlet for and expression of their spiritual yearnings.

Tekhinot were usually written in everyday language — Yiddish — and their content covered family matters, health, pregnancy and birth. They were designed to be said at women's rituals — such as candle lighting, Hallah baking, and *mikve* (ritual immersion bath). Today there is a revival of writing *Tekhinot* related to a renewed concentration on female spirituality and ritual creativity, but there is no reason why men cannot use these vehicles of religious expression.

Below you will find a variety of *Tekhinot* ranging from their traditional form in Europe to American compositions.

Issachar Ber Ryback, Russian-French cubist, 1917.
From *Shtetl, Mayn Khorerver Heym (The Jewish Shtetl, My Destroyed Home: A Recollection)*

Traditional Woman's Prayer

May it be Your will, God of our ancestors, that You grant my family and all Israel a good and long life. Remember us with blessings and kindness, fill our home with your Divine Presence. Give me the opportunity to raise my children and grandchildren to be truly wise, lovers of God, people of truth, who illuminate the world with Torah, good deeds and the work of the Creator. Please hear my prayer at this time. Regard me as a worthy descendent of Sarah, Rebecca, Rachel and Leah, our mothers, and let my candles burn and never be extinguished. Let the light of your face shine upon us. Amen.

A Prayer for Shabbat Happiness

May it be God's Will, that I be be privileged to receive this holy Shabbat with happiness and joy, with song and excitement. Protect me so that no sadness or depression, no anguish or worry will mar my Shabbat. May I be happy with all my soul, with all my heart and with all my strength. Let this happiness without limit encompass [the world], your people Israel, me, my spouse, and the members of my household. Amen.

— Rabbi Nachman of Bratzlav, Likutei Tefillot

Tikkun Olam — Mending the World

God, creator of Heaven and Earth, creator of humankind and of all living things, grant me the power to feel as others feel, the power to listen and to hear, to behold and to see truly, to touch and to be touched.

Keep fresh within me the memory of my own suffering and the suffering of Clal Yisrael (the whole community), not in order to stimulate eternal paranoia, but rather that I may better understand the suffering of strangers; and may that understanding lead me to do everything in my power to alleviate and to prevent such suffering . . . .

Enable me to be like Yourself — to feed the hungry, clothe the naked, tend the sick, comfort the bereaved. Guide me in the ways of *Tikkun Olam*, of mending the world. As I delight in a loving marriage of true minds, may I never forget the thousands of women battered and beaten by their spouses. As I rejoice in the bliss of my children and grandchildren, may I never forget the pleading eyes and swollen bellies of starving infants deprived of physical and emotional nourishment. May my woman's capacities for concern, compassion, and caring never be dulled by complacency or personal contentment. May my feelings always lead me to act.

— Alice Shalvi,
founder of Israeli women's lobby

A Contemporary *Tekhina*

We thank You, O God, for Your gift of Shabbat,
For the home in which we observe it,
And for the dear ones with whom we share it.
May the joy of Shabbat gladden our hearts,
And may its peace quiet our spirits.
As we observe Shabbat together,
May we understand its meaning and capture its mood.
Bring us closer to one another in love;
With laughter and soft words,
With shared concerns and mutual respect.
Help us make our home a sanctuary,
Warmed by reverence, adorned by tradition,
With family bonds that are strong and enduring,
Based on truth, trust, and faithfulness.
Keep us far from strife and anger;
May we be spared shame and reproach.
Help us so to live in the week ahead
That You may look upon all we have done
And find it good and worthy of Your blessing.

— Anonymous

My Mother-in-law's *Tekhina* — "The most moving prayers I have ever heard"

Even better than shul is my mother-in-law's Friday-night davening. Occasionally, she spends a Shabbat with us. As I lurk around a corner, and listen intently, I feel as if I am privy to a private audience with God. She finishes up the regular Friday-night prayers, and then, in a barely audible whisper, and looking into her Siddur all the while, she proceeds to carry on a one-way conversation with Him:

Welcoming Shabbat with my Wife and Son. (Los Angeles, 1981) Photo by Bill Aron.

With eighty-five years behind her, my mother-in-law brings God up to date on the whereabouts and doings of each child, grandchild, and great-grandchild, occasionally summing up past favors and events of yesteryear. Once, more than fifteen years after I had been married, she reminded God that her son had married a nice *yiddishe maidele* (a Jewish girl). After describing what each of us was doing, she turned His attention to the grandchildren — which school each attended, who was graduating, who was in a cast with a torn cartilage, and who was going to camp for a

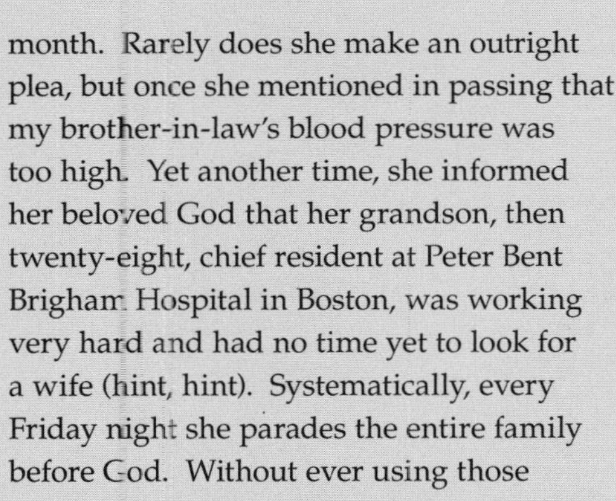

month. Rarely does she make an outright plea, but once she mentioned in passing that my brother-in-law's blood pressure was too high. Yet another time, she informed her beloved God that her grandson, then twenty-eight, chief resident at Peter Bent Brigham Hospital in Boston, was working very hard and had no time yet to look for a wife (hint, hint). Systematically, every Friday night she parades the entire family before God. Without ever using those words, it is a prayer of thanksgiving.

May I be forgiven for eavesdropping; hers are truly among the most moving prayers I have ever heard.

— Blu Greenberg

A person reaches
in three directions:
inward, to oneself
up, to God
out, to others.

The miracle of life is that
in truly reaching
in any one direction,
one embraces all three.

— *Rebbe Levi Yitzchak of Berditchev*

David Sharir, City of Angels,
Tel Aviv-Jaffa, 1969

שָׁלוֹם עֲלֵיכֶם

Shalom Aleichem

welcoming the angels of peace

1. SING the next few stanzas to welcome Shabbat into our homes, our families and our hearts. Often people repeat each verse three times and hold hands and sway while singing.
2. IMAGINE Shabbat as an angelic presence and welcome it.

Shalom Aleikhem	**שָׁלוֹם עֲלֵיכֶם**	Peace be upon you,
Malakhei ha-sha-reit	מַלְאֲכֵי הַשָּׁרֵת	angels in the Divine service,
Malakhei elyon,	מַלְאֲכֵי עֶלְיוֹן,	*malakhim* of the Supreme One,
Mi-melekh, malkhei ham'lakhim	מִמֶּלֶךְ מַלְכֵי הַמְּלָכִים	messengers from the Ruler above all rulers,
Ha-Kadosh Baruckh Hu!	הַקָּדוֹשׁ בָּרוּךְ הוּא.	the Holy One!
Bo-a-khem l'Shalom	**בּוֹאֲכֶם לְשָׁלוֹם**	Come, bring Peace,
Malakhei ha-Shalom	מַלְאֲכֵי הַשָּׁלוֹם	angels of Shalom,
Malakhei elyon,	מַלְאֲכֵי עֶלְיוֹן,	*malakhim* of the Supreme One,
Mi-melekh, malkhei ham'lakhim	מִמֶּלֶךְ מַלְכֵי הַמְּלָכִים	messengers from the Ruler above all rulers,
Ha-Kadosh Baruckh Hu!	הַקָּדוֹשׁ בָּרוּךְ הוּא.	the Holy One!
Barkhuni l'Shalom	**בָּרְכוּנִי לְשָׁלוֹם**	Bless me with peace,
Malakhei ha-Shalom	מַלְאֲכֵי הַשָּׁלוֹם	angels of Shalom,
Malakhei elyon,	מַלְאֲכֵי עֶלְיוֹן,	*malakhim* of the Supreme One,
Mi-melekh, malkhei ham'lakhim	מִמֶּלֶךְ מַלְכֵי הַמְּלָכִים	messengers from the Ruler above all rulers,
Ha-Kadosh Baruckh Hu!	הַקָּדוֹשׁ בָּרוּךְ הוּא.	the Holy One!
Tzeit-khem l'Shalom	**צֵאתְכֶם לְשָׁלוֹם**	Depart in peace,
Malakhei ha-Shalom	מַלְאֲכֵי הַשָּׁלוֹם	angels of Shalom,
Malakhei elyon,	מַלְאֲכֵי עֶלְיוֹן,	*malakhim* of the Supreme One,
Mi-melekh, malkhei ham'lakhim	מִמֶּלֶךְ מַלְכֵי הַמְּלָכִים	messengers from the Ruler above all rulers,
Ha-Kadosh Baruckh Hu!	הַקָּדוֹשׁ בָּרוּךְ הוּא.	the Holy One!

Our Guardian Angels

May God instruct the Divine angels to guard you
on whatever paths you take.

— *Psalm 91:11*

May Adonai guard your coming and going,
now and forever.

— *Psalm 121:8*

Shabbat is the choicest fruit and flower of the week.

The coming of the Queen transforms even the humblest home into a palace.

— *Judah Halevi, Kuzari III 5, Spain, d.1135*

If the angel deigns to come
it will be because
you have convinced her,
not by tears but by your humble resolve
to be always beginning; to be a beginner.

— *Angels Love Beginners, by Rainer Maria Rilke*

'The dove came back [to Noah on the seventh day] with an olive branch in its bill." (*Gen. 8:11*) Emile Prcbst, Cantecleer Bible, Netherlands, 1966.

Yiddish Rosh Hashanah Card, Warsaw-New York, 1920.
(Hayim Shtayer Collection, Beit Hatefutsot Photo Archives, Tel Aviv)

As the Jew enters the Shabbat, the Shabbat enters the Jew.

— Elliot Ginsburg

Welcoming sacred guests

"SHALOM ALEICHEM" is about welcoming and receptivity. After all the pre-Shabbat preparations to ready our home and our table, we now open our hearts and embrace our sacred guests. First, we welcome Shabbat personified as a queen, a feminine presence and a royal guest at our "banquet" meal. Sometimes we imagine that **Divine presence** in the form of a pair of angels, for whom the song *Shalom Aleichem* was composed in the 17th century. Then, of course, we also welcome **human guests**, making them feel honored. Metaphorically, they too represent the Divine presence; they are the bearers of the image of God among us. Perhaps our earthly visitors should be seen as human angels on a mission — guests who come to lodge briefly in our homes. *Shalom Aleichem* is not only used to greet angels but also to say "hello" (in eastern European parlance) whenever one Jew meets another. That is why one of the great Yiddish authors chose the pseudonym Shalom Aleichem; his short stories describe the many Jews whose paths he had crossed.

We are meant not only to be gracious hosts to those coming from afar — a heavenly queen and a distant traveler; we must also learn to welcome one another, **our friends and family.** This is a time to make peace with those whom we may have ignored or with whom we may have quarreled prior to Shabbat. To that purpose, this section contains selections about the Jewish goal of *Shalom Bayit* (domestic tranquility) and its special place on Shabbat.

Finally (and perhaps more effectively, before or simultaneous to the other welcomings), we must open ourselves to the often-ignored dimension of personal sanctity. That inner self is called the *Neshama Y'teira* — the extra Shabbat soul – or the sacred power at all times hidden within. It is to this extra soul, as much as to the angels, its symbolic bearers, that we now sing *Shalom Aleichem* — "Welcome, Come in Peace!"

Oseh Shalom — A Song for Peace in Israel and the Whole World

Oseh Shalom Bimromav, hu ya'aseh Shalom aleinu, v'al kol Yisrael v'imru Amen.	עֹשֶׂה שָׁלוֹם בִּמְרוֹמָיו הוּא יַעֲשֶׂה שָׁלוֹם עָלֵינוּ וְעַל כָּל יִשְׂרָאֵל וְאִמְרוּ אָמֵן.	May God who makes peace in the heavens, make peace for all of us and for all of Israel.

ℵ Guidelines

getting started

How do I initiate the welcoming of guests and the singing of *Shalom Aleichem* in my home?

Shalom Aleichem is a mini-play. We stand up as if greeting angels. We know that angels sing in the divine choir, so we greet them with song. For those celebrating Shabbat by themselves, the angels may give them a sense of companionship. (In fact, sometimes it is easier to focus on welcoming the divine presence into our hearts when we are alone.) When there are guests this moment may serve as an opportunity to make them feel fully at home, to welcome them and introduce them to those at the table, or even perhaps to learn their Hebrew names.

A musical rendition on a tape or a CD is an easy way to learn a new melody. Putting on the music for Shabbat in the car on Friday morning or in the kitchen on Friday afternoon not only sets a tone, but can help us learn the melody in advance — even for those who struggle with Hebrew.

At the table, you might begin *Shalom Aleichem* by humming the melody without words, while holding hands or with arms interwoven. Then try the words, which are repetitive and easy to learn. Just singing the *niggun*, the wordless melody, is also adequate. Do not feel obligated to sing all the four verses of *Shalom Aleichem*; it is not an official prayer or ritual requirement, just a lovely song. (Some intentionally skip the last verse which already speaks of the angels leaving, *Tzeitkhem l'Shalom*, since it is impolite to mention "leaving" to guests who have just arrived. It is more appropriate to sing that verse at Havdalah.)

Raphael, detail from Madonna Sistina, Italy, 16th century.

To set the peaceful mood appropriate for *Shalom Aleichem*, ask someone — especially one who prefers reading to singing — to read aloud a selection. For example, you might read the poem by Rainer Maria Rilke about angels who love beginners (like ourselves), the Hassidic story, "Making Peace with My Creator," or Larry Kushner's explanation of the human angels in our world, "Messengers of the Most High" *(page 43)*.

If you know the song/prayer ***Oseh Shalom***, you may prefer to sing it instead of — or in addition to — *Shalom Aleichem*. It may be combined with the activity, "War and Peace" *(page 41)*, which is designed to reinforce our connection to the State of Israel and its ongoing struggle for peace.

What Did You Do This Week to Prepare Your Home for Human and Divine Guests?

One great 19th century rabbi revealed the way he cleans the house for Shabbat:

"In our home it is customary to have the chairs already set around the table, all the beds made — even in the other rooms; everything swept up; the dishes and silverware clean and polished and even the cobwebs removed in honor of Shabbat as if an important guest were arriving." *(Aruch haShulchan, A.H. O.H. 262)*

Guidelines

parent-child corner

Shalom Aleichem is the common Jewish greeting for hello or welcome, so children may enjoy accompanying its singing with gestures of salutation. They may give everyone a "high five" while saying *Shalom Aleichem*. Or try bowing gently to one another as the Japanese do (also Abraham bowed before his three angelic guests). Or you might try the Sephardic custom of kissing your own hand after shaking each person's hand, as a sign of respect and affection. Actually children might like to say "goodbye" to the old week before they welcome the new one with all its hopes and fears.

You may wish to read aloud some of the **Tales of Peacemakers** at the end of this section and perhaps to mention quarrels and tensions to be removed as we enter Shabbat and a new week.

With your children, try imagining the angels. You may use questions, props and stories to evoke their involvement. You need not present angels as physical beings but they may be understood as symbols for spiritual realities. For this playful exercise pose evocative questions: what does your personal angel look like? Does the angel have a message or a task for us? Younger children might like to open the door for the angels and set them a place and a chair at the table. Maybe they could imitate the angels by standing with their feet together and bouncing on their toes three times or maybe by waving their "wings" like an angel taking off. (In the synagogue when reciting the *Kedusha* in the *Amidah*, it is customary to bounce on our toes that way while repeating the angelic praise: "Holy, Holy, Holy!").

Develop the conversation with them based on Biblical stories of angels that also express values. Read the children the story from Genesis 18 about the surprise noon visit of three mysterious men (actually angels on a mission) to Abraham and Sarah's tents. Imagine for a moment that the angels are approaching from the desert at the hottest hour of the day. They appear dressed as human beings but their faces are illuminated with an inner light. How would you greet them? Perhaps with a slight bow or even a kiss on the cheek? While you might not offer to wash their feet as Abraham did, imagine other ways to make them feel at home. What blessing or good tidings would you ask that they give your home? (The angels in the Torah predicted the birth of Isaac, whose name means "laughter," who would be born to his parents at age 100 and 90, respectively.) You may also wish to read in Genesis 28 about Jacob's dream of the angels ascending and descending the ladder to heaven. Then set your Shabbat table with props from that story like a toy ladder or popsicle sticks with an image of an angel attached.

Jacob Wrestles with the Angel, by Bencjon Benn, *Visions of the Bible*, 1954

Try to keep a playful spirit. The point is not to teach children to believe in angels as a scientific cause but to treat them as literary messengers of important ideas.

A New/Old Custom: Add Sweet Fragrances

Many people, of course, bring home flowers on Shabbat. But did you know there is a Sephardi and Hassidic custom of preparing fragrant cuttings of flowers or branches for Shabbat that has ancient roots? The Shabbat bouquet is first mentioned in the story of Shimon bar Yochai, the rabbinic mystic, to whom the writing of the Zohar is attributed. *(Talmud Shabbat 33b)*

War and Peace

Review the week's news relating to conflict and its resolution, in Israel and worldwide. Remember that no private Jewish celebration is permitted unless we keep in mind the memory of Jerusalem and the hope for a redeemed world *(Psalm 137)*. Think of Jews whom you know in the State of Israel and let us pray that God will spread the Sukkah of Shalom over them, over Jerusalem and over the whole world.

Reflections כַּוָּנוֹת
on themes of Shalom Aleichem

Making Peace with the Divine: Welcoming God's Angels

Higher than the Angels

The virtue of angels is that they cannot deteriorate; their flaw is that they cannot improve.

The flaw of human beings is that they do deteriorate; their virtue is that they can improve.

— Hassidic saying (quoted by Leo Rosten)

This Time You Are God's Hosts

When we enter a synagogue's sanctuary, we are the guests. As in the home of an influential human being, for example, the White House, we are likely to feel awed by the occasion and the setting. Perhaps we are self-conscious about how we are dressed and anxious lest we violate the rules of protocol. We are honoured to be in God's place but as Jacob said when awaking from his dream of the ladder with the angels, "How awesome is this place! How frightening! This is the house of God!" When entering the Temple understood as the Divine residence of the Sovereign of the world, there is a mitzvah to show *yirat hamakom* — respect for the sanctity of the place — which means we do not feel at home.

However, since the destruction of the Temple, *Beit HaMikdash*, we have become God's hosts and the Divine presence pays a visit to our home, sanctified for Shabbat. We are to make God and the angels feel at home, as it were, by making our home resemble their home — the Temple. Our candles recall God's menorah; our table recalls the altar with its meat offering and salt; our Hallahs on the table resemble the twelve show breads put out each Shabbat in the Temple; our singing imitates the Levis' choir in the earthly House of God or the angelic choir in the heavenly House. If we bless our children using the priestly blessing, then that too might make God "feel at home." The Zohar suggests that we regard our human guests — especially ones in need of hospitality, like the poor — as God's representatives on earth and honor them as we would God.

Welcoming Angelic Inspectors

The world is like the eve before Shabbat, and the next world is like Shabbat itself. If one does not prepare for the Shabbat, then what will there be to eat? *(Ruth Rabba 3:3)*

The Talmudic Rabbi Yossi ben Yehuda used to say: "There are two of God's ministering angels who accompany one home on Shabbat evening from the synagogue to his home — one is good and one is evil. If when entering the house, one finds a candle lit, a table set and a bed made — the good angel declares: 'May it be Your will, God, that next Shabbat be just like this one.' The evil angel is required, even against his will, to say 'Amen.' However, if the household is not prepared, the malicious angel declares: 'May it be Your will, that next Shabbat be just like this one.' Then the beneficent angel is required, even against his will, to say Amen. *(Talmud Shabbat 119b)*

More Angelic Inspectors

Imagine that the angels who came on Shabbat were not concerned merely with whether you set the table beautifully on God's seventh day, but whether you have merited the continuation of the world God created on the six days. Have you justified God's risky experiment in creating the human being? Here I am referring to one of the earliest debates in rabbinic tradition when Hillel and Shamai disagreed whether it was good that God created human beings.

"For two and a half years the school of Shamai and the school of Hillel debated.

"Shamai's school said: It would have been better for humans not to have been created, than to have been created.

"Hillel's school said: It is better for humans that they were created, than it would have been had they not been created.

"Finally they voted and it was decided: It would have been better for humans not to have been created. However now that humans have been created, let them examine what they have done in the past [and repent]. Some say: Let them examine what they are about to do [and reconsider]." *(Talmud Eruvin 13b)*

What might the angels think of you and what you have done to restore our faith in the goodness of humanity?

— Levi Lauer,
director of Atzum, fund for terror victims

Making Peace with Friends and Family: *Shalom Bayit*

Marriage with peace is the world's paradise;
With strife, this is life's purgatory.

— Folk Proverb

The Angels of peace do not just come on their own but demand that we make an effort to make our homes tranquil and our relationships more welcoming and validating one of another, thereby deserving their attention. Rabbi Nachman's prayer for peace (at right) sets an important tone for Shabbat eve.

The Messenger from on the Most High has Arrived with Your Very Own Puzzle Piece

On Angels and Messengers*

Each lifetime is the pieces of a jigsaw puzzle.
For some there are more pieces.
For others the puzzle is more difficult to assemble.

Some seem to be born with a nearly completed puzzle.
And so it goes.
Souls going this way and that
Trying to assemble the myriad parts.

But know this. No one has within themselves
All the pieces to their puzzle.
Like before the days when they used to seal
jigsaw puzzles in cellophane insuring that
All the pieces were there.

Everyone carries with them at least one and probably
Many pieces to someone else's puzzle.
Sometimes they know it.
Sometimes they don't.

And when you present your piece
Which is worthless to you,
To another, whether you know it or not,
Whether they know it or not,
You are a messenger from the Most High.

— Lawrence Kushner

* In Hebrew they are the same word.

Rabbi Nachman's Prayer for Shalom

Master of Shalom, Sovereign Possessor of Peace!

Make Shalom among the people of Israel and multiply Peace among all dwellers of the world.

Let there be no more hatred, jealousy, competitiveness and triumphalism between one another. Rather let there be love and great peace among all of us.

Each one will be aware of the love for the other until we are capable of uniting and gathering everyone together.

Then we will talk one with the other and explain the truth one to another.

Master of Shalom, bless us with peace. Amen.

Shalom Aleichem

How Are You?

"Shalom Aleichem" is a daily greeting like "How are you?' Are you at peace? One does not ask mourners at the Shivah, "how are you?" — for we know that they are not at peace and our task is to comfort them. With our everyday acquaintances and family we perfunctorily ask "how are you?' without really waiting for an answer. On Shabbat, however, we have time to find out. During Shabbat make time to really talk with a family member, a friend or a guest. Set aside a private moment when you are listening with your heart, and ask sincerely, "are you at peace?'

Once the Gerer Rebbe decided to question one of his disciples: "How is Moshe Yaakov doing?" The disciple didn't know. "What!" shouted the Rebbe, "You don't know? You pray under the same roof, you study the same texts, you serve the same God, you sing the same songs — and yet you dare tell me that you don't know whether Moshe Yaakov is in good health, whether he needs help, advice or comforting?"

Making Peace with Ourselves: Welcoming the *Neshama Y'teira* and Peace of Mind

You cannot find peace anywhere, save in yourself.

— Rabbi Simcha Bunam

An Onomatopoeia — A Word that Sounds What it Means

It sounds like it means. "Buzz" sounds like it means. So too the word for soul in Hebrew is derived from the word for breathing — *Neshama*. As we welcome the extra Shabbat *Neshama*, pronounce its name slowly and distinctly. Perhaps hold your hand before your mouth to feel the force of your breath when saying the Hebrew *Neshama* or the Latin-based equivalent *Spirit* (as in re-spira-tion, in-spira-tion).

The Psychology of the "Extra Shabbat Soul"

The 20th century rationalist thinker Mordecai Kaplan explained the mystical notion of *Neshama Y'teira* in psychological and poetic terms:

"The sense of enhancement of personality, which the Jew experienced on the Shabbat, gave rise to the tradition of his acquiring on that day a *'neshama y'teira,'* an additional soul."

David Sharir, The Sabbath Queen, 1969

What "additional soul" meant for the Jew is perhaps best set forth by Emerson in his essay on the "Oversoul." "There is a difference," says Emerson, "between one and another hour of life in their authority and subsequent effect. Our faith comes in moments; our vice is habitual. Yet there is a depth in those brief moments which constrains us to ascribe more reality to them than to all other experiences."

What is the Self?

"Adonai formed the human from humus, (Adam from the earth, Adama) and blew into the human's nostrils Nishmat Haim, *the breath of life."* (Genesis 2:7)

You are (like everyone else who is not crazy) a barely coherent hodgepodge of contradictory thoughts, feelings, and deeds. What keeps you "together" is an imaginary center called a "self." The parts may not organize themselves gracefully, but their totality is literally "you." Without a "self" you would literally disintegrate.

We speak about our self as if it were real even though it possesses neither substance nor location. It is precisely the same way with God. God is the self of the universe. To say, "There is a God," is to say that creation has some inner coherence and integrity that can make sense. For this reason, our innermost self and God are related. In the same way, our alienation is self-estrangement and estrangement from God.

The old joke about the madman who thought he was God and explained his delusion by observing that whenever he prayed to God he always wound up talking to himself is more than a joke. Our "self" is the "part" of us we share with God and every other human being, just as it may be what remains of our soul.

— Lawrence Kushner

Tales of Peacemakers

Making Peace with My Creator

A Hassidic story tells of a rebbe who saw that there was, of late, a problem in his relationship with God: there was no peace between himself and his Creator. So he began to reflect more deeply on his life:

First, he discovered that there was also no peace between his people and other nations.

Further there was no peace with fellow Jews.

Further there was no peace with his Hassidim, his students and followers.

Further there was no peace with his wife. Further there was no peace within himself.

So the rebbe made peace with himself. Then he discovered that he could also make peace with his spouse, then with his Hassidim, then even with his whole people. Further he could even make peace with other nations. Finally he discovered that he had made peace between himself and his Creator.

Save Me A Place in Heaven Next to the Jesters

It was in the marketplace that Elijah the prophet often appeared to Rabbi Berokha. Once Rabbi Berokha asked Elijah: Is there anyone in the market who has a share in the world to come? While they were conversing two people passed by and Elijah remarked: Here, these two have a place in the world to come!

Rabbi Berokha approached them and asked: What is your calling? They replied: We are jesters! Whenever we see people who are depressed we try to cheer them up, and whenever we see people quarrelling, we make every effort to make peace between them. *(Talmud Taanit 22a)*

Aaron, the Rabbinic Peacemaker

"Hillel says, 'Be among the followers of Aaron; for Aaron loved shalom and pursued shalom. He loved humanity and brought people close to Torah.'" (Pirkei Avot 1:12)

If two people were feuding, Aaron would walk up to one, sit down next to him and say, "My child, don't you see how much your friend is tearing his heart out and rending his clothes?" The person would then say to him/herself: "How can I lift up my head and look my friend in the face? I would be ashamed to see him; I really have been rotten." Aaron would remain at his/her side until s/he had overcome resentment.

Afterwards, Aaron would walk over to the other person, sit down next to him/her and say: "Don't you see how much your friend is eating his/her heart out and tearing his/her clothes?" And so this person too would think to her/himself: "O, my God! How can I lift up my head and look my friend in the eye. I am too ashamed to see him/her." Aaron would sit with this person too until s/he had overcome resentment. And finally when these two friends met, they embraced and kissed each other. *(Avot d' Rabbi Natan "A" Chapter 12)*

The Hassidic *Shalom Bayit* Kugel

My son told me the following story after I got into a pointless argument with my wife just before candle lighting.

He explained: One hassidic group is known for serving kugel twice on Friday night — at the beginning after Hallah and at the end for dessert. The following tale explains the custom. Once a married couple had terrible fights over the Shabbat Kugel. She complained that he never ate her kugel, which she prepared with such exceptionally rich ingredients according to her mother's recipe. He responded that he in fact loved his wife and loved the kugel but had no room to eat it at the end of the meal. He insisted it be served first as was customary in his parents' home while she insisted it be served as dessert as her family did.

The rebbe weighed this difficult matter — so small and yet so irritating to their Shabbat tranquility. He ordered that the Shabbat kugel be served twice at the meal both immediately after Hallah and immediately before *Birkat Hamazon*. Thereafter it was known fondly as the *Shalom Bayit* Kugel that is eaten in such a way as to maximize peace between family members.

— Noam Zion

A Holy Spirit Open to All Who Earn It

I [God] call heaven and earth to bear witness that whether one is a Jew or a Gentile, a male or a female slave, everyone — according to the merit of one's deeds — can have the holy spirit rest on them. *(Elijah Rabbah 9)*

Shalom Aleichem

"This was the child I prayed for." (I Samuel 1:27)
Hannah brings her son Samuel to the High
Priest Eli to begin his service to God.
Frank W. W. Topham, late 19th century.

Believe in a love that is being
stored up for you like
an inheritance,
and have faith that in
this love
there is a strength and a
blessing so large
that you can travel as far
as you wish
without having to step
outside it.

— Rainer Marie Rilke

Blessing our children is loving
their best selves as their
true inner selves.

— Mordechai Gafni

Who of us is mature enough
for offspring before the
offspring themselves
arrive? The value of
marriage is not that
adults produce children
but that children produce
adults.

— Peter de Vries

בִּרְכַּת בָּנִים

Birkat Banim

blessing our children — and one another

Blessing Children

For a boy or man of any age:		
MAY GOD MAKE YOU	**יְשִׂמְךָ אֱלֹהִים**	Y'sim-kha Elohim
like Ephraim and Menashe.	כְּאֶפְרַיִם וְכִמְנַשֶּׁה.	k'Ephraim v-khi-Menashe.
For a girl or woman of any age:		
MAY GOD MAKE YOU	**יְשִׂמֵךְ אֱלֹהִים**	Y'si-meikh Elohim
like Sarah, Rivka, Rachel and Leah.	כְּשָׂרָה רִבְקָה רָחֵל וְלֵאָה.	k'Sarah, Rivka, Rachel, v-Leah.
For all:		
MAY ADONAI BLESS YOU and guard you.	**יְבָרֶכְךָ יְיָ** וְיִשְׁמְרֶךָ.	Y'va-re-kh'kha Adonai v-yish-m'rekha.
May Adonai's face shine on you	יָאֵר יְיָ פָּנָיו אֵלֶיךָ	Ya-er Adonai panav ei-lekha
and be gracious unto you.	וִיחֻנֶּךָּ.	vi-khun-e-ka.
May Adonai's face smile at you	יִשָּׂא יְיָ פָּנָיו אֵלֶיךָ	Yisa Adonai panav ei-lekha
and grant you peace.	וְיָשֵׂם לְךָ שָׁלוֹם.	v-yasem lekha Shalom.

1. PLACE your hands on the head of a child.
2. RECITE the blessings, as appropriate for a boy or a girl.
3. REPEAT for each child.

Acknowledging Our Blessings for this Week

Invite the guests at the table to report on some good news, *Besorot Tovot*, that they wish to share. Afterwards recite together the *bracha* for reaching a special occasion:

Blessed are You, Adonai,	**בָּרוּךְ** אַתָּה יְיָ	Barukh ata Adonai
our God, Ruler of the Universe,	אֱלֹהֵינוּ מֶלֶךְ הָעוֹלָם	Eloheinu Melekh ha-olam
who has kept us alive,	שֶׁהֶחֱיָנוּ וְקִיְּמָנוּ	Sheh-heh-kh'yanu v'ki-y'manu
and brought us to this moment.	וְהִגִּיעָנוּ לַזְּמַן הַזֶּה.	v'hi-gee-anu la-z'man ha-zeh.

"Jacob kissed and hugged his grandchildren. 'I never expected to see your face again, Joseph, and now God has shown me your offspring.'" (*Genesis 48:11*)

Rembrandt van Rijn, Jacob Blessing his Grandchildren Ephraim and Menashe, the sons of Joseph. (Holland, 1656)

Renewing Connections

> Whether a person really loves God can be determined by the love that person shares with others.
>
> — Rebbe Levi Yitzchak of Berditchev

Shabbat at home is about reinforcing our relationships — with our spiritual selves and with the Divine, with the Creation of nature and with all we have created during the week. Yet first and foremost it is about renewing our deep connection with our family and friends — with our parents, our siblings and our children, and all those with whom we have chosen to share our lives. That is the concept of *Shalom Bayit,* making peace at home, an essential part of the sanctity of the day. It was only natural that Shabbat became a day for blessing one's children and an occasion to offer our blessings to others close to us.

Blessing one's children was ordained in the Torah, when Jacob gave two of his grandchildren and then twelve of his children a personalized blessing. In the Middle Ages it became customary on Yom Kippur eve for parents to bless their children before *Kol Nidrei.* That is a time when we are all particularly aware of our mortality and our need to leave a legacy to the next generation as well as to make our peace with those whom we may have hurt. In recent centuries many parents have begun to bless their children on every Shabbat and holiday eve. Using the words of the priestly benediction they place both hands on the head of each child.

For that reason, it is a time of particular poignancy — and sometimes pain — for those without children, or whose children are far away physically or emotionally. With that in mind, we have offered ways to expand the circle of blessing along with the traditional practice of blessing one's children. One may bless friends and students and pray for the blessing of healing.

Blessing Children

> There are only two lasting bequests we can hope to give our children. One of these is roots; the other, wings.
>
> — attributed to many authors

Mi Sheh-bei-rakh מִי שֶׁבֵּרַךְ

Mi-sheh-bei-rakh avoteinu
M'kor habrakha l'imoteinu
May the source of strength
Who blessed the ones before us
Help us find the courage
To make our lives a blessing
And let us say, Amen.

Mi-sheh-bei-rakh imoteinu
M'kor habrakha l'avoteinu
Bless those in need of healing
With *r'fu-a sh'leima*
The renewal of body
The renewal of spirit
And let us say, Amen.

— Debbie Friedman

A Prayer for Healing

While Shabbat is not traditionally a time to dwell on our needs and to make requests from God, it has become a universal practice to ask for Divine blessing for those in need of physical and emotional healing. Similarly, while no mourning is permitted, comforting the mourner is a mitzvah on Shabbat. At this point at the beginning of our meal when parents often bless their children, we may ask for God's blessing for all those in need. Debbie Friedman's version of that blessing offers a musical expression of that prayer. It allows us an occasion to share our concern for those whose illness may mean that they cannot join us for this Shabbat dinner. After reciting the request for God's blessing, the appropriate greeting is **R'fuah Shlemah** *— "May there be a complete recovery!"*

Logo at right by Dan Reisinger
for the Israeli Society for the Protection of Children

א Guidelines

getting started

How do I initiate my family into the practice of blessing our children?

Shabbat dinner at home is the ideal time to show love for friends and children — in words and in physical gestures. Eating is not the only physical need we have to fill. We also long for touching our loved ones and offering them emotional nourishment.

For Children and Grandchildren: Shabbat dinner is a magnificent time to celebrate and express love for our children and grandchildren. Younger children are very appreciative of being stroked or having us lay our hands on their head for a blessing; adolescents, however, may prefer maintaining distance and avoiding intimacy especially at the table. If you feel awkward blessing older children, try to explain the idea in advance, but try not to put them on the spot at the table. Some children are very reluctant to try new things, so do not force them, but start with the ones ready to join in.

Lay your hands on their head and recite a blessing in Hebrew or English (and perhaps add a personal blessing or read an appropriate quote). The blessing can be given whenever you like — at candle lighting, after Shalom Aleichem, or after Kiddush before hand washing.

In formulating a personal blessing, you may wish to acknowledge what you most admire in your child or express a particular wish for that child. Some blessings must remain in our hearts — unsaid, lest they embarrass the children. Often they are conveyed in a whisper with or without the Hebrew priestly benediction. Persevere one way or another for a month and the blessing for children can become an accepted (and expected) part of your Shabbat.

יהדות
בדרכי נועם
ובנתיבות שלום

Haim Ron, Priestly Hands of Benediction,
from *Midrasha L'Moreshet Hayahadut* of MK Menahem HaCohen, Old City of Jerusalem

When children or grandparents are not home: A parent or grandparent whose children and grandchildren are not present may feel particularly emotional at this moment. Yet they can use it to create a positive (if long distance) moment of intimacy. Sometimes children leave and will not stay for Shabbat dinner, so my wife is careful to bless each child before they leave the house or to call them on Friday and bless them by telephone. One grandparent tells his young grandchildren that wherever they may be in the world, they can look up and see the same moon that their grandparents see. The grandchildren should know that every Friday night as they look up at the moon, or at the Kiddush cup on the Shabbat table, their grandparents will be sending them their blessings. Develop your own family customs like a particular *niggun* or melody you whistle every Shabbat when blessing the children.

Guidelines

parent-child corner

Some families make this intimate weekly moment of blessing their children into a "secret communication." The mother picks one special quality or behavior of her children in the last week and whispers to them her praise for them. But no one else is allowed to hear the secret admirer.

Other families, whose children or nephews and nieces are far away, call them before candle lighting to give them a blessing via the telephone. E-mail blessings with virtual flowers or singing messages can also follow our globetrotting relatives around the globe every Shabbat.

Younger children like to imitate their parents by putting their own hands on the head of the parent and offering their own version of the blessing.

A wonderful story about his four-year old daughter is told by a Jewish educator from Canada who spent many months a year working in Russia with the newly liberated Soviet Jews. He would loyally call home every Friday afternoon to pronounce the blessing over the phone. Spontaneously his daughter would put the receiver on her head to simulate her father's hands that would otherwise have rested on her head.

Jacob Blesses His Grandchildren, by Bencjon Benn, *Visions of the Bible*, 1954

"May God's Face Shine Upon You"

We are the object of God's gaze, but this means more than just that God is looking at us. God's shining face is an open face; it inspires openness in us, the object of the gaze. Being open creates possibilities, the possibility for a true I-Thou encounter, a spiritual connection with God.

Along with this closeness goes the knowledge of each other and a potential for mutual inspiration. The image of two lovers looking at each other comes to mind or of a mother gazing lovingly at her child. These images not only evoke feelings of intimacy but also a sense of safety, of being protected by the one whose face and love shine on us.

— Sabine Y. Meyer

The Rabbi's Blessing, by Moritz Daniel Oppenheim (Germany, c. 1866)

Reflections כַּוָּנוֹת

extending the circle of blessing beyond the children at the table

The Torah channels God's blessings through the priests — *Kohanim* — who were originally to recite those words and invoke God's name only in the place where God's name will be mentioned — in the Temple. However, since the Middle Ages parents have taken over priestly roles as have synagogue rabbis, who often bless their congregations using those words. Human beings have the power to call down Divine favor on those they love and on those whose behavior evokes praise and blessing. Neither the giver nor the recipient of our good wishes need be restricted to the parent-child relationship. One Hillel rabbi on a college campus used to bless all the students at the Shabbat table one at a time. He explained that he was the parent away from home, in loco parentis, even if not all the parents were accustomed to bless their children in that way. Some grandparents, uncomfortable with the traditional Hebrew, express their blessing in their own words.

To Bless Each Other in God's Name

The Kabbalists believe that every one has a special spark, a potential uniquely their own — a special blessing and destiny to cultivate. At the Shabbat table, commenting on someone's special gifts can be the basis of our personalized blessings for each other. This is one way to welcome each person into the circle of the Shabbat table. The host warmly greets each of the guests and introduces them by acknowledging the blessings they have brought to the world and in particular to this table.

Not only parents and children may find Shabbat a time for blessing. As in the days of Ruth and Boaz, everyone is invited to bless one another in the name of God. They too can cite a quality which they recognize in those sharing the Shabbat meal with them. For example, Boaz said to Ruth:

"I have been told about all you did for your mother-in-law after the death of your husband and how you left your father and mother and the land of your birth and came to join a people whom you had not previously known. May the Lord reward your deeds and may you have all you deserve from the God under whose wings you have sought refuge." (Ruth 2:11-12)

Acknowledging Qualities of Others that Surpass my Own

I never met persons in whom I failed to recognize some quality superior to myself.

If they were older, I said they had done more good than I; if they were younger, I said they had committed far less wrongs than I. If richer, I said they had given far more Tzedakah; if poorer, I said they had suffered more. If wiser, I paid them honor for their wisdom; if not wiser, I said their faults should be judged less severely. Take this to heart, my son.

— *Judah ben Jehiel Asher's Ethical Will (1250-1327)*

Adopt a Child or "Rent a Grandparent"

At Shabbat dinner my 82-year-old father, "Opa" Moshe Sachs loves to offer any of the younger guests (younger than 82) his priestly benediction along with his biological children and grandchildren. Many "children" of all ages whose parents are not at the table enjoy taking him up on the offer and even call him "Opa" (grandfather, in Dutch).

On his grandson's bar mitzvah he gave a sermon to his congregation, which has many retired members but few grandchildren. He proposed they begin a "Rent a Grandparent" program for the sake of both children and the elderly whose corresponding biological grandparents or grandchildren do not live in the same city.

— Noam Zion

Hello God!

Calling out "the name" is evoked world over in greetings. The Spanish hello — *"olah"* — originated in Arab Spain from the term *"O'Allah"* — Allah of course being the Arab appellation of God. In Austrian German they say *"Gruss Gott."* In Hebrew, the common response when asked how you are doing is *"Barukh Hashem"* — Praise God, or Thank God. The Hebrew greeting *"Shalom"* is actually a name of God. In English, we still follow this custom when we part from someone and say "God speed" or "God be with you."

— Mordechai Gafni, *The Mystery of Love*

Bless your Students

The Talmud considers all one's students to be one's children. In fact, the teacher-student, mentor-apprentice relationship,

"May God raise her to Torah, to Huppah (the wedding canopy), and to a life of good deeds." (Traditionally this blessing is used for boys at their circumcision.)
A Wimpel — A Birth Wrapping by Marcelle Zion for her daughter Eden Zion, Jerusalem, 1988

takes priority over the biological parent-child relationship, for a spiritual mentor helps us give re-birth to ourselves as adolescents and as adults.

Therefore anyone who has taught anything significant to another, even just one letter of the alphabet, is honored as a teacher. Therefore it would not be too bold to suggest that anyone who has taught someone some wisdom for life may take on the priestly and parental prerogative to bless his students at the Shabbat table.

For the Child without a Parent

After overcoming our denial and redefining ourselves, we must then attempt to conquer the most insidious emotion that our misfortunes may be produced within us: envy.

It's easy and natural to feel envious when you are in pain and your friends are not. It's difficult not to be bitter when you are suffering from a serious illness, wondering whether you will live or die, and your friends are healthy, unburdened by such worries. When your business is failing and you're struggling just to make ends meet, it's hard to like your friends who are succeeding. When you have spent years long praying that you will find love, marriage, and babies and your friends are happily married with a brood of children, it's almost impossible to wish them well. The same is true when you have lost a loved one and your friends have never experienced that level of grief and loss.

When I was in high school, after my father's death, my friend Susan invited me to sleep over at her house on a Friday night. We played piano, sang and gossiped for hours. Her mother was cooking the Sabbath dinner, and the sumptuous smell of roast chicken and onions filled the air. Then her father arrived, and we were summoned to the dinner table . . . We lit the Sabbath candles and stood up as Susan's dad recited the blessing over the wine. I had forgotten what it felt like to have a father's presence at the dinner table. At my home, the responsibility of presiding over all the Sabbath blessings had fallen on me. Afterward Susan's father hugged her, kissed her lovingly on top of her head, and said, "Good Shabbas to you, my little angel." I could see that Susan was embarrassed. In my presence she wanted to seem adult and mature, yet her father was treating her like a little girl. She rolled her eyes at me, the way teenagers do, as if to say, "I'm so above this childishness." But I could have given anything to have my father's hug and kiss once more. At that moment my heart was filled with envy. My eyes started to fill up with tears, but I bit my bottom lip until the hurt passed.

— Naomi Levy

Blessing One's Children on Shabbat Evening, by Moritz Daniel Oppenheim (Germany, c. 1866)

For the Adult without Children

Blessing one's children and grandchildren on Shabbat is a moment of intimacy but also one of longing both for those whose children are far away or have passed away and for those without children. The medieval Hassidim of Ashkenaz (GERMANY, 13TH CENTURY) were particularly sensitive to the feelings of those vulnerable. In Yehuda HeHasid's book *Sefer Hasidim* (section 102) the following tale is told based on an ancient Jewish custom still widely practiced in Afro-Asian families that when the father completes an *aliyah* to the Torah, his children congratulate him by kissing his hands and giving him a hug.

"In a particular city a father commanded his son not to kiss him after his *aliyah* to the Torah, for there were many people there without children and he did not want them to suffer anguish. Similarly, if someone's young son or daughter has passed away, leaving them no other small children, then other parents should not parade their own young children before the bereaved at a time close to the bereavement, lest it cause them to remember their sorrow."

Baby Moshe Protected by his Sister Miriam and his Mother Yocheved, by Simeon Solomon, 1866, England.

A Contemporary Blessing: May You Be Yourself

The custom of blessing one's children on the eve of the Shabbat and holidays is an especially tender moment in Jewish ritual life. The actual content of the blessing, however, is puzzling. Based on words said by Jacob to his grandsons in Genesis 48:20, it asks God to make the male child like Ephraim and Menashe; an adaptation for girls asks that they be like the foremothers Sarah, Rebecca, Rachel and Leah. Why Ephraim and Menashe, one cannot help but wonder — indeed, why any particular ancestors at all? In its specificity, this blessing seems restrictive rather than expansive: it doesn't open out to the range of possibility and promise that ought to characterize youth.

I am reminded, in this context, of the famous Hassidic story about the righteous Rabbi Zusya:

"One day his disciples found him weeping and they asked him why. Rabbi Zusya explained that he trembled at the thought of being asked at the end of his life, as he approached the gates of heaven, not the question, 'Zusya, why were you not Moses?' but 'Zusya, why were you not Zusya?'"

It doesn't seem from this story that Zusya would have been at peace having lived the life of Ephraim or Menasheh — and why should we expect that he would?

Indeed, why should we wish for a child to be anything other than her or his best self? Not living one's own life, not being true to the unique configuration of gifts and potential that nourish the self from within-is a tragedy. Yet letting a child be herself, himself — letting go of expectations that do not emerge from the reality of who the child is — is one of the hardest lessons parents have to learn. So once a week, at the onset of the Sabbath just after lighting the Sabbath candles, I remind myself gently, as I kiss my son's hair, what it is I really want for him. "Abraham Gilead," I say, "be who you are, heyeyh asher tihyeh." The Hebrew words deliberately echo the biblical voice of divinity announcing (IN EXODUS 3:14) *ehyeh asher ehyeh*, "I am that I am," which I understand as the ultimate expression — the very model — of authentic being.

— *MARCIA FALK*

The Ritual of Touch: Laying on of Hands

There are two ways to check for a fever. One is with a thermometer. The other is to rest your hand or lips against a warm forehead. Both methods are fairly accurate. But one leaves us with nothing more than a number. The other leaves us with the seeds of healing.

That touch conveys so much more than a simple temperature reading: it conveys the power of comfort, the assurance that all will be well. That loving touch, all by itself, makes us feel a little better.

Once, in a university class I was teaching on spirituality, I asked my students to tell me about the most powerful religious experience they'd ever had. Before I even completed my sentence, one man in my class called out, "That's easy." He told us that his son had been born in critical condition and had immediately been placed in the neonatal intensive care unit. The student explained that he had always promised himself that if God ever gave him a child, he would bless his child every Sabbath eve. Well, it was Friday night, and my student knew what he needed to do. He walked into the neonatal ICU and stared at his tiny, vulnerable son lying before him. The doctors couldn't tell if the boy was going to live or die. The man knelt over his baby's crib, placed his big hands over his child's little head, and uttered the words of the priestly blessing: "May God bless you and watch over you. May God's countenance shine upon you and offer you grace. May God's presence be with you and grant you peace."

The student suddenly shuddered and once again seemed to be at with all of us in the class. It was as if he were waking up from a nightmare. Then he said, "That's it. That was the most incredible religious experience I've ever had."

If you have never laid your hands in blessing upon your child or upon anyone you love, try it. You cannot imagine the love that is transferred at the moment. If you have never been blessed by someone's hands, ask someone to do it. The feeling is extraordinary. Physical connection between human beings is like a bridge that transfers holiness and healing from one person to another.

We can't cure illness with our touch, but we can bring healing and comfort and blessing. With a touch we can also mend differences, resentments, and hatred. When there is deep estrangement between friends or family members, sometimes words are of no use. We find ourselves arguing the same points over and over again. But an embrace can convey the love that lies beyond all the bickering and miscommunication. We don't have to love our enemies in order to make peace with them, but we do have to be willing to extend a hand, a touch.

— *Naomi Levy*

"The long-barren Rachel kissing her first-born Joseph," by Abel Pann, Jerusalem, 20th century. (Mayanot Gallery and Itiel Pann).

Three things have delighted me and they are desirable before God and humans:

(1) the bonds of brotherhood

(2) the fondness of friends

(3) and man and woman for they achieve completeness.

— *Ben Sira 25:1, second century BCE, Eretz Yisrael*

Love at First Sight: Jacob and Rachel, by Harry Milcham (d. 1957)

שִׁיר הַשִּׁירִים and/or אֵשֶׁת חַיִל

Song of Songs — renewing our love

Eishet Hayil — praising a strong woman

One who loves brings God and the world together.

— MARTIN BUBER

Introduction

Renewing our Love (with the *Song of Songs*) or Honoring the Home-maker (with *Eishet Hayil*)

The Shabbat evening ritual script may include three types of love and appreciation: *Song of Songs, Eishet Hayil* (both ancient Biblical poems adapted in the medieval era to express affection between loving partners on Friday night) and a contemporary prayer for a loving family.

1. **Solomon's Song of Love** *(see page 59)*. Selections from the Biblical *Song of Songs* may be recited as a verbal renewal of one's love. For a couple, here is the chance to reaffirm formally their love for one another and the sanctity of their mutal commitment, something too often taken for granted in the course of a busy week. While the tradition of the Middle Ages had a married couple in mind, this poem may also serve to confirm committed love between partners not officially married. After all, the orginal *Song of Songs* describes a wondrous loving relationship in the fields, not in a middle class family seated around the table.

2. ***Eishet Hayil*** *(see page 61)*. This second Biblical poem literally, "in praise of a strong and accomplished woman," was adapted for use on Friday nights by the 16th century mystical tradition of Safed. They directed this earthly poem to the Divine Feminine presence, the *Shekhina*, but they also included the woman homemaker as the Shekhina's earthly embodiment in our world.

   As gender roles change and what was once a compliment may become an insult, some women do not want this traditional praise. Sometimes the women are no longer the primary homemakers. Sometimes they may still be the chief cook and bottle washer, but they do not think that a role to be praised. The Rabbis recognize that the one who is honored has the right to forego gestures of respect and deference as long as they are offered by the ones who need to be appreciative. Let the homemaker — male or female — decide whether to recite *Eishet Hayil* or to prefer the *Song of Songs*.

3. **A Family Prayer: To Love and To Care** *(see page 59)*. A final option that avoids the gender question is a contemporary prayer in thanks to God for a loving family.

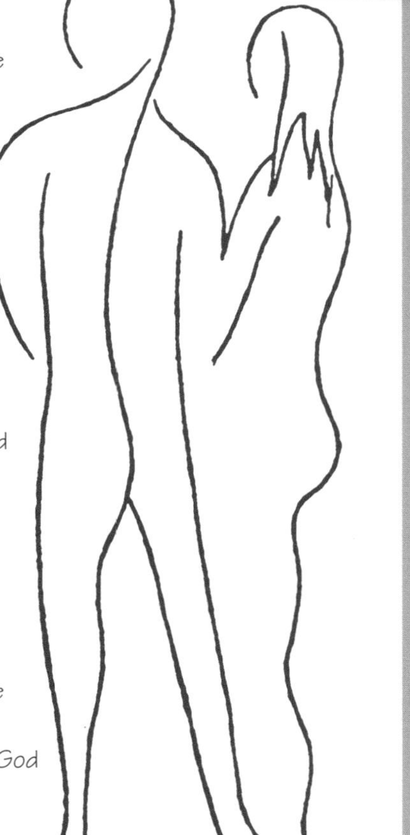

"Therefore a man will leave his father and mother and hold onto his wife and they become one flesh." GENESIS 2:24

by Benecjon Benn, *Visions of the Bible*, 1954

Marc Chagall, Lovers on the Promenade, 1917, © ADAGP Paris 2004

Shir haShirim

Solomon's Song of Songs — Renewing our love

Songs from the Tanakh for my Partner in Love

A couple recites together or responsively:

I AM COMMITTED TO MY BELOVED	אֲנִי לְדוֹדִי	Ani l'dodi
and my beloved is committed to me.	וְדוֹדִי לִי.	v'dodi li.

— Song of Songs 6:3

One might also add the most beautiful Biblical verse of marital commitment composed by the prophet Hosea.
He uses the human ceremony of engagement to represent God's renewed love and loyalty to Israel after a period of estrangement:

I WILL BE ENGAGED TO YOU FOREVER	וְאֵרַשְׂתִּיךְ לִי לְעוֹלָם
I will engage you by living the qualities of justice and equity,	וְאֵרַשְׂתִּיךְ לִי בְּצֶדֶק וּבְמִשְׁפָּט
by a life of kindness and mercy.	וּבְחֶסֶד וּבְרַחֲמִים.
I will engage you by a life of faithfulness	וְאֵרַשְׂתִּיךְ לִי בֶּאֱמוּנָה
And then you will know God.	וְיָדַעַתְּ אֶת יהוה.

— Hosea 2:21-22

A Blessing for One's Beloved

I love the light in your eyes, the smell of your hair, the sound of your voice. I love the goodness in your heart and the kindness of your deeds. I love our conversations, our home, the family we have created together. I love you. You are a blessing from God.

May God bless you, as you have blessed me, with joy and light and love. Amen.

— *Naomi Levy (from Talking to God)*

A Family Prayer: To Love and To Care

We thank You, God, for our family and for what we mean and bring to one another. We are grateful for the bonds of loyalty and affection which sustain us, and which keep us close to one another no matter how far apart we may be.

We thank You for implanting within us a deep need for each other, and for giving us the capacity to love and to care.

Help us be modest in our demands of one another, but generous in our giving to each other. May we never measure how much love or encouragement we offer; may we never count the times we forgive. Rather, may we always be grateful that we have one another and that we are able to express our love in acts of kindness.

Keep us gentle in our speech. When we offer words of criticism, may they be chosen with care and spoken softly. May we waste no opportunity to speak words of sympathy, of appreciation, of praise.

Bless our family with health, happiness, and contentment. Above all, grant us the wisdom to build a joyous and peaceful home in which your spirit will always abide.

— *from Sydney Greenberg, Likrat Shabbat*

Although I conquer
all the earth,

Yet for me there is
only one city.

In that city
there is for me
only one house;

And in that house,
one room only;

And in that room,
a bed.

And one woman
sleeps there,

The shining joy
and jewel of all
my kingdom.

— *Sanskrit poem*

A Modern Woman of Valor,
Israeli paratrooper.
Photo by David Perlmutter.

Eishet Hayil — 22 biblical women of valor

Praising a strong and accomplished woman

BY MOSHE SILBERSCHEIN AND NOAM ZION

אֵשֶׁת חַיִל

"Just as God gave the Torah to Israel using all 22 letters of the alphabet, so God praised worthy women with 22 letters."

— *Rabbi Yitzchak bar Nachmani, Yalkut Shimoni*

	MIDRASHIC ASSOCIATIONS		
א	**Naamah**, Noah's wife, mother of humankind	What a rare find is a woman of valor — Her worth is far beyond that of rubies.	אֵשֶׁת חַיִל מִי יִמְצָא, וְרָחֹק מִפְּנִינִים מִכְרָהּ.
ב	**Sarah**	Her husband puts his confidence in her, And lacks no fortune.	בָּטַח בָּהּ לֵב בַּעְלָהּ, וְשָׁלָל לֹא יֶחְסָר.
ג	**Rebecca**[1] or **Tsipora** Moshe's wife	She repays his good favors, but never his harm All the days of her life.	גְּמָלַתְהוּ טוֹב וְלֹא רָע, כֹּל יְמֵי חַיֶּיהָ.
ד	**Leah**	She seeks out wool and flax And sets her hand to them willingly.	דָּרְשָׁה צֶמֶר וּפִשְׁתִּים, וַתַּעַשׂ בְּחֵפֶץ כַּפֶּיהָ.
ה	**Rachel**	She is like a merchant fleet Bringing her food from afar.	הָיְתָה כָּאֳנִיּוֹת סוֹחֵר, מִמֶּרְחָק תָּבִיא לַחְמָהּ.
ו	**Bitya** Pharaoh's Daughter	She rises while it is still night, and supplies provisions for her household, The daily fare of her maids.	וַתָּקָם בְּעוֹד לַיְלָה, וַתִּתֵּן טֶרֶף לְבֵיתָהּ וְחֹק לְנַעֲרוֹתֶיהָ.
ז	**Yocheved** Moshe's Mother	She sets her mind on an estate and acquires it; She plants a vineyard by her own labors.	זָמְמָה שָׂדֶה וַתִּקָּחֵהוּ, מִפְּרִי כַּפֶּיהָ נָטְעָה כָּרֶם.
ח	**Miriam** Moshe's Sister	She girds her loins with strength; Her limbs she applies to the task with resolve.	חָגְרָה בְעוֹז מָתְנֶיהָ, וַתְּאַמֵּץ זְרוֹעֹתֶיהָ.
ט	**Hannah** or **Tamar**	Her good judgement makes her business thrive; Her lamp never goes out at night.	טָעֲמָה כִּי טוֹב סַחְרָהּ, לֹא יִכְבֶּה בַּלַּיְלָה נֵרָהּ.

Continued on page 63 →

1 Rebecca's verse means *"the good wife returns good for good but does not hold a grudge and revenge a husband's negative behavior in kind."*

The Four Matriarchs by A. Calderon and M. Prague (1977). Courtesy of the Israeli Philatelic Society.

Ray Frank (1861-1948)
first woman to preach in synagogue

Gertrude Weil (1879-1971)
suffragist and social reformer

Justine Wise Polier (1903-1987)
New York State Family Court Justice and child advocate

Ten modern-day women of valor

A 20th century gallery

from the files of the Jewish Women's Archive www.jwa.org

Jewish Women's Archive
jwa.org
where history lives and grows

Henrietta Szold (1860-1945)
pioneering Zionist and founder of Hadassah, the Women's Zionist Organization of America

Bella Abzug (1920-1998)
activist and Congresswoman,
© by Dorothy Marder.

Hannah Senesh (1921-1944)
Israeli poet, halutz and parachutist who was tortured and killed by Nazis in Budapest

Bobbie Rosenfeld (1904-1969)
Olympic athlete in track and field, Canada's Sports Hall of Fame

Anna Sokolow (1910-2000)
modern dancer and choreographer

Gertrude Elion (1918-1999)
Nobel Prize in medicine

Emma Goldman (1869-1940)
radical activist

2. Michal is known for saving her husband David from her father King Saul, when Saul sent his soldiers to capture and subsequently execute David (I Samuel 19:12). Thus she proved her love as well as her ingenuity and courage. But Michal was also unique in rebuking her husband in public when she thought he was besmirching the dignity of the anointed king by dancing wildly before the women of Israel during the procession of the ark to Jerusalem. She is also known among the Rabbis as the first woman to wear Tefillin (Midrash Hagadol on Proverbs 31). Other women followed in her footsteps in 13th century Ashkenaz and Italy and again in the modern period.
3. Rashi explains that the clothes she weaves make her husband well-known.
4. Serach bat Asher, Jacob's granddaughter, is regarded like Elijah as a figure who never dies and carries good tidings and secret traditions from generation to generation.
5. The prophet Ovadya 's wife is otherwise unknown; however there were prophetesses like Hulda.
6. The great woman of Shunem was wealthy and generous. She supported the prophet Elisha who then brought her news that she would finally have a child. When later the son had a medical emergency, Elisha cured the child. (II Kings 4:8ff)

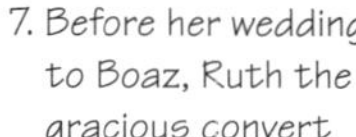

7. Before her wedding to Boaz, Ruth the gracious convert to Judaism, King David's great grandmother-to-be, was blessed by the people of Bethlehem and called an *Eishet Hayil*: "May the Lord make the woman who is coming into your house like Rachel and Leah, both of whom built the house of Israel. Be strong and accomplished/Hayil!..." (Ruth 4:11)

Eishet Hayil — A Woman of Valor

Continued from page 61

י	**Yael** Sisera's assassin	She extends her hands to spin yarn Her palms support the spindle.	יָדֶיהָ שִׁלְּחָה בַכִּישׁוֹר, וְכַפֶּיהָ תָּמְכוּ פָלֶךְ.
כ	**Naomi** Ruth's mother-in-law	She spreads out her palm to the poor; She extends her hands to the needy.	כַּפָּהּ פָּרְשָׂה לֶעָנִי, וְיָדֶיהָ שִׁלְּחָה לָאֶבְיוֹן.
ל	**Rahab** Jericho's prostitute	She does not fear for her household in the face of snow, For her entire household is dressed in crimson.	לֹא תִירָא לְבֵיתָהּ מִשָּׁלֶג, כִּי כָל בֵּיתָהּ לָבֻשׁ שָׁנִים.
מ	**Bathsheba**	She makes warm clothes for herself; Her clothing is linen and purple.	מַרְבַדִּים עָשְׂתָה לָּהּ, שֵׁשׁ וְאַרְגָּמָן לְבוּשָׁהּ.
נ	**Michal**[2] Saul's daughter	Her (well-dressed[3]) husband is well-known in the city gates, As he sits among the elders of the land.	נוֹדָע בַּשְּׁעָרִים בַּעְלָהּ, בְּשִׁבְתּוֹ עִם זִקְנֵי אָרֶץ.
ס	**Hatslelponi** Samson's mother	She makes cloth and sells it, And offers a sash to the merchant.	סָדִין עָשְׂתָה וַתִּמְכֹּר, וַחֲגוֹר נָתְנָה לַכְּנַעֲנִי.
ע	**Elisheba** Aaron's wife	She is clothed in strength and majesty; She looks to the future cheerfully.	עֹז וְהָדָר לְבוּשָׁהּ, וַתִּשְׂחַק לְיוֹם אַחֲרוֹן.
פ	**Serach Bat Asher**[4]	She opens her mouth in wisdom And teaching (a Torah) of kindness is on her tongue.	פִּיהָ פָּתְחָה בְחָכְמָה, וְתוֹרַת חֶסֶד עַל לְשׁוֹנָהּ.
צ	**Ovadiya's wife**[5]	She oversees the ways of her household And never eats the bread of idleness.	צוֹפִיָּה הֲלִיכוֹת בֵּיתָהּ, וְלֶחֶם עַצְלוּת לֹא תֹאכֵל.
ק	**The Wealthy Woman of Shunem**[6]	Her children rise to honor her; Her husband praises her.	קָמוּ בָנֶיהָ וַיְאַשְּׁרוּהָ, בַּעְלָהּ וַיְהַלְלָהּ.
ר	**Ruth**[7]	Many women have shown valor (Hayil), But you surpass them all.	רַבּוֹת בָּנוֹת עָשׂוּ חָיִל, וְאַתְּ עָלִית עַל כֻּלָּנָה.
ש	**Vashti**	Grace is deceptive, beauty is ephemeral; A woman of piety is to be praised.	שֶׁקֶר הַחֵן וְהֶבֶל הַיֹּפִי, אִשָּׁה יִרְאַת יְיָ הִיא תִתְהַלָּל.
ת	**Esther**	Credit her for the fruit of her hands, And in the city gates let her works praise her.	תְּנוּ לָהּ מִפְּרִי יָדֶיהָ, וִיהַלְלוּהָ בַשְּׁעָרִים מַעֲשֶׂיהָ.

Controversial Faces of *Eishet Hayil*

During the six days of the work week, the public realm dominates. But on Shabbat we come home. We gather around the table. Traditionally, the woman — mother, wife, home organizer and emotional ballast — was the one who held the household together. Even today, multi-tasking Jewish professional women often remain the mainstay of the home while also working outside the home. Sometimes a mother holds her far-flung family together simply by keeping each member in mind, tracking their locations like UPS tracks packages sent from place to place. Being "my brother's keeper" may begin with this concern for the whereabouts and hence the welfare of one's biological family. Homes do not just happen; they are made. Thus if the woman still fills this anchoring role in one's life and grants the family inner peace and security, it is most appropriate to use at least part of *Eishet Hayil* to express appreciation for that.

Eishet Hayil honors her for her economic contribution and her organizational skills inside and outside the home (while the husband is not described as a breadwinnner at all). While a woman should not be reduced or restricted to such roles, she may be honored for the ones she fulfills. These are essential roles not to be denigrated. They model for children an appreciation of all that is done to create a warm supportive home in which to mature. However, many modern women reject the workaholic "superman" model. Note: the Israeli version of "Wonder Woman" is called *"Eishet Hayil."*

Obviously, in many contemporary households, men serve these essential homemaking roles happily and comfortably. They are *Ish Hayil* just as women may be *Eishet Hayil.* Both terms are associated with a general strength typical of dignified men and women. That is why a few contemporary ritual innovators have suggested hymns to the man of the house.

Guidelines

getting started

Should I initiate the recitation of *Eishet Hayil* in my household?

Some people do not like the stereotypical views of the woman praised in the biblical poem, usually translated as the "Woman of Valor." A closer reading of the poem might change their minds, but there is no reason to force this issue since, unlike Kiddush over the wine and *HaMotzi* over Hallah, *Eishet Hayil* is simply a poem. Its use on Shabbat began only in the last 400 hundred years, usually in circles influenced by Jewish mysticism, who regarded it as praise for the Divine woman — the Shabbat Queen — not necessarily for the woman of the house.

You may wish to use *Eishet Hayil* or other readings to set aside a few minutes at the Friday night table to honor Jewish women in general or the homemaker of the house in particular (who has often worked very hard cooking this meal and performing other unsung domestic tasks).

Singing the whole of *Eishet Hayil* itself may be quite a challenge both for one's Hebrew pronunciation skills as well as musical ability. Furthermore with little children at home, the length of *Eishet Hayil* may be an obstacle. Pragmatically, my father used to reduce his expression of appreciation to my mother to one line adapted from the opening verse: "A woman of valor? I have found her!" Some families sing merely the first or last verse. One innovative family sings each of the alphabetized verses that spell out the wife/mother's name.

— Noam Zion

A Yiddish Cupid — New Year's Card, Warsaw-New York, 1920s

Guidelines

parent-child corner

Happy Mother's Day

One's mother and father as well may be honored as persons of valor, especially by young children. One father in Atlanta asks each child to recount one thing that their mother has done for them each week.

Remarking on a Remarkable Woman

Think of an important woman in your life, or in the books you have read, or someone you have encountered this week. What are her significant traits? Share with the others some of these "women of valor," these women of character and courage. Perhaps read a thumbnail biography of this woman at the table. *(See stories of Golda Meir, Hannah Senesh, and Bella Abzug in* A Different Light, *the Hanukkah books edited by Noam Zion and Barbara Spectre.)*

Recruitment poster, 1943, for Jewish women from Palestine to join the British army (PATS) in its war against the Nazis. Note the picture of Prime Minister Winston Churchill. (Zionist Archive)

Two Rays of Light Merging

From every human being there emerges a ray of light that reaches into heaven. When two soul mates destined for one another find each other, their streams of light flow together into a single, even brighter light that illuminates the heavens.

— Baal Shem Tov, founder of the Hassidic movement

Golda on "Grace is deceptive, beauty is ephemeral" (Proverbs 31)

I was never a beauty. There was a time when I was sorry about that, when I was old enough to understand the importance of it and I overheard people referring to it. Looking in any mirror, I realized it was something that I was never going to have. Then I found what I wanted to do in life and being called pretty no longer had any importance. It was only much later that I realized that not being beautiful was a blessing in disguise. It forced me to develop my inner resources. I came to realize that women who cannot lean on their beauty and need to make something on their own have the advantage.

— Golda Meir

The Governor called her "a woman of valor"

> She opens her hands to the poor.
>
> — *Proverbs 31:20*

by Maya Bernstein

My grandmother, Freda Miriam Appleman Aranoff, still has traces of her southern accent. It's very faint now, but she's fond of telling us the story of when she was a teenager, a few years after she moved to Brooklyn with her family, from Evarts, Kentucky, in Harlan County, thick in the heart of mining country.

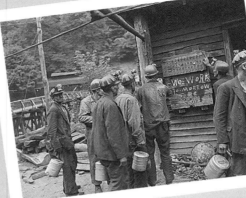

Harlan County, in the 1920s, was mining territory, with two opposing camps: the coal miners, and the mine owners. The miners were basically enslaved to the owners of the mines. They worked hard physical labor, day in, day out, and were paid in Scrip — the mine owner's version of money, a cheap paper certificate that could be exchanged for food only in the Company Store, owned, of course, by the mine-owners. (Recall the song "Sixteen tons and what do you get? Another day older and deeper in debt.") The coal company had its own police force, which was used to keep union organizers out of the coal camps, and to intimidate the miners who tried to join the union.

In 1932, in the midst of the Great Depression, the miners went on strike. They wanted to be unionized, and they refused to work until they were granted that right. The owners of the mine, like the Bible's Pharaoh, had hearts as hard as stone, that hardened at each request made by the miners — they would let the miners starve to death rather than allow them to join the union, and gain their freedom. The town was basically at war. Bullets flying in the streets, riots and vandalism.

By this time, Savta, my great-grandmother, and her husband had four children, and they had opened a clothing store, and were making a living. Savta baked her own bread each week, and the family ate fruits and vegetables and grains — they still kept strictly kosher. Twice a year, they could afford a chicken, which was ritually slaughtered according to Jewish law, and sent to them from Cincinnati, Ohio. They were extremely well respected in Evarts. Savta's husband was famous throughout the county for his honesty and kindness, and had even been asked to be a member of the town court. He refused — he didn't want to make decisions that would affect people's personal lives — but the judge said to him, "Mr. Appleman, if you were to be tried, wouldn't you want a fair trial?" "Yes, of course," he answered, "Then you will sit on this court," the judge said, "for you are a fair and honest man." And he did. (Recall the verse in *Eishet Hayil*: "Her husband is well-known, sitting in the city's courts of judgment." — *Proverbs 31:23*)

Harlan County photos from 1930s and 1940s courtesy C. Richard Matthews.

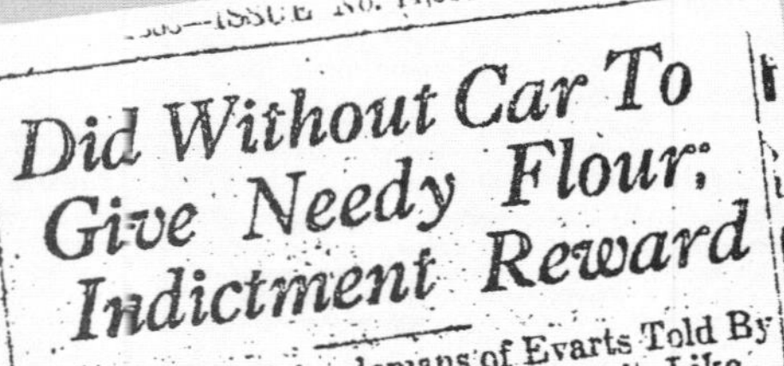

—ISSUE No. 14,364

Did Without Car To Give Needy Flour; Indictment Reward

Strange Case of Applemans of Evarts Told By Kentucky Commission; 'We Don't Like Your Giving Flour,' Said Prosecutor.

Editor's Note: This is the second of seven articles presenting the high spots of a 1200-page report by a commission appointed by the then Gov. Flem D. Sampson to investigate conditions in Harlan county. The commission only recently completed its investigation and was unable to present its report until the day before Sampson was succeeded by Gov. Ruby Laffoon. Altho Sampson did not have time to act on it, the report is expected to come before the next session of the Kentucky legislature.

By JOHN T. MOUTOUX

For 12 years Mr. and Mrs. Harry Appleman have been operating a general merchandise store at the little town of Evarts in Harlan county. It was to Evarts that coal miners flocked and took their families last spring when they were fired for joining the union. Their only source of income suddenly cut off, the miners lived on the little that aid committees would bring in from adjoining counties.

Testifying before former Governor Flem Sampson's commission was Mrs. Henry Appleman, 38-year-old mother of four children. She was born in Poland, and came to America when a child, was educated in Virginia, and later naturalized.

"Did you and your husband distribute a carload of flour here?" she was asked by one of the commissioners.

A—We did.

Files Circular

Q—Will you file this circular and make it part of your disposition.

The circular read:

LOOK

In accordance with the Jewish custom to remember the needy during the Passover Season, Mr. and Mrs. Harry Appleman will give away on Friday, April 17, at the Evarts depot a car load of flour.

The flour will be given away as long as it lasts, a 24-pound bag to a family. All needy from ... surroundings are

... its probative value lies in the detail of circumstances she relates. The commissioners taking her testimony were greatly impressed by her sincerity. It is the testimony of a good and truthful woman."

(TOMORROW: "Red raids" by deputies created reign of terror in mining towns of Harlan County).

WOMAN CHOSEN ARMS DELEGATE

Miss Woolley First of Sex to Be So Honored.

By Associated Press

WASHINGTON—The success of American feminism stood at new heights today thr...

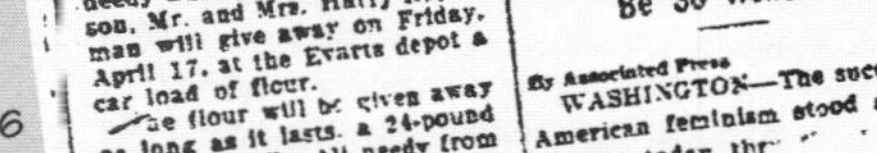

A Car Load of Flour.

The couple had been saving up money over the years to buy a car, and finally had saved enough — a small fortune in those frugal days. But people around them were starving. Children did not have shoes on their feet. They were not political people, but they could not live surrounded by such poverty, without doing what they could to help. And so in the spring of 1932, they opened a soup kitchen, and put an ad in the paper, which read: "**LOOK!** In accordance with the Jewish custom to remember the needy during the **Passover Season**, Mr. and Mrs. Harry Appleman will give away, on Friday, April 17, at the Evarts depot, **A Car Load of Flour**. The flour will be given away as long as it will last. A 24-pound bag to a family. All needy from Evarts and surroundings are welcome, regardless of **Color and Creed**."

They spent every last penny on flour — flour! And they gave out bag after bag after bag. There was such joy in the town. The joy of giving and receiving with honor — the joy that transcends color and creed, that transcends the particular, and enters the realm of the universal — the realm of the human. This had such an impact on the people of the town, that years later, when my grandmother visited the town with her siblings, she was amazed to find that young boys in Evarts, Kentucky were named "Harry Appleman," after her father.

The coal company wasn't happy, though. They bombed the soup kitchen in the middle of the night, sent bullets flying through the windows of the house, and then came to indict my grandfather for criminal syndicalism — supporting the miners and aiding their strike against the Company. Savta went to court the next day, to defend her husband. Savta explained, "The Jews have a holiday that is Passover. And on that holiday, whoever is hungry must be fed, even if he is a stranger. We were taking no sides, this way or that, in the strike, but when people are hungry, should it be said to them: no, you are strikers, and we can give you nothing to eat? There were so many children that had no bread . . . ." The case made its way all the way to Governor Chandler of Kentucky, who called Savta a "woman of valor," and said that hers was the testimony of "a good and truthful woman." But at the time, the Company Store owners continued to shoot through their windows, and the entire family escaped to West Virginia in the middle of the night, eventually making their way north to Brooklyn.

OOK!

In accordance with the Jewish custom to remember the needy during the

Passover Season

Mr. and Mrs. Harry Appleman will give away on Friday, April 17, at the Evarts depot

A Car Load of FLOUR

The Flour will be given away as long as it will last. A 24 pound bag to a family. All needy from Evarts and surroundings are welcome regardless of

Color and Creed

Harry and Bina Appleman, 1928, Evarts, KY, with children Freda (5), Joe (2), and Toby (7)

I want to know how God created this world. I am not interested in this or that phenomenon, in the spectrum of this or that element. I want to know God's thoughts; the rest are details.

— *Albert Einstein*

God is in the details.

— *Ludwig Mies van der Rohe, Bauhaus architect*

Olim/Immigrants from Ethiopia and Russia practice Shabbat in an Israeli kindergarten outside Jerusalem. Photo (1990) by Zion Ozeri.

Kiddush

sanctifying the day of Shabbat over wine

קִדּוּשׁ

(God saw all that had been made
and it was very good.
There was evening and there was morning):

(וַיַּרְא אֱלֹהִים אֶת כָּל אֲשֶׁר עָשָׂה
וְהִנֵּה טוֹב מְאֹד,
וַיְהִי עֶרֶב וַיְהִי בֹקֶר)

(Va-yar Elohim et kol asher asah
V'hinei tov me'od,
Va-y'hi erev va-y'hi voker)

the sixth day was complete.
The sky and the earth
and all their contents were completed.
On the seventh day God completed
all the skilled labor.
God ceased (shabbat)
from all skilled labor.
God blessed the seventh day
and declared it holy,
because on that day God ceased
from all the acts of creation.

יוֹם הַשִּׁשִּׁי.
וַיְכֻלּוּ הַשָּׁמַיִם וְהָאָרֶץ
וְכָל צְבָאָם.
וַיְכַל אֱלֹהִים בַּיּוֹם הַשְּׁבִיעִי,
מְלַאכְתּוֹ אֲשֶׁר עָשָׂה,
וַיִּשְׁבֹּת בַּיּוֹם הַשְּׁבִיעִי,
מִכָּל מְלַאכְתּוֹ אֲשֶׁר עָשָׂה.
וַיְבָרֶךְ אֱלֹהִים אֶת יוֹם הַשְּׁבִיעִי,
וַיְקַדֵּשׁ אֹתוֹ,
כִּי בוֹ שָׁבַת מִכָּל מְלַאכְתּוֹ,
אֲשֶׁר בָּרָא אֱלֹהִים לַעֲשׂוֹת.

Yom Ha-shishi.
Va-y'khu u Ha-shamayim v'ha-aretz
v'khol tz'va-am.
Va-y'khal Elohim ba-yom ha-sh'vi-i
m'lakhto asher asah,
va-yish-bot ba-yom ha-sh'vi-i
mi-kol m'lakhto asher asah.
Va-y'vareikh Elohim et yom ha-sh'vi-i
va-y'kadeish oto,
ki vo shavat mi-kol m'lakhto,
asher bara Elohim la'asot.

1 POUR Some people pour one big cup and pass it around; some pour a cup for each person at the table; some recite Kiddush over a big cup and then pour a little wine from it into many small cups offered to everyone after the Kiddush.

2 STAND OR SIT Some people stand for all or part of the Kiddush, while others sit for the entirety (SEE PAGE 74).

3 LOOK Kabbalists recommend that each person look deeply into their glass of wine (called "a cup of blessing") before reciting Kiddush. The leader then looks around into the face of each guest at the table, and sanctifies Shabbat on their behalf with the words of the blessing.

4 LIFT Some people hold the cup on the surface of their open hand. Openhandedness, as opposed to tightfistedness, is a sign of generosity and trust (DEUTERONOMY 15:7-8).

5 SING and BLESS The words of Kiddush officially declare this day holy and celebrate God's partnership with humanity. Some people sing it all together, some sing just a portion and some listen to the leader and reply "amen."

6 DRINK and ENJOY. L'Chaim!

Unless we believe that God renews the whole of creation every day, our prayers grow old and stale.
How difficult it is to say the same words day after day!
"Cast us not into our old age" *(Psalm 7:19)* — May the world never become too old for us.
When the world is experienced as "new every morning, then great is your faithfulness." *(Lamentations 3:23)*

— *Hasidic source,* Degel Mahaneh Efraim

Tully Filmus, Russian-American artist (born 1908), courtesy of his sons.

Happy are those who walk the streets of the world with the fragrance of Shabbos.

Friday night, when my heart is overflowing like the Kiddush wine, jealousy is wiped out from my heart and, hopefully, from the hearts of mankind.

You can keep every Shabbos to the letter of the law, but unless Shabbos reaches the deepest place in your heart, you haven't kept Shabbos.

— *Shlomo Carlebach*

Judaism does not divide life into holy and profane, but into the holy and the not yet holy.

— *Martin Buber*

Blessed are You, Adonai,
Our God, Ruler of the Universe,
Creator of the fruit of the vine.

בָּרוּךְ אַתָּה יְיָ
אֱלֹהֵינוּ מֶלֶךְ הָעוֹלָם,
בּוֹרֵא פְּרִי הַגָּפֶן.

Barukh ata Adonai,
Eloheinu Melekh ha-olam,
borei p'ri ha-gafen.

Blessed are You, Adonai
Our God, Ruler of the Universe,
who made us holy with your commandments
and favored us.
Your holy Shabbat
in love and favor,
You gave us as our heritage,
a reminder of the acts of Creation.
For it is first
among the days called holy,
a reminder of the Exodus from Egypt.
For You have chosen us to serve you
and set us apart
from all other peoples;
Your holy Shabbat,
with love and favor,
You have given us as our heritage.
Blessed are You, Adonai,
who makes Shabbat holy.

בָּרוּךְ אַתָּה יְיָ
אֱלֹהֵינוּ מֶלֶךְ הָעוֹלָם,
אֲשֶׁר קִדְּשָׁנוּ בְּמִצְוֹתָיו
וְרָצָה בָנוּ,
וְשַׁבַּת קָדְשׁוֹ
בְּאַהֲבָה וּבְרָצוֹן
הִנְחִילָנוּ
זִכָּרוֹן לְמַעֲשֵׂה בְרֵאשִׁית,
כִּי הוּא יוֹם תְּחִלָּה
לְמִקְרָאֵי קֹדֶשׁ,
זֵכֶר לִיצִיאַת מִצְרָיִם.
כִּי בָנוּ בָחַרְתָּ
וְאוֹתָנוּ קִדַּשְׁתָּ
מִכָּל הָעַמִּים,
וְשַׁבַּת קָדְשְׁךָ
בְּאַהֲבָה וּבְרָצוֹן
הִנְחַלְתָּנוּ.
בָּרוּךְ אַתָּה יְיָ
מְקַדֵּשׁ הַשַּׁבָּת.

Barukh ata Adonai,
Eloheinu Melekh ha-olam,
asher k -d'shanu b'mitz-votav
v'ratzah vanu,
v'shabbat kod'sho
b'ahavah u-v'ratzon
hin-khi-lanu
zikaron l'ma'asei v'rei-sheet.
Ki hu yom t'khilah
l'mikra-ei kodesh,
zekher litzi-at mitzrayim.
Ki vanu va-kharta
v'otanu kidashta
mikol ha-amim,
v'shabbat kodsh'kha
b'ahavah u-v'ratzon
hin-khal-tanu.
Barukh ata Adonai,
m'Kadeish ha-Shabbat.

Kiddush (evening)

עַל אַהֲבָתְךָ / For Your Love

I raise my cup in love of you,
Peace to you, Seventh Day!
Six days of work are like your slaves,
I work my way through them . . .
Because of my love for you,
Day of my Delight.

— *Yehuda Halevi, Spain, 11th century*

No rejoicing before God is conceivable
without wine.

— TALMUD PESACHIM 109A

An Opening Toast

Kiddush may be seen as an opening toast to God, our benefactor. It dedicates this holy day to recalling both the Creation of the world and the Exodus from Egypt — thus on Shabbat we celebrate both creativity and freedom. Kiddush is also our chance to thank God for a gift of love given us weekly — Shabbat, a day of rest and of joy.

Before drinking the wine, we recite two blessings, which together are called the Kiddush. One blesses the wine and one sets apart the day. The Hebrew words *Kiddush* and *Havdalah* both mean literally, "to separate" or "to distinguish," thus both set apart this Day Apart — making it special or holy. Performing these rituals at the opening and closing of Shabbat is mandated in the Ten Commandments: "Remember the day of Shabbat to make it holy" (*Zachor . . . l'kad'sho).* The words of the Kiddush (which may be recited in any language) — *M'kadesh HaShabbat,* — are our way of sanctifying this day — marking its entrance and its exit.

But why the wine? Why aren't words enough?

The wine and its blessing — *Borei p'ri hagafen* — were added by the Rabbis to express the celebratory nature of this invocation as a kind of toast to the day. The Rabbis chose to ally the blessing to the drinking of wine (which historically was one of the highest forms of human cultivation of natural foods).

Coconut shell kiddush cup inscribed with a scene of angels visiting Abraham to announce the birth of Isaac. (Probably 19th century; The Jewish Museum, London)

Guidelines *from tradition*

1. Kiddush is part of the meal so it should be recited at the table; however, we cover the Hallah during the Kiddush over the wine. Why? (SEE PAGES 74-75)

2. Generally try to use a large cup filled with wine.
   - One custom calls for letting the cup overflow a little onto a plate, for "a cup that runs over" is a sign of gratitude for abundant blessings.
   - Some people pour a little water into the wine. (In the Roman era, wine was a mixture of a thick essence of grape and pure water.) Kabbalists interpret that custom to signify a balance between justice (wine) and mercy (water).
   - Mystics also recommend we look deeply into the cup before reciting Kiddush and we hold the cup on the surface of the open hand (unlike *Havdalah* when we cup our hand before the flame).

3. "If one's desire to eat bread is greater than one's desire for wine, or if one has no wine, then first wash hands, then say the blessing *HaMotzi* and then the Kiddush and break and eat the bread." (RAMBAM, MISHNE TORAH, LAWS OF SHABBAT 29:1,6,9)

4. Some people stand for parts of the Kiddush and some people respond with the salutation *"L'Chaim"* before drinking (SEE KIDDUSH CHOREOGRAPHY, PAGE 74).

5. "Amen" is usually recited by those not singing the Kiddush in order to show their concurrence with the leader. If everyone sings the *bracha* (blessing) together, no one is required to say "Amen."

Logo at top by Dan Reisinger for the Israel Ministry of Tourism portrays spies bringing back enormous clusters of grapes from the land of milk and honey *(NUMBERS 13:23)*

Guidelines

getting started

How can I initiate Kiddush in my home?

Kiddush is a relatively easy custom to introduce, if we make it tasty, personal, and easy to read.

Tasty. If you'd like, ask a wine maven for suggestions about the best wines. But you need not go beyond a reasonable budget for your family. The Rabbis recommended we make our Shabbat fare like an everyday menu rather than draining ourselves financially by spending too much. Some families, even if they don't exclusively drink Kosher wine, endeavor to buy certified Kosher brands for Kiddush. But the wine need not be the sweet Concord grape variety. (Incidentally, if you do not like or do not have wine or grape juice, you may recite Kiddush over bread).

Grape juice should be available for those averse to alcohol for reasons of taste or for medical reasons.

Personal. Having a silver Kiddush cup for each person at the table makes Kiddush a personalized mitzvah *(hiddur mitzvah)*, but using any beautiful glass or cup is fine. Today some people make their own pottery cups for Kiddush. In my home we received as a gift a Kiddush cup for each child's birth and had the infant's name engraved on it.

Simple. For starters, some families simply recite the one-line blessing ending with *Borei P'ri Ha-gafen* — "Blessed is the Creator of the Fruit of the Wine." As you feel more comfortable, it is important to recite also the rest of the Kiddush, ending with *M'kadeish HaShabbat* — "Sanctifier of Shabbat," for Kiddush is more about sanctifying Shabbat than blessing the wine or grape juice. If Hebrew is a challenge, then it is perfectly acceptable to recite all or part of the Kiddush in English or any language.

— Noam Zion

Shabbat is celebrated in memory of Creation.

— Kiddush

"The universe works," proclaimed Dr. Rosenzweig on seeing the solar eclipse, "there's some satisfaction in that . . . ."

The sky got very dark, the horns of the crescent sun shrank . . . as the sun disappeared and the leading edge of the moon's shadow swept over them at 1,500 miles an hour. He looked up at a blank circle [the moon] surrounded by a pure white ring of light [the sun's corona] . . . .

"I've been crying . . . I am absolutely awed . . . ." Dr. Rosenzweig stood up and started clapping. "Encore! Encore!" he shouted. And then, upon reflection, "Author! Author!"

— Ludwig Mies van der Rohe

Customs explained

Why Cover the Hallah?

We usually cover the Hallah during the Kiddush over the wine. Why?

Problem: On the one hand, bread is the "staff of life," the primary ingredient of the daily meal — and is generally honored by the first blessing. (The ingredients of bread — wheat or other grains — are the first to be mentioned in the list of seven species grown in the Biblical land of milk and honey even before grapes are mentioned — *Deuteronomy 8:8*).

On the other hand, the opening invocation of the Shabbat meal is the Kiddush, the sanctification of the Shabbat, which has been attached to the drinking of a cup of wine. So what takes priority — basic nutrition or a spiritual toast?

Solution: By covering the Hallah, we "pretend" that it is not on the table, and thus can recite Kiddush over wine first. Then, after washing hands, we uncover the Hallah and break bread with all who are hungry.

That is the legal and historical answer to why we cover the Hallah during Kiddush. Some people also enjoy the folk-explanation that the Hallah will be embarrassed to see the wine receive its blessing first. So we cover the Hallah's eyes so she will not be shamed.

The Rezhiner Rebbe's Protective Coin, turned into a Kiddush Cup. (19th Century Poland, The Gross Family Collection, Tel Aviv.)

Kiddush Choreography — When to Stand, When to Sit, and Why

Do we stand or sit for Kiddush?
What is the proper decorum, and why?

Four different views on Kiddush choreography offer four different symbolic perspectives. Each one invites us to participate in a different script simply by specifying different bodily gestures:

(1) Please be Seated: The Dignity of Dinner

Sitting down for the whole Kiddush shows that we are at a banquet and of course dignified dinners call for everyone to eat while seated and the wine is part of the meal and an essential part of the mitzvah of *Oneg Shabbat*/enjoying oneself in honor of seventh day.

(2) Please Rise to Honor God's Name (Y-H-V-H)

To welcome both God's presence and honor the Shabbat Queen, many people stand at least for the four words of the introductory verse "**Y**om **H**aShishi **V**a-y'khulu **H**ashamayim" (its initial letters spell out God's holiest name). Some whisper the first part of the sentence *[Vay'hi erev vay'hi voker — Genesis 1:31]* and emphasize out loud the relevant four words spelling out God's name while standing.

(3) Please Rise to Solemnly Bear Witness

Standing up for the first paragraph *Vay'khulu* is akin to a witness bearing testimony before a judge. For in reciting the summary of God's creation *(Genesis 2:1-3)*, we publicly declare our belief in the Divine origin of the world and become partners in God's work. After standing for this paragraph, some people then sit down (seeing Kiddush as part of the meal); others sit down only after the entire Kiddush, to drink.

(4) Please Rise for the Wedding Ceremony

A Kabbalist interpretation views the entire Kiddush as the betrothal ceremony at a mystical marriage of the male and female aspects of the Divine, and at weddings it was customary to stand. The Zohar sees the Kiddush as marking the moment when the Bride (the Shabbat Queen) steps under the canopy *(huppah)*; the wine symbolizes the overflowing blessing/*shefa*, and the meal which follows is the marital feast/*seudat sheva berachot* accompanied by song and festivity. The greeting *"l'chaim*/to life" is our blessing to the bride.

L'Chaim — To Life!

There are many explanations that illuminate the custom of saying *L'Chaim* before drinking the wine at Kiddush.

From a **legal** point of view, the person reciting Kiddush wishes to confirm that the participants want the leader to represent them in reciting Kiddush. Often the leader evokes the salutation *L'Chaim* from the people for whom Kiddush is being said. The leader turns to them by saying the phrase *savrai*/"do you agree" and thereby invites the participants at the table to join with the Kiddush. They respond by saying *L'Chaim*. For a more **poetic** understanding, read this beautiful Kabbalist explanation. It connects the drinking of the wine to the Tree of Life and to the mystical *Sefirot*:

"As Israel below is sanctifying the day, the Tree of Life *[Tif'eret]* rouses. Its leaves rustle as a breeze comes forth from the World-to-Come [sefirotically, *Binah*]. The branches of the Tree sway and waft forth the scent of the World-to-Come. The Tree of life is further aroused and at this moment, brings forth holy souls which it gives to the world. Souls exit and they enter, each rousing the other. They exit and they enter, and the Tree of Life is filled with joy. All Israel is wreathed with crowns, which are these holy souls. Now the cosmos is joyous, and at rest." *(Zohar 3: 173a)*

On Shabbat the Tree of Life rules, while on weekdays the Tree of Knowledge of Good and Evil rules. Life in exile from the Garden of Eden, everyday life, is marked by distinctions between good and bad, forbidden and permitted, while redemptive existence unites all opposites and suspends the opposition between good and bad, *asur umutar.*

However, there are more ominous explanations that are associated with the dark side of wine and inebriation. Some Rabbis identified the forbidden fruit of the Tree of Knowledge — that brought humanity both wisdom and death — as the fruit of the vine *(Genesis Rabbah 15:8)*. In fact, the first time wine is explicitly mentioned in the Torah, Noah, who planted the first vineyard, promptly got drunk. This leads him to curse one of his children (Genesis 9:21). Wine also has more negative associations because it is also the mainstay of consoling mourners in the Talmudic period. It was even used as a tranquilizer in the last meal of a prisoner condemned to death *(Talmud Sanhedrin 43a)*. Nevertheless, at Kiddush on Shabbat wine celebrates a joyful occasion and we declare that it is "For Life!" — not for death.

Havdalah from *Sefer Minhagim* (Amsterdam, 18th century)

In regard to external gifts, to outward possessions, there is only one proper attitude — to have them and to be able to do without them. On Shabbat we live, as it were, independent of technical civilization: we abstain primarily from any activity that aims at remaking or reshaping the things of space. Man's royal privilege to conquer nature is suspended on the seventh day.

— *Abraham Joshua Heschel, The Sabbath*

Guidelines

parent-child corner

Kiddush is a wonderful opportunity for children to show what they know and to become full participants. Even if an adult recites the Kiddush, each child may be invited to recite it themselves — as much as they know. Having their own Siddur or book of blessings, their own cup and their turn, guarantees each child a place at the Shabbat table and in the family celebration.

European Kiddush Cup for the seder, displaying the wise child.

Wine may not be a delicacy for younger children but grape juice is usually very popular. Yet this joy can turn into tears when the cup is overturned and the stained tablecloth makes parents angry or anxious, especially around guests. Parents must make their peace with the possible spills before the wine or grape juice is poured, so that they and their children will not be anxious. (Some parents cover the area around the child's plate with plastic, some use a simple white tablecloth that may be bleached easily and others use white grape juice that does not stain. Some parents even kiss their children after they spill to reassure them that they will not be angry with them on Shabbat. Others make no big deal at all — but they keep a supply of salt available to pour on wine stains and prevent them from setting). Most important is to keep the joy of the family Shabbat uppermost in our minds.

Don't Cry over Spilt Wine

☛ **A Public Message**
from the Hosts
to all the Guests
and all the Children:
Don't cry over spilt wine!

Rabbi Akiba Aiger *(German, 18th century)* used to be very strict about the mitzvah of hospitality. Once on Shabbat one of the guests happened to spill a cup of wine. The clean white tablecloth was stained and the guest was visibly embarrassed. So Rabbi Aiger himself bumped the table so as to spill his own glass of wine. He exclaimed: "Oh, this table must be off-balance!"

Modern Swedish Kiddush Cups by Sigvard Bernadotte, 1987, photographed by Karl Gabor.

The Week in Review: Accounting for Our Last Six Days of Creation

Kiddush marks the conclusion of the six days of work and beginning of Shabbat. God looked back at all that had been accomplished in one week, saw its completeness and its harmony and exclaimed, "It is very good." Here lies an idea for a weekly activity of retrospective evaluation. It is our chance to survey and grade our achievements as well as share them with our family and friends.

Joseph Telushkin writes of the meaningful experience he had witnessing a congregation's collective week-in-review:

"Some years ago, I attended a Shabbat service conducted by my friend Rabbi Leonid Feldman in Palm Beach, Florida. Before the service began, he wished everyone "Shabbat Shalom," and asked if anyone in the congregation had good news that had occurred over the preceding week, which he or she wished to share with others. People stood up and announced engagements, anniversaries, the first words spoken by a child or grandchild, a book's publication, the visit by a family member or friend whom they hadn't seen in many years, the completion of a degree, and more.

"My wife decided to bring this ritual into our home. At the beginning of the Friday-night Shabbat meal, she asks family members and guests to share their achievements."

The first reported such week-in-review activity goes back to the year, 1575, and to the place, Safed, where so much of the Friday night ritual was created. The innovator was Rabbi Elazar Azikri, a Kabbalist and author of the still popular song *Yedid Nefesh*. He founded a "Holy Havurah" in order to worship God and study traditional texts with intensity and devotion. As part of the Havurah's weekly routine, Rabbi Azikri conducted a weekly spiritual week-in-review for all *haverim* (members). The mystics met in the synagogue before Shabbat and discussed their spiritual behavior during the past week — the good and the bad. After that, they proceeded to greet the Shabbat Queen.

You may incorporate this custom — without its mystical aspects or its harsh self-scrutiny — simply by offering your own brief review of your achievements and experiences and then ask others to share them as well. You might even ask people to present projects that they are now considering and ask for advice about the worlds that they have created during the week or intend to create in the coming weeks.

Revisiting our Week Day by Day: Guided Meditation

Just as God reviewed all that had been created in six days before resting and sanctifying the seventh day, so we may review our week by using a guided meditation.

Close your eyes for a full two minutes and try to revisit each day of your week — since last Shabbat. Where were you emotionally and physically last Shabbat? Where did you journey on Sunday, Monday and so on? What events or accomplishments or frustrations filled those days? Which of these do you want to gather in yourself and carry forward and which do you prefer to leave behind as Shabbat begins.

— Laura Geller

All Professions are Equal

All forms of labor should be appreciated as we sum up our creativity during the week. Intellectual pursuits are not necessarily to be given greater honor. As the Rabbis of Talmud used to say:

> **I am a creature** [of God] and my fellows are also creatures [of God].
>
> **My work** is in the city and others' in the field.
>
> **I rise early** to go to my work and others rise early to theirs.
>
> **As they do not** deign to do my work, I do not deign to do theirs.

But should you think: "I do much [study of Torah] and they do little," we have learned: "Doing more or doing less, it matters not, so long as one's heart is directed toward Heaven [doing God's work on earth]." *(Talmud Berakhot 17a)*

Reflections כַּוָּנוֹת

on being co-partners in creativity and freedom

שׁוּתָּף בְּמַעֲשֵׂה בְרֵאשִׁית

Sanctity of life means that humans are partners, not sovereigns, that life is a trust, not a property. To exist as a human is to assist the Divine.

— *Abraham Joshua Heschel,* The Insecurity of Freedom

"Co-Partner in Creation"

Talmud Shabbat 119

"And the heaven and the earth were finished . . . "

— *Genesis 2:1-3*

Rabbi Joseph B. Soloveitchik taught that the recitation of *Vay'khulu* — the passage from the Torah preceding the Kiddush — lets us testify to two things: God's work on earth and our job to go with it. We state that God started the work of Creation — and it is the human task to complete it. We're in a partnership with the divine: our part is to complete and transform the domain of chaos into a perfected, beautiful reality.

Soloveitchik writes: "The creator, so to speak, made the world deficient in order that mortal man could repair its flaws and perfect it . . . So the human task is to 'fashion, engrave, bond, and create,' and transform the emptiness of being into a perfect and holy existence, bearing the imprint of the divine name . . . The peak of religious ethical perfection to which Judaism aspires is the human as creator."

— *Rav Joseph B. Soleveitchik,* Halachic Man

To Be Fully Free: The Meaning of the Sabbath

The Sabbath ritual has such a central place in the biblical religion because it is more than a "day of rest" in the modern sense; it is a symbol of salvation and freedom. This is also the meaning of God's rest; this rest is not necessary for God because he is tired, but it expresses the idea that great as creation is, greater and crowning creation is peace; God's work is a condescension; he must really "rest," not because he is tired but because he is free and fully God only when he has ceased to work. So is man fully man only when he does not work, when he is at peace with nature and his fellow man; that is why the Sabbath commandment is at one time motivated by God's rest and at the other by liberation from Egypt. Both mean the same and interpret each other; "rest" is freedom.

— *Erich Fromm, psychoanalyst*

Mark Chagall, 1946

A *Kavana*/Meditation on a Shattered World

How did the world begin?

For Jewish mystics the world began with an act of withdrawal. God did *Tzimtzum*. God contracted to leave a space for the world to exist. After this *Tzimtzum*, "withdrawal," some divine energy entered the emerging world, but this divine light, this divine energy was too strong, overpowering the worlds that tried to contain it, and the universe exploded with a cosmic bang. Shards of divine light, holiness, were scattered everywhere in the universe. The sparks of holiness are often buried deep in the cosmic muck of the universe, they are difficult to behold and yet they are everywhere, in everyone, in every situation. They are the life and meaning of the universe.

We live in this world of shattering. We feel in our bodies and in our souls the brokennness of the world, and we feel at times the resonance in ourselves of that initial cosmic shattering. Our bodies, like that primordial world, try not to contain, but rather to hold on to the divine light and energy flowing around us and in us. But, as in the world's origin, our bodies are too frail, made only frailer with the passage of time, and so we begin to leak our divine image/energy. Perhaps, then, illness is really the leaking of our souls. In this world of shattered hopes and expectations, we search for wholeness.

Moses shattered the first set of tablets, the first set of the Ten Commandments. And then he got a second set that he helped to write. When the ark was constructed for the sanctuary, the Rabbis tell us not only the whole second set of tablets was put into the Holy Ark, but the pieces of the first set as well.

Shabbat Kiddush Cup (Augsburg, Germany, 17th century).

Otto Geismar, Spies with their Grapes from the Promised Land. (*Numbers 13:23*) (Germany, 20th century)

Wholeness comes not from ignoring the broken pieces, or hoping to magically glue them back together. The shattered coexists with the whole; the divine is to be found amid the darkest depths and the heaviest muck of the universe. Every moment has the potential for redemption and wholeness. Our brokenness gives us that vision and the potential to return some of the divine sparks scattered in the world.

— *Michael Strassfeld*, A Book of Life

Creation is Constantly Becoming, Evolving, Ascending

An epiphany [a personal revelation] enables you to sense Creation not as something completed, but as constantly becoming, evolving, ascending. This transports you from a place where there is nothing new to a place where there is nothing old, where everything renews itself, where heaven and earth rejoice as at the moment of Creation.

— *Rav Abraham Isaac Kook*

Sharing our Bread — Jews in Ethiopia.
Photograph by Aliza Urbach, 1991.

Oneg Shabbat: The Childhood Pleasures of an Unforgettable Family Meal

By age twelve I already knew what foods I love to eat and what I hate. However, I never imagined that food could give me such pleasure *(Oneg)* — so deep and sharp. Not only my tongue and inner cheek of my mouth, but also my throat, my stomach and the ends of my fingers released little bundles of taste. The aroma filled my nose, saliva flooded my mouth. Even though I was still a child, I knew I would never forget this meal that I had eaten.

— MEIR SHALEV, ISRAELI NOVELIST
(FROM KAYAMIM AKHADIM)

The Memories Carried by the Sensations of Eating

The French Jewish novelist, Marcel Proust, identifies the most fundamental ground of human memory in sensory experience.

By themselves alone, smell and taste linger on for a long time like souls — remembering, waiting, hoping . . . They carry without trembling, wafted almost airborne, the whole colossal structure of human memory.

— FROM REMEMBRANCE OF THINGS PAST

Hallah

חַלָּה

washing our hands and sharing our bread

After washing and drying your hands:

BLESSED ARE YOU, Adonai	**בָּרוּךְ** אַתָּה יְיָ	Ba-rukh ata Adonai,
our God, Ruler of the Universe,	אֱלֹהֵינוּ מֶלֶךְ הָעוֹלָם,	Elo-hei-nu me-lekh ha-olam,
who has sanctified us	אֲשֶׁר קִדְּשָׁנוּ	asher ki-d'shanu
by commanding us	בְּמִצְוֹתָיו וְצִוָּנוּ,	b'mitz-votav v'tzi-vanu,
to wash our hands.	עַל נְטִילַת יָדָיִם.	al n'tilat yadayim.

1. **POUR** clean water over your hands from a pitcher or glass.
2. **DRY** the hands.
3. **RECITE** the blessing.
4. **SHHH!** no talking until after taking a bite of bread.
5. **HOLD** both loaves up.
6. **RECITE** the blessing over bread *(hamotzi lekhem min ha-aretz.)*
7. **EAT** a bite of bread dipped in salt or honey.

detail from Swedish Hallahs photographed by Karl Gabor, page 91

Raise both loaves and say:

BLESSED ARE YOU, Adonai	**בָּרוּךְ** אַתָּה יְיָ	Ba-rukh ata Adonai,
our God, Ruler of the Universe,	אֱלֹהֵינוּ מֶלֶךְ הָעוֹלָם,	Elo-hei-nu me-lekh ha-olam,
who brings out bread from the earth.	הַמּוֹצִיא לֶחֶם מִן הָאָרֶץ.	ha-motzi lekhem min ha-aretz.

Introduction to Handwashing

Pouring water over the hands has an enormous symbolic significance. Hands are our tools for manipulating the world. Both Hebrew and English phrases use the imagery of the hand liberally. The Latin root for hand is *"manus"* — as in manual, manipulate, manuscript, manufacture. We are *homo faber* — humans involved in fabricating our world. In Hebrew, *"yad,"* meaning "hand," is the chief image for Divine work — God's hand in history. *"Yad"* also means memorial; with our hands we leave a mark on the world. We sanctify those creative hands by pouring water over them. In Genesis, the world emerges from water; thus immersing our hands signifies a process of rebirth. Our hands bring forth bread from the earth but we eat that bread only after sanctifying those same hands with water. Both cleanliness and ritual purity contribute to achieving the sanctity of a spiritual life. Hand washing prepares the way to transform everyday eating into a form of communion with God. Our table becomes a Divine altar. Eating that serves our bodies are complemented by blessings that nourish our souls.

Introduction to Eating

Food is a sacred gift. We eat it to keep ourselves healthy and to enhance the pleasure of life's happy events. By reminding yourself and your children who the food is from (God), what it is for (to fuel us to be of service to others), and what attitude we should have toward it (both self-discipline and full enjoyment), you will have a useful perspective for dealing with many of the food struggles that may arise in your family.

Moderation, celebration, and sanctification are invaluable touchstones in this process. If you learn to practice moderation, you can approach food with interest and enthusiasm rather than obsessions or fear. By celebrating a wide variety of the foods God has provided, you can let go of unreasonable guilt and teach your children both self-regulation and delight. Finally, sanctifying food by sitting down together and saying a blessing puts the mealtime back in its proper place, as a means by which to appreciate your good fortune and God's bounty.

— *Wendy Mogel*, The Blessing of a Skinned Knee

Honoring A Family Recipe

"Although [the tradition of] cooking is fragile because it lives in human activity, it is not easily destroyed. It is transmitted in every family like genes, and it has the capacity for change and for passing on experience from one generation to another." *(Joan Nathan, Jewish Cooking in America)*

God does not eat, but God is honored by gifts brought on the altar like choice flour mixed with oil and baked or roasted lamb. They create a sweet smell for God. Our food should also be appreciated for its associations and the care that went into its preparation as much as for its nutrients. "**Preparing a meal is a tangible offering of love** . . . Celebrating and sanctifying a meal requires that we take the time to appreciate the cook's work and creativity" *(Wendy Mogel)*. After reciting *HaMotzi*, honor the cooks and bakers who contributed to this meal. Ask them if the recipes used have special memories. Recall your favorite family recipes.

"PEANUTS" by Charles Schultz, © United Features Syndicate

Handwashing

Guidelines
getting started

Some households wash their hands ritually with a cup, pouring water over each hand in turn, and providing a hand towel next to the sink. This can create an aura of sanctity: both water and hands have deep associations in our culture, though we seldom pay attention to them.

Initially some guests at the table may be uncomfortable waiting during the hand washing, but that variation from "diving into the food" forces them to take this meal seriously and to note its special standing. Even if only one person leaves the table to wash hands after Kiddush and before the blessing over the bread, *HaMotzi*, it may contribute to an atmosphere of expectation as the others wait to eat. It is customary to halt conversation from the hand washing until after saying *HaMotzi* (and eating a bit of bread). This unusual silence draws even more attention to the act of eating as a sacred moment removed from the rush of events at the table.

Guidelines
from tradition

1. Remove rings from the fingers to return hands to a pristine natural state. Then using clean water, pour water 1, 2 or 3 times over hands (first right and then left), up to fingers or over the whole hand up to the wrist (depending on the rabbinic authority you follow). In this way we reenact at home the life of the priests who washed before eating the twelve loaves of bread from God's table in the Temple each Shabbat.
2. With clean and pure hands, the blessing is recited over the washing.

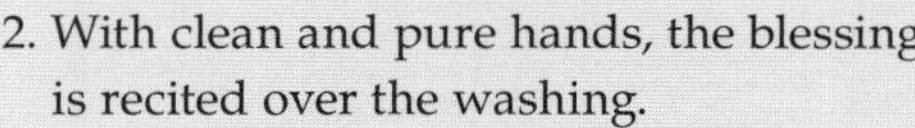

3. Then, between washing hands and eating the bread, no conversation is begun. This is in order to keep everyone's attention on the act of eating the bread, which is the sole reason for hand washing. (However, speaking about topics related to the bread — such as asking for a knife or some salt — is permitted since it does not distract us from eating.) Some people hum a wordless *niggun* to set the mood while waiting for everyone to finishing washing their hands before saying *HaMotzi* over the Hallah.

Yaacov Greenvurcel,
Netillat Yadaim.
www.greenvurcel.co.il

Hallah

THEY MAY BUILD MIGHTY BRIDGES, OR HEAL THE SICK, OR HIT HOME-RUNS, OR WRITE SOUL-STIRRING NOVELS!

THESE ARE HANDS WHICH MAY SOMEDAY CHANGE THE COURSE OF DESTINY!

THEY'VE GOT JELLY ON THEM!

Guidelines
getting started

How can I introduce a blessing over the bread into my home?

Breaking bread together is an ancient tradition, but often contemporary meals (especially with diet-conscious people) involve no bread at all. Many families do not eat together during the week, since individual schedules and tastes are so diverse. On Shabbat, however, sharing a meal beginning with wine and two loaves of Hallah can transform the act of eating into a social — and even spiritual meal.

However, some changes may be needed in the typical eating patterns in many homes. This involves a ritualization of the opening of the meal with the Kiddush and *HaMotzi*. Try to have the table set in advance with two Hallah loaves on a breadboard or beautiful plate covered with a nice napkin (or Hallah cover) and flanked by a knife and salt. If you forget to buy two Hallahs, then use an uncut regular loaf of bread. Even two slices of the best bread in the house are enough to set the scene.

Before reciting *HaMotzi* some families hold up the two loaves for a moment of silence or humming — a melody may help create a concentrated atmosphere. Others ask everyone sitting at the table to extend a hand and touch the loaf being shared as the blessing is recited. Then they recite the blessing and cut or tear the bread into multiple smaller pieces, dip each in salt (or honey) and pass them around in a plate or basket. The host may sometimes hold the whole loaf and go around the table to offer it to each of the guests consecutively so they may tear off a piece for themselves.

Shabbat Electricity

Try this: Everyone either holds the Hallah, or else holds onto someone who is holding onto the Hallah (or onto someone who is holding onto someone . . .). Children enjoy holding onto an elbow or a knee.

The Shabbes Dog

One dog lover has trained his dog — a valued member of the family — to come and stand at attention at the Shabbat table, and to beg for a piece of Hallah when *HaMotzi* is said.

Guidelines
from tradition

1. The peak of this process of physical and spiritual preparation is the sharing of the two loaves of Shabbat Hallah. The blessing is often recited by the host of the meal who — in distributing bread to each guest — symbolizes his or her hospitality.
2. The host may preface the blessing/*bracha* with a verse from the Ashrei *(Psalm 145:16)* **"God, You open Your hand and satisfy every living creature to its heart's content"** and then say *HaMotzi* and sprinkle salt over the bread or dip it in salt or honey.
3. The host eats the first bite right away, so that there will not be too great a delay between blessing the bread and consuming some of it. Usually the host breaks or cuts the loaf so as to give out generous portions.

No Leftovers for Shabbat

On every day of his life Shammai ate in honor of Shabbat. How? When he chanced upon a nice piece of meat [in the market, he would purchase it and] declare, "This is for Shabbat." If, on the following day, he found an even more desirable piece of meat, he would set the second piece aside [for Shabbat] and eat the first [during the week].

— *Talmud Beitza 16a*

Guidelines

parent-child corner

Hot Dogs and Jello for Shabbat

There is no mitzvah to eat kugel and gefillte fish, chicken soup and matza balls. Eating favorite foods that maximize our culinary pleasure is recognized as the mitzvah of *Oneg Shabbat* (enjoying Shabbat pleasures). One mother served her young children hot dogs and jello every Shabbat while they wore their prettiest pajamas. That was a cardinal source of their love for Shabbat. Even take-out pizza may serve the goal if framed properly as a way to honor Shabbat. However you do it, make it special.

Delegating Honors

In synagogues, especially on the High Holidays, there is a preassigned division of every task (even opening and closing the ark). Each act becomes "an honor." Similarly, children as well as adults can be honored at the table with tasks from passing out the books of blessings or the kippot, to reciting the Kiddush, to washing hands and providing a guest towel to dry them, to uncovering the Hallah (perhaps ask the youngest child), to picking a favorite melody for a Shabbat song.

Assign someone to read or even act out some of the Bread Tales *(page 91)*.

Specially Shaped Hallah

Bread bakers often involve their children in making special Hallah. It might be a chocolate chip Hallah or one shaped like a cartoon figure.

Overwrought Parents at the Shabbat Table

"The Jewish mother betrays an unusual amount of concern about the problem of feeding her children. In general, she should stop worrying so much about how much they eat and what they wear."
(Froyen Zhurnal, *an American Yiddish magazine for women, 1923)*

Beware of the "life and death struggle over food," says Wendy Mogel, in her wise and practical book on parenting, *The Blessing of a Skinned Knee.* She explains that "among many of the families I know, love, power and food have been bound together . . . Parents become very involved in what their children are and are not eating. Intuitively, children recognize this as the perfect place to seize power. When it comes to food, few modern parents are clear, calm, and authoritative. Put all this together and **food becomes a battlefield** . . . The ambivalence about food and eating and the resulting tension over self-control, guilt and sensual pleasure get passed along to children, even if we don't voice our worries out loud."

On Shabbat, when eating is to be a pleasure including extravagant fattening treats (which the traditional Shabbat songs praise), parents might best call a moratorium on control. The emotional health of a day without power conflicts at the table might be worth making an exception once a week from an otherwise healthy and balanced diet. Moderation is still called for, but not asceticism. "In Judaism there is a place for nutrition and for delight."

The Surprise Under the Hallah Cover

In my family the Hallah cover often hid little gifts purchased for our children. They were forbidden (futilely) to peek under the cover until after *HaMotzi.*

If you eat matza balls, try hiding a raisin in one matza ball and whoever finds it receives a small gift (or small task: telling a story, washing the dishes). Janus Korczak, the great Jewish educator from Warsaw who ran an orphan's home, would hide a chestnut in a matza ball at the Seder and reward the child who found it with a gift and much needed attention. A docent at the Holocaust museum in Kibbutz *Lochamei HaGhettaot* once showed an elderly man around and mentioned this story. The man pulled out his wallet and removed the chestnut that he had received from Korczak before the war. He had never forgotten that token of love.

— Noam Zion

Children and Misunderstanding Rules

At the home of friends who have recently become very observant, parents reminded their 5-year-old not to talk after *netilat yadayim*, and then asked him to recite *"Hamotzi."* He stood there frozen, while we all waited, wondering why he was stalling. He looked uncomfortable, and started humming, while we started nudging him, "nu . . . ." Finally he burst out: "How am I supposed to say the *bracha* if I'm not allowed to talk?!"

— Baruch Sienna

Hallah

Reflections כַּוָּנוֹת

on the sanctity of our hands and of our tables

Blessed Be These Hands

Blessed be the works of your hands, O Holy One.
Blessed be these hands that have touched life.
Blessed be these hands that have nurtured creativity.
Blessed be these hands that have held pain.
Blessed be these hands that have embraced with passion.
Blessed be these hands that have tended gardens.
Blessed be these hands that have closed in anger.
Blessed be these hands that have planted new seeds.
Blessed be these hands that have harvested ripe fields.
Blessed be these hands that have cleaned, washed, mopped and scrubbed.
Blessed be these hands that have become knotty with age.
Blessed be these hands that are wrinkled and scarred from doing justice.
Blessed be these hands that have reached out and been received.
Blessed be these hands that hold the promise of the future.
Blessed be the works of your hands, O Holy One.

— Diann Neu, Earth Prayers

Ritual Handwashing —Ceremonial or Real?

Do we wash our hands before eating bread primarily for the sake of ritual holiness or for physical hygiene? At times, the rabbis emphasize cleanliness as primary. They recommend that people rub their hands together to remove the dirt during washing. They complain that it is disgusting to eat with dirty hands, as well as with wet hands, therefore one must be sure to dry one's hands with a towel after the handwashing.

Other times, the Rabbis explain that the model for handwashing is the priests who removed ritual impurity before eating the food sanctified in the Temple. Aaron and his sons "washed"/*ra-khatzu* actively with their own power *(koach gavra)* and with a special vessel, so we too must pour water over our hands from a vessel, not merely dip them into the water. (For lovers of winter sports, note that one may dip one's hands in snow for the purpose of ritual handwashing). As is the case with a ritual immersion in the *mikveh,* to remove impurity there cannot be any obstructions between the water and one's body. Therefore, people remove their rings before hand washing (some families even have ring-holders on the table for this purpose!).

A Pitcher for *Netillat Yadayim*: Generosity is the Art of Receiving and Giving

What is the ethical message behind the requirement to wash our hands before eating bread using a *kli* — a pitcher — rather than just the water from the faucet?

The French-Israeli philosopher and scholar Marc-Alain Ouaknin suggests that the key to **Jewish ethical eating is the ability to receive with appreciation and to give to others with grace**. Metaphorically, the pitcher that receives water from the faucet and empties itself out on the hands of one about to eat bread is a model for human receiving and giving. This can be compared to the biggest bodies of water in drought-prone Israel: the Kineret (the Sea of Galilee), with its sweet water, and the Dead Sea (the Salt Sea). The Jordan River carries the sweet water from the Kineret to the Dead Sea.

Why is one sea sweet and one sea salty (30% minerals)? The secret is to understand that life is a flow of energy and that when it is stopped up then we have illness and death. The Kineret receives and then gives away its water, while the Dead Sea exclusively receives and never gives away its water to another source until it "dies." As the Dead Sea evaporates, it drops its sediments and salts, leaving a residue of undrinkable water. So all human beings should see themselves as pitchers appreciating the life flow into themselves from the love of others and generously passing on this treasure to others. Stagnation means death whether for the individual or the community. Then purity becomes impurity. After this act of purifying our hands with water from a pitcher, the hosts share their bread generously with the guests, for the hosts know that they are recipients of God's grace and therefore they owe it to pass it on to others.

— based on Marc-Alain Ouaknin,

The Heavenly and the Earthly

Originally the holy *(kadosh)* meant that which is set apart, isolated, segregated. In Jewish piety it assumed a new meaning, denoting a quality that is involved, immersed in common and earthly endeavors; carried primarily by individual, private, simple deeds rather than public ceremonies. "Humans should always regard themselves as if 'the Holy One is within you' *(Hosea 11:9)* — therefore one should not mortify the body." . . . Judaism teaches us how even the gratification of animal needs can be an act of sanctification. The enjoyment of food may be a way of purification. . . . Sanctification is not an unearthly concept. There is no dualism of the earthly and the sublime. All things are sublime. They are all created by God.

— *Abraham Joshua Heschel*

Marianna Kirschstein, silk Hallah Cover. Austria, late 19th century. (HUC Skirball Cultural Center, Museum Collection.)

The Table is Like an Altar

How can our home become a sacred space?

In Biblical and Rabbinic tradition the Temple is called *HaBayit* (the House) — the home of God who dwells in the midst of the human community. The portable "Temple," the Tent of Meeting that was in the desert, is called the *mishkan* (the Dwelling), the place of God's immanent *Shekhina* that dwells among us (God said: "Make Me a *mikdash*, a sanctified structure — and I will dwell, *shakhanti*, among them." — *Exodus 25:8*).

When the Temple was destroyed, the Rabbis sought to establish a place for the Divine Presence *(Shekhina)* inside the Jewish home. The Kabbalist Isaiah Horowitz *(17th century)* summarizes a symbolic view that dates back to the Talmud:

"The table substitutes for the altar, one who eats stands in for the priest, the food replaces the sacrifice."

Therefore Jewish tradition — whether as law or as custom — established patterns of table life to sanctify the otherwise animal function of feeding our bodies and to make it an occasion for communion with God and sharing with one another. This communal meal helps bring atonement with God and humans. Rabbis Yochanan and Elazar used to say: "In the era of the Temple we had the altar to atone for Israel. Now each person's table atones for him or her" *(Talmud Brachot 55a)*.

Reflections כַּוָּנוֹת

on the meaning of eating and sharing bread

Grief can take care of itself, but to get the full value of a joy you must have somebody to divide it with.

— Mark Twain

Open Channels between the Dining Room and the Gates of Heaven

Every *bracha* could be translated as: Stop, take three breaths, bring your being together, try to become aware of the significance of what you are about to do or to witness. Now: slowly, deliberately, utter the words that connect your intentions with what you are actually about to do. Pause, make yourself spring forth wholly, and connect yourself to the rest of the universe, and to the Source of Holiness and Being itself.

"Praised are you, O Lord our God, Ruler of the Universe" has become religious duckspeak. What we ought to do is create radically new translations of that formula which says, for example:

"I now voluntarily and with holy intention slow down what I am doing and contemplate the awesome potential of what I hope to do;" or "by the act that I am about to do — by putting food in my mouth — I hope somehow to turn my table into an altar." Or "by the act of lighting these candles, I hope to open channels between this dining room and the gates of heaven."

— Lawrence S. Kushner

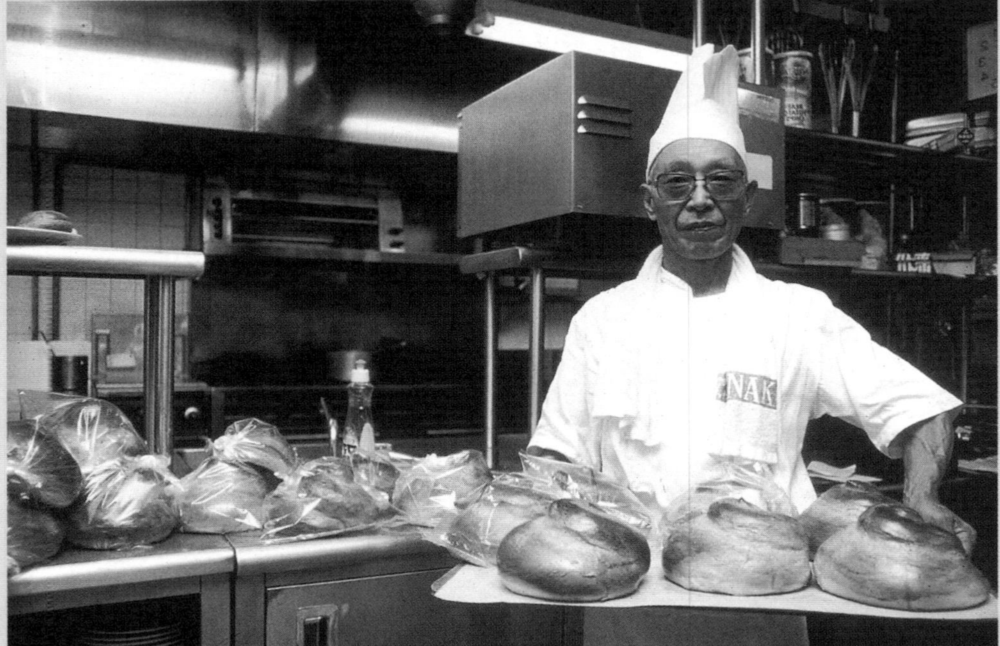

Selling Hallah at the JCC in Tokyo, 1983, by Ehud Malez. (Beit Hatefutsot Photo Archive, Tel Aviv)

The Sacred and the Everyday

It has often been said that Judaism is a religion of the everyday. It is not that we are intent on transforming the everyday into the sacred. It is that the sacred exists around every ordinary bend in life's journey. Our daily prayer acknowledging the miracles of God, for instance, does not specify the spectacular instances of the hand of God. Instead, you find mention of "Your miracles which are with us daily, the wonders and goodness that occur all the time — morning, noon and night." . . . Jews are trained to look for God in ordinary places: faces on the street, blossoms on a tree, a simple loaf of bread. Remember Elijah [who discovered God in the still small voice, not the earthquake].

Blessings are our own still small voice, the best approximation we have to being Godlike ourselves. They are an act of creation, that convert the ordinary into the extraordinary, not because they are a kind of verbal alchemy turning leaden experience into gold, but because they reveal the sacred in the everyday.

— Lawrence Hoffman

Tearing Bread

When God created the world, God made everything a little bit incomplete. Instead of making bread grow out of the earth, God made wheat grow so that humans might bake it into bread. Instead of making the earth of bricks, God made it of clay so that man might bake the clay into bricks. Why? So that humans could become God's partner in the task of completing the work of creation.

The altars of the Temple had to be built of unhewn stones, that is, no tool which could also double as a tool of warfare could be used in building the altar, a symbol of peace. As such, many families today do not use a knife to cut the Hallah; they tear it with their hands instead. Others keep the knife under the Hallah cloth until ready for use.

— Shira Milgrom

Bread and Behavior: The Ethics of Covering the Hallahs

While on a lecture tour, the nineteenth-century Rabbi Israel Salanter accepted a man's invitation for Shabbat dinner. As he and his host were preparing to sit down for the meal, the man threw an angry fit at his wife for forgetting to cover the Hallahs. Wounded by her husband's words and ashamed in the presence of their distinguished guest, the woman ran off to the kitchen and remained there. Rabbi Salanter, shocked by the man's behavior, leaned over and said to him, "Excuse me, but I'm getting older and my memory is weakening. Could you remind me of the reason we cover the Hallahs until after we recite the kiddush [over the wine]?"

The man, proud to be hosting so prominent a sage, explained the symbolism behind the custom; the Hallahs are covered so that they be spared the "embarrassment" of being exposed while all the ritual attention is being focused on the wine (normally, bread is the first item on the table to be blessed). After he finished,

Continued on next page →

Collecting Manna in the Desert, by Dieric Bouts (Flemish, 1420-1475)

Rabbi Salanter rose and rebuked him: "You are so meticulous about a mere custom of not 'embarrassing' a loaf of bread. And yet you are so quick and ready to dishonor your wife and hurt her feelings. I cannot eat with you." Only when the man hurried into the kitchen and pleaded with his wife to forgive him did Rabbi Salanter consent to remain.

People are often far crueler to their spouses than to strangers. Yet while the Torah obliges us to "love your neighbor as yourself," concerning one's wife, the Talmud teaches, "honor her more than yourself" *(Yevamot 62b)*.

— *Joseph Telushkin*

Breaking Bread — The Essence of Human Giving

To love is the art of knowing how to give and to share. Love consists essentially in giving and not in receiving. Giving is the source of more joy than receiving, because one's vitality is expressed in the gift. It constitutes the highest expression of power. In the very act of giving, I feel myself as superabundant, spending, living, free and hence joyful. *Pirkei Avot* teaches: "Who is rich? The one who is happy with his/her share." Shlomo Rotnemer has suggested another possible translation: "Who is rich? The one who is happy in sharing."

In the sphere of material relations, giving signifies that one is rich — not that the person who has a lot is rich, but that the person who gives a lot is rich. The miser who anxiously tortures himself with the thought of losing something is, psychologically speaking, a poor man, impoverished, as wealthy as he may be. People capable of giving of themselves are rich.

— *Rabbi Marc-Alan Ouknin*

Animals First!

Noah's Ark and the Mitzvah to Feed Your Animals First, then the Needy and Yourself Last

Before we ourselves begin to eat we are obligated to feed the domesticated animals whose lives depend on us *(Talmud Berachot 40a)*. That set of priorities is hinted at in the Shema where it says: "I shall provide grass in your field for your cattle." Only afterwards does the Torah declare: "and you will eat and you will be satisfied" *(Deuteronomy 11:15)*. But how does that relate to Noah's ark and more broadly to the needs of the poor? Here is a rabbinic story that draws them all together:

[Abraham] asked [the legendary king of Jerusalem] Malki Tzedek: 'What righteous act did you and your family do to merit surviving [Noah's] flood?'

Malki Tzedek responded: 'Because we gave *Tzedakah* in the ark.'

Tanya Zion

Abraham then said: 'How is that possible? There were no poor people on the ark — only Noah and his family. To whom did you give *Tzedakah*?'

Malki Tzedek replied: 'We gave it to the cattle, beasts and birds. We never slept because we were always setting food before one animal or the other.'

Abraham then reasoned, if they survived the flood because of their *Tzedakah* to animals, then how much greater will be my deed if I am charitable to my fellow man! At that time he immediately planted an **E-Sh-eL** tree in Beersheva *(Genesis 21:33)* — meaning [symbolically, that he offered all travelers passing by his home]: **E** = *ekhol* = food to eat, **SH** = *shtiya* = drink and **L** = *liviya* = a protective escort [to their next destination because of the danger on the roads].

— *Midrash Tehillim (Buber), Psalms 37; 110; Adapted from Joseph Telushkin*

My Grandfather Feeding the Cats

Tanya Zion

My grandfather Reb Elyah Pruzhaner [Feinstein] would always insist on feeding the cats before he ate. It was not so simple, for you had to find out where the cats were in the house. After all, the cats did not know that my grandfather was about to eat. Nevertheless, he would not sit down to eat until food was placed before the cats! The alarm would go on throughout the Feinstein household to search for the cats. This is not an allegory, but it is an exact account of what took place in my grandfather's home.

— *Rav Joseph B. Soloveitchik*

Bread Tales

Bread is the "the most historic, romantic, humane of all the foods."

— *Meir Shalev, Esau, p.352*

"May All Who Are Hungry" — The Hands of God

The following story is told by Rabbi Zalman Schacter Shalomi:

A long time ago in the northern part of Israel, in the town of Safed, the richest man in town was sleeping, as usual, at the synagogue through Shabbat morning services. Every now and then, he would almost wake up, try to get comfortable on the hard wooden bench, and then sink back into a deep sleep. One morning he awoke just long enough to hear the chanting of the Torah verses from Leviticus 24:5-6 in which God instructs the children of Israel to place twelve loaves of Hallah on a table in the ancient wilderness tabernacle.

When services ended, the wealthy man woke up, not realizing that all he had heard was the Torah reading about God's commandment to place twelve loaves in the *Mishkan* (the sacred tent in the desert). He thought that God had come to him in his sleep and had asked him personally to bring twelve loaves of Hallah to God. The rich man felt honored that God should single him out, but he also felt a little foolish. Of all the things God could want from a person, twelve loaves of Hallah did not seem very important. But who was he to argue with God? He went home and baked the bread that night.

Upon returning to the synagogue, he decided the only proper place for his holy gift was alongside the Torah scrolls in the ark. He carefully arranged the loaves and said to God, "Thank You for telling me what You want of me. Pleasing you makes me very happy." Then he left.

No sooner had he gone than the poorest Jew in the town, the synagogue janitor, entered the sanctuary. All alone, he spoke to God. "O Lord, I am so poor. My family is starving; we have nothing to eat. Unless You perform a miracle for us, we will surely perish." Then, as was his custom, he walked around the room to tidy it up. When he ascended the bimah and opened the ark, there before him were twelve loaves of Hallah! "A miracle!" exclaimed the poor man. "I had no idea You worked so quickly! Blessed are You, O God, who answers our prayers." Then he ran home to share the bread with his family.

Minutes later, the rich man returned to the sanctuary, curious to know whether or not God ate the Hallah. Slowly he ascended the bimah, opened the ark, and saw that the Hallahs were gone. "Oh, my God!" he shouted. "You really ate my Hallahs! I thought You were teasing. This is wonderful. You can be sure that I'll bring another twelve loaves — with raisins in them too!"

Swedish Hallahs
photographed by Karl Gabor
(from the Swedish Jewish cookbook, *Judisk Mat i Svenskt Kok*, 2002)

The following week, the rich man brought a dozen loaves to the synagogue and again left them in the ark. Minutes later, the poor man entered the sanctuary. "God, I don't know how to say this, but I'm out of food again. Seven loaves we ate, four we sold, and one we gave to charity. But now, nothing is left, and unless You do another miracle, we surely will starve." He approached the ark and slowly opened its doors. "Another miracle!" he cried. "Twelve more loaves, and with raisins too! Thank You God. This is wonderful!"

The Hallah exchange became a weekly ritual that continued for many years. And, like most rituals that become routine, neither man gave it much thought. Then, one day, the rabbi, detained in the sanctuary longer than usual, watched the rich man place the dozen loaves in the ark and the poor man redeem them.

The rabbi called the two men together and told them what they had been doing.

"I see," said the rich man sadly. "God does not really eat Hallah."

"I understand," said the poor man. "God has not been baking Hallah for me after all."

They both feared that now God no longer would be present in their lives.

Then the rabbi asked them to look at their hands. "Your hands," he said to the rich man, "are the hands of God giving food to the poor. And your hands," said the rabbi to the poor man, "also are the hands of God, receiving gifts from the rich. So you see, God can still be present in your lives. Continue baking and continue taking. Your hands are the hands of God."

— Lawrence Kushner

The Twin Loaves, Twin Friends

Two youths who were deeply devoted to one another used to go to Rabbi Naftali together to sit at his table. When he distributed the bread, for such was his custom, he always gave the two friends twin loaves clinging each to each.

Once they were vexed with each other. They did not know how this feeling had entered their hearts and could not overcome it. Soon after when they again went to Roptchitz and were seated at the rabbi's table on the eve of the Sabbath, he took the twin loaves, cut them apart, and gave one to each of the youths.

On their way home from the meal they were overcome with emotion and both cried out in the same breath: "We are at fault, we are at fault!" They went to an inn, ordered schnapps and drank a toast to each other.

The next day at the midday meal of the Sabbath, Rabbi Naftali again put twin loaves into the hands of the friends.

The King's Loaves, an Afghani Folktale

Once there were two beggars who went daily to the palace to beg at the king's gate. Every day the king gave each of them a loaf of bread. One of the beggars would always thank the king for his generosity. But the other thanked God for giving the king sufficient wealth to give *tzedakah*.

The second beggar's words always hurt the king. So the king decided to teach him a lesson. The king ordered his baker to bake two identical loaves, but in one he had him conceal precious jewels. Then he instructed the baker to give the loaf with the hidden jewels to the beggar who always thanked the king for his *tzedakah*.

The next day the baker went to the king's gate and handed the two loaves to the beggars. He took great care not to confuse the two, for he feared the king's wrath if he should make a mistake.

When the beggar with the special loaf felt how heavy and hard it was, he concluded that it was poorly made and asked the other beggar to exchange loaves with him. The second beggar, always eager to help a friend, agreed. Then they went their separate ways.

When the second man bit into the loaf, he discovered that it was filled with jewels. He thanked God for his good fortune, grateful that he would no longer have to beg for his bread.

The next morning the king was surprised to find only the first beggar at the palace gate. He had the baker brought before him and asked him, "Did you mix up the two loaves I had you bake?"

"No, your majesty," answered the baker. "I did exactly as you commanded."

The king turned to the beggar and asked, "What did you do with the loaf you received yesterday?"

The man replied, "It was hard and poorly baked, so I gave it to my friend in exchange for his."

Then the king understood that all his riches had indeed come from God, and that only the Holy One can make a poor man rich and a rich man poor. Not even a king can change the will of heaven.

"Let Them Eat Cake"

When told about the shortage of bread for the poor in France, an insensitive French queen who lived just before the French Revolution once responded: "If the people have no bread, let them eat cake." *(J.J. Rousseau, Confessions)* In her luxurious style of eating, she lacked all sensitivity to the poor's hunger. One might conclude that the rich should eat the food of the poor and then become more sensitive to their needs. Yet a Hassidic rebbe concluded the opposite.

He used to urge the rich to maintain their luxurious cuisine. "Let the rich eat cake; otherwise if they are satisfied with mere bread, then they will expect the poor to be satisfied with even less."

"And God Braided Eve's Hair"

When Eve saw the day getting darker on the sixth day of creation, she said: "This is all my fault. The world is returning to a state of unformed chaos because of me!" Then God came and braided Eve's hair and taught her how to kindle light to usher in the Shabbat Bride. And ever since then Eve's daughters have brought light where there is darkness by lighting Shabbat candles at the end of the sixth day of each week. And we eat braided Hallah on Shabbat to remember God's kindness, how God comforted Eve by braiding her hair.

— *Moshe Silberschein*

Bread and Creativity: The Innovative Baker as the Model of Jewish Continuity

Once there was a king with two servants whom he loved with a complete love, so he gave them each a bushel of wheat and a sheaf of flax to guard.

What did the clever one do? He took the flax and wove it into a table cloth.

He took the wheat and made it into fine flour by winnowing it and grinding it. He then kneaded the flour, baked it and placed the loaves on the table, over which he had spread the table cloth. He left his prepared table for the king.

What did the stupid one do? He did nothing [but guard them].

When the king arrived at home and he said to them, "My sons, bring me what I gave you."

One brought forth the wheat in a [strong] box and the sheaf of flax on top. The other brought out the table [with the table cloth] and the fine quality bread on it . . . *[Which one do you think is the more beloved one?]*

— *Midrash Seder Eliyahu Zuta*

Baking Hallah in Hot Springs, Arkansas. Photo by Bill Aron.

A Weekly Test: What Have You Learned? By Moritz Daniel Oppenheim (Germany, 19th century)

D'var Torah
Shabbat table talk

דְּבַר תּוֹרָה

Introduction

Shabbat has its own narrative — just as Pesach has the Haggadah and Purim has the *Megillah* of Esther. It is not unlike a serial soap opera: The 54 weekly Torah readings (*Parshat Hashavua*) follow our ancestors' stormy love lives and parent-child conflicts. The Shabbat narrative is also a travelogue we relive. One week we are in the Garden of Eden and several weeks later Joseph's brothers are selling him down to Egypt. The final episode describes Moshe — at age 120 — looking over toward the Promised Land. But before we enter the happy ending, the reruns begin and we roll back our scroll to the beginning to retell it all anew. The Shabbat table is the setting for an interactive rendition in which all are encouraged to participate.

The study of Torah is the right of every Jew

The Jewish people were given three crowns:
the crown of Torah, the crown of priesthood and the crown of sovereignty.
The crown of priesthood was given to Aaron and his descendants . . . .
The crown of sovereignty was given to David and his descendants . . . .
But the crown of Torah is for every Jew.
Whoever desires may come and claim it . . . it is the greatest crown of all.

— *Maimonides, Mishne Torah, Laws of Learning Torah 3:1*

Guidelines
parent-child corner

The *Shema* tells every parent to teach Torah in the course of everyday life — "when you walk by the way and when you sit in your house." *(Deuteronomy 6:7)* On Shabbat in Eastern Europe, fathers would often test their children on their weekly studies at school. That test could be quite ominous, but it did provide parents a good sense of what the teacher — the parents' stand-in for Jewish education — was doing. Today's Shabbat table should not be a "testing ground" for children, but it might provide an opportunity for the younger children to share what they have learned and display art, perform songs or tell stories. This reinforcement is essential for them to take their studies seriously.

For middle-school children, quizzes with prizes work wonders in helping them enjoy the Shabbat Torah talk. Prepare for them (or ask them to prepare) ten questions about the weekly portion or the upcoming holiday, and then quiz (or be quizzed) by everyone at the table.

For teenagers, try presenting an ethical dilemma: this invites their participation and allows them to argue either side of the case without a right answer being forced upon them. Then bring some Jewish responses. Bibliodrama is also very exciting; participants speak in first person in the name of a Biblical character at a dramatic moment. *(See A Different Night, The Leader's Guide, "Bibliodrama" by Peter Pitzele or his books, Scripture Windows or Our Fathers' Wells.)*

Guidelines

getting started

How do I initiate a Torah discussion at my table on Shabbat?

The Rabbis teach that every time at least three Jews sit at the table together, they are expected to exchange words of Torah. Every Shabbat, devote five minutes to Torah at your table. But don't worry. You need not be a scholar. Use Hillel as your paradigm. A minimally inquisitive non-Jew came to him and asked merely: Explain your whole Torah while standing on one leg. Often that is all the time and interest you can count on at your table. Do the best you can and hope to plant seeds for further learning. Hillel's response was: "Whatever is hateful to you, do not do unto others. The rest is commentary, go and learn." *(Talmud Shabbat 20b)* You need not be the rabbi who knows all the answers and defends the piety of the Torah. Your task is to facilitate these Torah exchanges, not to be a scholar yourself. Let the participants at the table know in advance that after the main course and before dessert there will be a five minute Torah break.

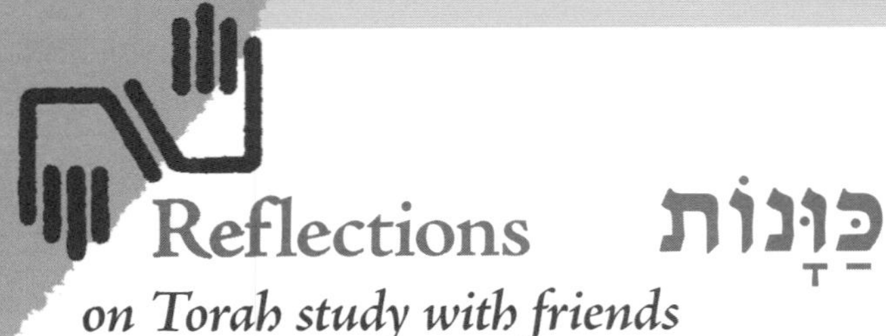

Reflections כַּוָּנוֹת

on Torah study with friends

Jews Love Books and Fight with Books

Some traditional Jews begin studying by kissing the book. Then they open it with a sense of awe and reverence. Once they begin learning they often beat on top of the book with their fists in the fervor of their arguments with their study partners. At the end of the learning they close the book — which aroused such hot debate — and kiss it farewell.

— Adin Steinsalz

Leading a Shabbat Table Talk

Shabbat table conversation need not be restricted to intellectual treatments of classical texts. Just sharing personal memories and dreams goes a long way to bonding among the guests and the members of the household. **Value clarification exercises, reading short stories especially hassidic ones, raising ethical dilemmas for discussion (such as those recounted in Joseph Telushikin's many wonderful books) or just talking about the most significant event of the last week** serve to build *Shalom Bayit* — the social peace of the household. The Rabbis describe students of Torah as sharing all aspects of their lives together not merely their formal learning. That is their definition of friendship — of *hevruta*. These discussions also allow guests to share.

Here are a just few topics of the many that might be raised:

A. **Remembering.** Ask everyone to report on something positive they have done in their line of work, their contribution to the world God created in six days. Then again one might describe the worst aspect of their week, and try to understand the difference between creative and fulfilling work and degrading or disheartening work. Or focus on leisure time and recall some of the best places of recreation or the most interesting Shabbat experiences one has shared. It is best to model this idea by going first in answering the question you pose. Allow people to pass or to chime in later, so no one will feel on the spot.

B. **Oneg Shabbat Dreamshop.** Imagine the best spots for Shabbat *menucha*/rest and relaxation. Is a mountaintop or a seashore better? A book or a game of tennis?

C. **Getting back in touch with the Creation.** Describe a beautiful aspect of nature; take out nature books.

The Philosophers' Shabbat for Everyone

Medieval Jewish philosophers like Rabbi Abraham ibn Ezra from the Golden Age of Moslem Spain added a new understanding to Shabbat: "Shabbat was given so that we might contemplate the Creation of God and ponder the Torah." *(Ibn Ezra commentary on Exodus 2:8)* "On this day the power of procreation is in the body and the power of insight and understanding in the soul are renewed" *(Ibn Ezra on Genesis 2:3)* "for God sanctified this day and prepared it so that souls might receive more wisdom than on any other day." *(Ibn Ezra on Exodus 20:8)* That added intellectual acumen is the meaning of what the Rabbis called the *Neshama Y'teira* — the added soul of Shabbat. However unlike elitist cultures, Judaism — with Shabbat — offers the pleasures of philosophy to all classes.

The Mystics' Shabbat

Where do all the extra Shabbat souls go when they depart this world after Havdalah?

When all the souls that had settled upon Israel [during Shabbat] ascend [after Havdalah], they go up and present themselves before the holy Sovereign and the Blessed Holy One asks them all: "What new interpretation of Torah did you discover in that world?"

Happy is the person whose *Neshama Y'teira* — extra soul — can tell God an original interpretation of the Torah! What great joy the soul causes! The Blessed Holy One brings in the divine retinue and says: "Listen to the original interpretation that the soul of so-and-so has just related!" But if they have nothing new to add, then the heavenly assembly is grief-stricken.

— *Zohar III 173a*

A Noisy Torah Argument

Judaism is a noisy religion. The faithful are rarely silent. The prophet Hosea said, "Take with you words," and this commandment at least has been well kept. And if their mouths are not enough, Jews also use their hands as they speak, argue and discuss. They do this with each other, and they do the same with God.

Jews even study divine law traditionally in pairs, so that they can argue better. How can one argue with oneself?

Many feel uneasy with this vehement approach to religion. Surely God, they say, should be sought in silence, head reverently bowed, mind an inviting blank, eyes reverently closed. How can one seek the Divine in the atmosphere of a holy prize-fight?

Yet this is the meaning of the name "Israel" — "one who struggles with God." It was not given to Jacob after quiet meditation, but after prolonged and realistic struggle with a messenger of God. Jews, even in their religion, assert the humanness of humans, the arguing, contradictory, passionate side to our nature that God put in us. We are not holy vegetables, bits of religious asparagus, quietly growing upwards, complying with divine requirements, in a dull earthy silence.

— *Lionel Blue*

Heder (Hebrew School)
from *The Book of Hebrew Letters*
by Mark Podwal, © 1972, 1992

Shabbat, a "Pause Between the Notes"

A great pianist was once asked by an ardent admirer:

"How do you handle the notes as well as you do?"
The artist answered: "The notes I handle no better than many pianists, but the pauses between the notes — ah! That is where the art resides."

In great living, as in great music, the art may be in the pauses. Surely one of the enduring contributions which Judaism made to the art of living was the Shabbat, "the pause between the notes." And it is to the Shabbat that we must look if we are to restore to our lives the sense of serenity and sanctity which Shabbat offers in such joyous abundance.

— *Abraham Joshua Heschel*

Zemirot — Music from the Shtetl
from *The Book of Hebrew Letters*
by Mark Podwal, copyright © 1972, 1992

Zemirot . . . soul singing at the table

זְמִירוֹת

Singing Together

Alone,
I cannot lift my voice in song.
But when you come near and sing with me,
Our prayers fuse and a new voice soars.
Our bond is beyond voice and voice.
Our bond is one of spirit and spirit.

— ADAPTED FROM REBBE PINCHAS OF KORETZ

Introduction

During Shabbat meals Jews have sung songs about the food, the company and the Shabbat experience. This Shabbat book is not large enough to contain the whole range of songs from Biblical to medieval to contemporary Israeli and American Jewish. Those are available from many existing organizations. On the following pages are three aids to Shabbat singing:

a) inspirational quotes about the significance of this characteristically Jewish singing experience.

b) how-to advice on getting started

c) a sampler of a few songs of different types

However beyond these teasers, we have prepared many other aids available by writing to us by electronic mail. These include an annotated list of Shabbat musical CDs, practical advice for singing with younger children, and a complete annotated translation and commentary on the traditional Zemirot that are so seldom understood.

A few short songs: biblical, medieval, modern

אֶשָּׂא עֵינַי אֶל הֶהָרִים,	**Esa einai** el he-harim,
מֵאַיִן יָבוֹא עֶזְרִי?	mei-ayin yavo ez-ri?
עֶזְרִי מֵעִם יְיָ,	Ez-ri mei-im Ha-shem,
עוֹשֵׂה שָׁמַיִם וָאָרֶץ.	oseh shamayim va-aretz.

I raise my eyes to the mountains: from where will my help come?
My help comes from Adonai, creator of heaven and earth.

— PSALM 121:1

אֵלֶּה חָמְדָה לִבִּי	**Ei-leh khamdah li-bi**
חוּסָה נָא וְאַל נָא תִּתְעַלֵּם.	khusah na v'al na tit-a-lem.

These are the desires of my heart.
Have mercy and do not turn away.

— ELAZAR AZIKRI, 16TH CENTURY MYSTIC POET, SAFED

אֵלִי, אֵלִי,	**Eili, Eili,**
שֶׁלֹּא יִגָּמֵר לְעוֹלָם,	shelo yi-gameir l'olam,
הַחוֹל וְהַיָּם,	Ha-khol v'ha-yam,
רִשְׁרוּשׁ שֶׁל הַמַּיִם,	rish-roosh shel ha-mayim,
בְּרַק הַשָּׁמַיִם,	B'rak ha-shamayim,
תְּפִלַּת הָאָדָם.	t'filat ha-adam.

O Lord, my God, I pray that these things shall never end,
The sand and the sea, the rush of the waters,
The lightning of the sky, the prayer of human beings.

— HANNAH SENESH (KIBBUTZNIK, POET AND PARATROOPER, 1942.
REPRINTED BY PERMISSION OF ACUM AND THE AUTHOR.

Songs/ Zemirot

Menucha v'Simcha: Past, Present, & Future

Menucha v'Simcha invites us to explicate three issues — one past, one present and one future:

(1) PAST — Jews are called upon to standup and bear witness to the Creation of the world in the beginning of time and to clarify our shared responsibility in taking care of our environment for the future.

(2) PRESENT — Jews are invited to transform this day of rest into a day of taking joy in the here and now;

(3) FUTURE — Observers of Shabbat are promised that they will recover the Divine light once hidden and saved for the future.

"Stand By Me": Bearing Witness to the Creator and Bearing Responsibility for the Creation

Like many of the Shabbat Zemirot, *Menucha V'Simcha* reminds us of the key Shabbat observances beginning with Kiddush. We stand *(omdim)* for the Kiddush when we recite *Vay'khulu*/"God finished the Heaven and the Earth" on Friday night and *V'Shamru*/"Observe the Shabbat" and *Zakhor*/"Remember the Shabbat" on Shabbat morning.

Why is it important to stand up for Kiddush? "Standing" is the posture of a witness, so in standing for the Kiddush it is as if we are testifying publicly that God is the Creator.

> Anyone who keeps Shabbat bears witness before the One whose words called the world into existence, that God created the world in six days and rested on the seventh. "You are my witnesses, says Adonai" *(Isaiah 43:10)*, *(Mekhilta Yitro)*.

How did the Rabbis arrive at this interpretation of Kiddush as bearing witness?

Noticing that the two tablets of the Ten Commandments are easily divided into 5 and 5, the Rabbis were struck with the symmetry between the 4th commandment ("Remember the Shabbat day to make it holy/*kodesh*") *(Exodus 20:8)* and the 9th one — "You shall not bear false witness" *(Exodus 20:16)*. Both require human beings to bear witness to the truth. Hence anyone who fails to acknowledge the Creator and to mark this day as *kodesh*/holy by both reciting this and observing it is in effect bearing false witness against the Creator, implying that God did not create the world *(Mekhilta Yitro)*.

Bearing Witness and Ecology

Bearing witness involves, however, not only a belief about God, but also a behavior showing restraint and respect for the created world that God made.

> Rabbi Shimon ben Elazar says: Anyone who rips up his clothes when in a rage or smashes dishes in a rage, or throws away coins in rage — should be viewed as an idol worshipper.
>
> Rabbi Abin explains the verse: "You shall have no foreign god in your midst." Who is that foreign god in the midst of the human body? It is the evil inclination. *(Talmud Shabbat 105b)*

We destroy the world out of our own frustration as if it did not have value in itself and as if it did not have a Creator. We treat the world as our own creation — to be disposed of at will based on the whims of the god of aggressive drives within us. Therefore in bearing witness to the Creator we must accept the need to honor that Creation — independent of the ups and downs of our personal feelings.

Our responsibility to preserve the ecology of God's Creation is expressed beautifully in this Midrash:

> When the Holy One created the first human, God took Adam and conducted a tour of all the trees in the Garden of Eden. God said: "Do you see how beautiful and how superb these are?
>
> Well, all of what I created, I created for you. Pay attention so that you do not ruin or destroy My world. For if you ruin it, who will ever be able to repair it after you? *(Midrash Ecclesiates Rabbah 9)*

God is the Creator and therefore we must become reliable trustees of the Creation celebrated now.

Menucha: The Art of Resting

Not only must we sing about rest, but we need to learn from the idea of musical rests how to develop a Shabbat cadence to one's life. Oscar Castro-Neves is an accomplished guitarist and composer. He writes musical scores for movies. He says it is common in a dramatic scene to gradually bring the music to crescendo, and then stop – rest – silence. "Whatever is spoken on the screen in that silence is heard more clearly, more powerfully; the words are lent an additional potency, because they are spoken out of the silence. When you listen to music, " he counsels me, "listen to the cadence of rest." Then he gives me an example I can understand, one from Martin Luther King's most famous speech. "Listen to the cadence: Free at last. *(Rest)* Free at last. *(Rest)* Thank God almighty, we are free at last." *(Sabbath: Restoring the Sacred Rhythm of Rest, Wayne Muller, 1999)*

מְנוּחָה וְשִׂמְחָה *Menucha v'Simcha — rest and joy by Moshe*

(Moshe is an anonymous medieval poet whose name is contained in the acrostic of the first three stanzas. He composed the poem in the early 16th century.)

מְנוּחָה וְשִׂמְחָה אוֹר לַיְּהוּדִים,
יוֹם שַׁבָּתוֹן יוֹם מַחֲמַדִּים,
שׁוֹמְרָיו וְזוֹכְרָיו הֵמָּה מְעִידִים,
כִּי לְשִׁשָּׁה כֹּל בְּרוּאִים וְעוֹמְדִים.

Rest and joy, that is the "light for the Jews." (Esther 8:16)
The Shabbat day is the Divine day of delight.
Those who "keep" it and "remember" it bear witness that:
At the end of the six days altogether. Those created were standing . . .
[as established features of the world. Among them the greatest include:]

שְׁמֵי שָׁמַיִם אֶרֶץ וְיַמִּים,
כָּל צְבָא מָרוֹם גְּבוֹהִים וְרָמִים,
תַּנִּין וְאָדָם וְחַיַּת רְאֵמִים,
כִּי בְּיָהּ יְיָ צוּר עוֹלָמִים.

The sky, the earth and the seas;
All the legions of heavenly bodies, lofty and high;
The sea-monster, the humans and even the great wild ox. (Job 39:9)
Yet "we can trust in Adonai, the Rock of Eternity"
[who can demote even powerful heavenly creatures at will]. (Isaiah 26:4-6)

הוּא אֲשֶׁר דִּבֵּר לְעַם סְגֻלָּתוֹ,
שָׁמוֹר לְקַדְּשׁוֹ מִבּוֹאוֹ וְעַד צֵאתוֹ,
שַׁבַּת קֹדֶשׁ יוֹם חֶמְדָּתוֹ,
כִּי בוֹ שָׁבַת אֵל מִכָּל מְלַאכְתּוֹ.

God told his treasured people:
"Keep Shabbat and sanctify it" (Deuteronomy 5:12), from its arrival to its departure.
Shabbat is sacred, a day of delights,
"For on that day God ceased from all his labor." (Genesis 2:3)

בְּמִצְוַת שַׁבָּת אֵל יַחֲלִיצָךְ,
קוּם קְרָא אֵלָיו יָחִישׁ לְאַמְּצָךְ,
נִשְׁמַת כָּל חַי וְגַם נַעֲרִיצָךְ,
אֱכֹל בְּשִׂמְחָה כִּי כְבָר רָצָךְ.

In reward for observing the mitzvah of Shabbat, God will strengthen you.
So get up [early] to petition God and God will be equally quick to grant you courage.
[Sing the Shabbat morning prayers:] Nishmat and Na'aritzakh
Then "eat with joy,... for God has already found you acceptable." (Ecclesiastes 9:7)

בְּמִשְׁנֶה לֶחֶם וְקִדּוּשׁ רַבָּה,
בְּרֹב מַטְעַמִּים וְרוּחַ נְדִיבָה,
יִזְכּוּ לְרַב טוּב הַמִּתְעַנְּגִים בָּהּ.
בְּבִיאַת גּוֹאֵל לְחַיֵּי הָעוֹלָם הַבָּא.

With two loaves of bread and the Great Kiddush [recited on Shabbat morning],
With plenty of delicacies and a spirit of sharing and generosity,
All those who enjoy themselves on Shabbat will earn overflowirg goodness
When the Messiah arrives for the World-to-Come.

„והיה באחרית הימים"—
א ריקודל גאר מיטן קנאק
עס וועלען ערשט טאנצען צוזאמען
בונדיסט, ציוניסט און חסיד'אק...
לשנה טובה תכתבו
A happy New Year

Bitter ideological enemies singing together: a Jewish socialist Bundist, a Zionist, and a Hasid — New Year's card, Warsaw-New York, 1900s. Reprinted by permission of Beit Hatefutsot Photo Archive, Tel Aviv, from the Jewish Natonal and University Library in Jerusalem.

Introduction to *Tzur Mishelo:* An Overture to *Birkat HaMazon*

Tzur Mishelo is a preview of the *Birkat HaMazon.* Like an overture before a symphony, the song introduces briefly all of the major motifs and key literary phrases which will echo in our ears as we recite the blessings after our meal. Most appropriately, *Tzur Mishelo* is often the last of the zemirot sung before *Birkat HaMazon,* since it corresponds to the *Birkat's* first three *brachot.* The refrain parallels the *mezuman* in which everyone is invited to recite *Birkat HaMazon. Tzur mi-shelo akhalnu barchu* recalls *Nevarekh she-akhalnu mishelo*/" Let's Bless the One from whose bounty we have eaten." In the poem God is referred to as a *tzur*/ rock, not primarily to represent God's strength, but the divine ability to nourish Israel under any circumstances, even in the desert, even from a rock. When Moses struck the rock to satisfy a thirsty, tired and despondent people *(Exodus 17:6; Numbers 20:11)*, "God fed them honey from a rock and oil from a stone" *(Deuteronomy 32:13).* The miracle of God's abundant gift of food is that even after we have eaten our fill *(sava-nu)* we have bread left over *(hotarnu).* It is traditional to leave bread on the table during *Birkat HaMazon,* for an empty table is not suitable for a blessing.

הִנֵּה מַה־טּוֹב וּמַה־נָּעִים	**Hi-nei mah tov** u-ma-naim
שֶׁבֶת אַחִים גַּם יָחַד.	Sheh-vet akhim gam yakhad.

How pleasant it can be
For brothers and sisters to live together. — *Psalm 133:1*

צוּר מִשֶּׁלּוֹ *Tzur mishelo akhalnu — the divine rock that feeds us*

Refrain:

צוּר מִשֶּׁלּוֹ אָכַלְנוּ בָּרְכוּ אֱמוּנַי.
שָׂבַעְנוּ וְהוֹתַרְנוּ כִּדְבַר יְיָ.

***Tzur*, the refrain, corresponds to the Zimun, the Invitation to Birkat HaMazon:**

Let us, my faithful friends, bless (Barchu) the Divine Rock whose food we have eaten.

For we have eaten our "fill" (Deuteronomy 8:10) "and even have food left over,
as God promised." (Elisha, II Kings 4: 43-44; see II Chronicles 31:10)

1

הַזָּן אֶת־עוֹלָמוֹ רוֹעֵנוּ אָבִינוּ,
אָכַלְנוּ אֶת־לַחְמוֹ וְיֵינוֹ שָׁתִינוּ.
עַל כֵּן נוֹדֶה לִשְׁמוֹ וּנְהַלְּלוֹ בְּפִינוּ,
אָמַרְנוּ וְעָנִינוּ אֵין קָדוֹשׁ כַּיְיָ. צוּר מִשֶּׁלּוֹ . . .

***Hazan* corresponds to the first bracha of the Birkat HaMazon:**

The Provider of food for the world is our Shepherd and our Parent.

We have eaten God's bread and drunk God's wine.

Therefore, let us acknowledge (Nodeh) the Divine name and praise God with our mouths.

We declare in song: "There is no one as holy as Adonai."
(Hannah, the prophet Samuel's mother, I Samuel 2:2)

2

בְּשִׁיר וְקוֹל תּוֹדָה נְבָרֵךְ לֵאלֹהֵינוּ,
עַל אֶרֶץ חֶמְדָּה טוֹבָה שֶׁהִנְחִיל לַאֲבוֹתֵינוּ,
מָזוֹן וְצֵידָה הִשְׂבִּיעַ לְנַפְשֵׁנוּ,
חַסְדּוֹ גָּבַר עָלֵינוּ וֶאֱמֶת יְיָ. צוּר מִשֶּׁלּוֹ . . .

***B'Shir* corresponds to the second bracha of the Birkat HaMazon:**

With song and sound of thanksgiving let us bless our God

For the "desirable land" (Jeremiah 3:19), for the "good land" (Deuteronomy 8:10);
that God granted to our ancestors as an inheritance.

With food and provisions God has filled our souls,

"God's kindness has overwhelmed us, Adonai is true and reliable." (Psalms 117:2)

3

רַחֵם בְּחַסְדֶּךָ עַל עַמְּךָ צוּרֵנוּ,
עַל צִיּוֹן מִשְׁכַּן כְּבוֹדֶךָ, זְבוּל בֵּית תִּפְאַרְתֵּנוּ,
בֶּן דָּוִד עַבְדֶּךָ יָבוֹא וְיִגְאָלֵנוּ,
רוּחַ אַפֵּינוּ מְשִׁיחַ יְיָ. צוּר מִשֶּׁלּוֹ . . .

***Rakhem* corresponds to the third bracha of the Birkat HaMazon:**

Our Divine Rock, be kind to your people.

Be merciful to Zion, your dwelling, our splendid Temple (I Kings 8:13).

Let your servant David's descendant come and redeem us —

"[The messiah] is the breath of our life, Adonai's anointed one." (Lamentations/Eicha 4:20).

4

יִבָּנֶה הַמִּקְדָּשׁ, עִיר צִיּוֹן תְּמַלֵּא,
וְשָׁם נָשִׁיר שִׁיר חָדָשׁ וּבִרְנָנָה נַעֲלֶה,
הָרַחֲמָן הַנִּקְדָּשׁ יִתְבָּרַךְ וְיִתְעַלֶּה,
עַל כּוֹס יַיִן מָלֵא כְּבִרְכַּת יְיָ. צוּר מִשֶּׁלּוֹ . . .

***Yibaneh* corresponds to the Cup of Blessing poured before and drunk after the Birkat HaMazon:**

May the Temple be rebuilt and the city of Zion be filled
(just as this cup is filled with wine of blessing and joy) (Isaiah 33: 5).

There we will sing a "new song" (Psalms 98:1) and make joyful pilgrimages.

May the Merciful one (HaRakhaman), whom we sanctify, be blessed and praised.

Over this cup of wine which is full "like God's blessings" to us. (Deuteronomy 16:17).

— by an anonymous medieval poet, probably from northern France in the 14th century

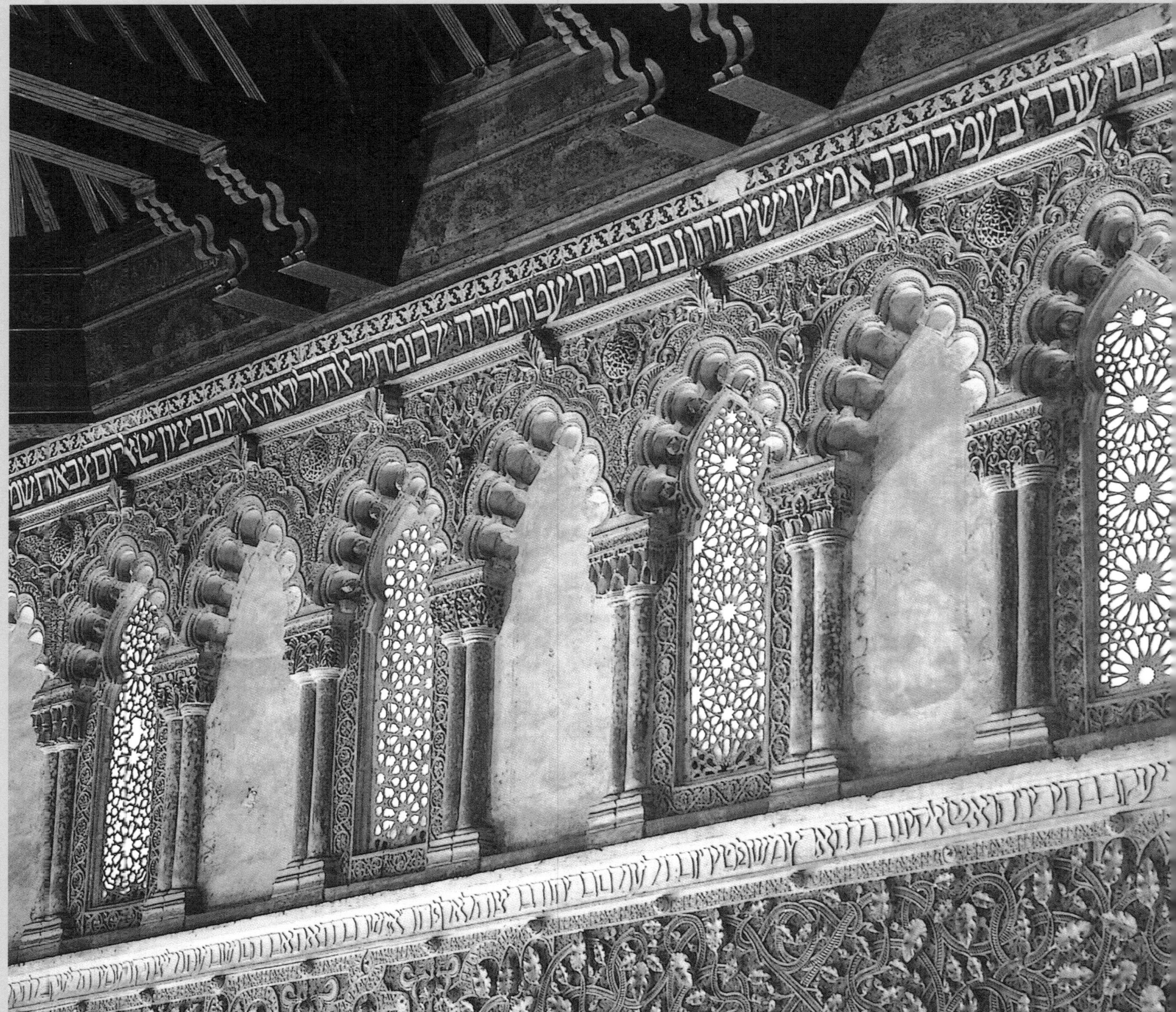

דְּרוֹר יִקְרָא

Dror yikra — "let liberty be proclaimed"

דְּרוֹר יִקְרָא לְבֵן עִם בַּת
וְיִנְצָרְכֶם כְּמוֹ בָבַת
נְעִים שִׁמְכֶם וְלֹא יֻשְׁבַּת
שְׁבוּ נוּחוּ בְּיוֹם שַׁבָּת.

Dror — God will proclaim liberty for man and woman alike
(For Shabbat is a time of liberty from labor, just as the Jubilee year proclaims the liberation of all slaves, male and female alike). (Leviticus 25:10, Jeremiah 34:8-9)
God will guard you like the apple of God's own eye (Psalms 17:8; Deuteronomy 32:10; Zecharia 2:12).
And your name will be pleasing and your fame will never cease (Isaiah 56: 5).
Just sit down and relax on Shabbat.

דְּרוֹשׁ נָוִי וְאוּלָמִי
וְאוֹת יֶשַׁע עֲשֵׂה עִמִּי
נְטַע שׂוֹרֵק בְּתוֹךְ כַּרְמִי
שְׁעֵה שַׁוְעַת בְּנֵי עַמִּי.

[God], seek the well-being of my Temple and [its] sacred entryhall.
(Reverse the sad state of abandonment that Jeremiah describes: "Zion, no one seeks her" – Jeremiah 30:17)
Make me a sign that you will bring redemption.
Plant a choice vine in my vineyard (an image of the people of Israel planted in Eretz Yisrael, Isaiah 5:1-2).
Respond to the cry for help from my people.

דְּרוֹךְ פּוּרָה בְּתוֹךְ בָּצְרָה
וְגַם בָּבֶל אֲשֶׁר גָּבְרָה
נְתוֹץ צָרַי בְּאַף עֶבְרָה
שְׁמַה קוֹלִי בְּיוֹם אֶקְרָא.

Trample the grapes in the city of Botzra (ancient capital city of Edom, the mortal enemy of Israel, symbolizing Rome, who destroyed our Second Temple, and its Christian heirs who persecuted the Jews, Isaiah 63:1),
Also trample Babylonia which has achieved hegemony (for it destroyed our First Temple, with the help of Edom, and its powerful military heir is the Arab Empire centered in Baghdad, where the poet Dunash was born).
Smash (Jeremiah 1:10) my enemies with angry rage!
"Hear my voice on the day I call." (Psalm 27:7)

אֱלֹהִים תֵּן בַּמִּדְבָּר הָר
הֲדַס שִׁטָּה בְּרוֹשׁ תִּדְהָר
וְלַמַּזְהִיר וְלַנִּזְהָר
שְׁלוֹמִים תֵּן כְּמֵי נָהָר.

In the midst of desolation, God, replenish the Mountain [of Zion] (Isaiah 51:3)
"with myrtle, acacia, cypress and elm trees." (as Isaiah promised the Jews who returned from Babylonia) (Isaiah 41:19)
To the one that cautions people (to observe Shabbat) (Ezekiel 3:21) and to the one who takes heed,
Grant a great peace that streams like a river. (Isaiah 48:18, 66:12,23)

הֲדוֹךְ קָמַי אֵל קַנָּא
בְּמוֹג לֵבָב וּבִמְגִנָּה
וְנַרְחִיב פֶּה וּנְמַלְאֶנָּה
לְשׁוֹנֵנוּ לְךָ רִנָּה.

Zealous God, knock down my enemies that rise up against me.
[May they flee] in fear and depression.
"Then may we open our mouths wide, filling them [with praise]." (Psalm 81:11)
"Our tongues will sing to You." (Shir HaMa'alot Psalm 126:2)

דְּעֵה חָכְמָה לְנַפְשֶׁךָ
וְהִיא כֶתֶר לְרֹאשֶׁךָ
נְצוֹר מִצְוַת קְדוֹשֶׁךָ
שְׁמוֹר שַׁבַּת קָדְשֶׁךָ.

"Know that wisdom [that is, Torah,] is good for your soul" (Proverbs 24:14)
and it will be a crown for your head. (Proverbs 4: 4,7,9)
Guard the mitzvah of your Holy One:
"Keep Shabbat," your holy day. (Deuteronomy 5:12)

— Dunash ben Labrat (Babylonia and Spain, 920-990)

Samuel Halevi built this private synagogue (14th century) in Toledo, Spain. Samuel Halevi was an enormously wealthy fiscal advisor to the king who later betrayed his counselor, imprisoned, tortured and finally executed him. Some think Halevi's mansion later became the home of El Greco the painter. Later (during the Inquisition) the synagogue was turned into a church called El Transito.

A Thematic Commentary on *Dror Yikra*

The poem *Dror Yikra* — "Let Liberty be proclaimed" — is almost brutally direct in its powerful petitional prayer to the Lord of history. The poem demands a crushing military defeat of Israel's enemies and a glorious political redemption from exile for God's people. The Baghdad-born Spanish poet **D-U-Na-Sh** ben Labrat, whose name is inscribed in its acrostic, uses his thorough knowledge of the prophecies of Isaiah to weave together the unexpected themes of a tranquil family Shabbat with a messianic Shabbat of Divine justice.

The first and last stanza, the bookends of the poem, celebrate the personal "liberty" from labor granted to Shabbat observers and their opportunity to pursue wisdom for their souls. The middle stanzas insist that God smash our enemies and reestablish our Temple. How do these themes meld together? The "secret" connection is the Biblical context of Isaiah's prophetic poetry. The second half of the book of Isaiah is written from the perspective of the Jews who, after the destruction of the first Temple, were exiled to Babylonia (today's Iraq and the birthplace of Dunash). Isaiah praises Shabbat as the greatest source of our joy and makes its honoring prerequisite for bringing our national redemption and honor. "If you call Shabbat 'a delight/*oneg*' and God's holy day 'honored/*m'khubad*,' then you will have delight with God and God will place you on the heights of the earth . . ." *(Isaiah 58:13-14)*. The Rabbis later formulate this prophecy as a promise: "If Israel observes two *Shabbatot*, then redemption will come" *(Talmud Yerushalmi Taanit 1:1)*.

Dror Yikra and the Liberty Bell

Liberty/*Dror* is the gift that God grants in the Jubilee/*Yovel*, the fiftieth year (after a complete cycle of seven sabbatical years). In the jubilee year, each slave goes free and returns to family and to their respective ancestral tribal lands in Israel; this is analogous to the Jewish people's liberation from enslavement in exile and a messianic return to the land of Israel. The verse describing the Jubilee, "Proclaim liberty throughout the land unto all the inhabitants thereof" *(Leviticus 25:10)*, was inscribed on the Liberty Bell cast by the colony of Pennsylvania to celebrate its 50th anniversary year in 1751. The colony had been established by the Quaker William Penn as a haven free of religious persecution and committed to religious liberty. Later the Liberty Bell was reinterpreted as referring to the political liberty of the United States whose Declaration of Independence from English tyranny was proclaimed in Philadelphia, Pennsylvania, in 1776. Still later in the 1840s the abolitionist movement used the Liberty Bell as symbol of the personal freedom from slavery for all human beings. In its fullest meaning this kind of liberty involves liberation from economic, social and national oppression and the provision of land to ensure the self-sufficiency of each liberated slave.

Dunash translates the *Dror*/liberty in personal terms. The freedom from labor that Shabbat provides applies to man and woman alike — both within the family hierarchy and the economic one. The Ten Commandments establish Shabbat for all: "Do not do any work — you, your son and your daughter . . . so that your male and female slave may rest/*lanu-akh* like you do." *(Deuteronomy 5:14-15)* By virtue of our keeping /*n'tzor* Shabbat secure, God keeps us/*v'yin-tzor-khem* secure "like the apple of his eye." *(Zecharia 2:12)* Fortunately, we earn this liberation at the end of every seven-day week and not just in sabbatical years (or in every jubilee year — the fiftieth year after seven seven-year cycles of sabbatical years).

However, Dunash also looks forward to a political liberation, as prophesied by Isaiah to the Jews who were exiled in Babylonia:

> "God has anointed me to announce good news to those who have been humbled, to bandage up the broken-hearted, to proclaim liberty/*likro Dror* to the captives . . . and to proclaim a year of God's goodwill, a day of divine justice to comfort the mourners . . . of Zion."
> *(Isaiah 61:1-3)*

Inscription on the Liberty Bell, Pennsylvania, 1751.

What are zemirot? — soul singing at the table

When you pray, choose a tune you like, then your heart will feel what your tongue speaks. For it is song that makes your heart respond.

— Yehuda HeHassid (d. 1217, Sefer HaHassidim)

In the Shabbat Psalm it says, "It is good to sing to God." This means, it is good if a person can bring the God that is within to sing.

— Rebbe Elimelch of Lizhensk

Zemirot are table songs describing the pleasures of celebrating Shabbat — food, drink, rest, and hope for a better day. They are a unique Jewish invention halfway between folksongs and sacred poetic prayer. While synagogue-based services have a sacred formality rigorously governed by Jewish law and community custom, the singing around the Shabbat table that developed between the 10th and 16th centuries in Europe, has a light, supple use of melodies and an openness to contemporary additions. The songs are not obligatory, though the printing of the *Zemirot* in the *Siddur* in the last few centuries has created a sense of formal structure and has assigned the classic poems to each of the three Shabbat meals as if that is their required place. Nevertheless many families choose and vary their singing repertoire spontaneously. They search incessantly for new melodies often drawn from contemporary non-Jewish sources including Disney and Broadway show tunes, just as their ancestors in Safed who wrote *Zemirot* like *Yah Ribon* used melodies from the then popular Turkish love songs. In addition to the classics, many Jews now sing short Israeli, Hassidic and popular folk songs.

This creative mixture of sacred and secular, piety and sociability, mystical or scholarly allusions and folk creations is unique. In medieval Christian lands, for example, the hymnals were sung in church and clearly reserved for sacred occasions. In contrast, the troubadours' love songs and drinking songs around the table were in style and content very secular. In *Zemirot* for Shabbat the act of eating and drinking is integrated with a celebration of holiness. The earthly pleasures *(oneg)* are Divinely mandated. For the Kabbalists, who wrote and sang many of the *Zemirot* from the 16th century on, the language of human love could serve unabashedly as a metaphor for Israel's love of God and for the interrelationship of the male and female aspects of the Divine.

Borrowing Musical Melodies

Zemirot have always been enriched by the musical culture of the host country, though today we are unaware of those old fashions of musical and poetic form.

In Moslem Spain all the Hebrew poetry was structured on Arabic classical forms, so for example, *Dror Yikra* is based on the standard Arab meter called *"Hazaj,"* while *Ki Eshmara* is based on *"Mujtath."* In Provence in southern France the *canso redonda* inspired *Ma Yafit.* In Germany march rhythms shaped *Hamavdil* and *Menucha v'Simcha*, while chorale melodies and even drinking songs are models for *Tzur Mishelo.*

Yisrael Najara in Safed used Spanish, Turkish and Arabic popular songs for lyrics and melodies such as *Yah Ribon.* Hassidic dynasties wrote their own tunes based on shepherd songs or Polish, Moldavian, and Ukrainian folk dance tunes including waltzes. During the Napoleonic wars military marches and even the French national anthem *La Marseillaise* were adopted with an appropriate Hasidic explanation that singing the tunes of the non-Jews redeems the Divine sparks within them. In Western Europe even Beethoven and Shubert were fair game for the search for new tunes, especially for songs like *Tzur Mishelo* that are so easily adapted to many different melodies.

Unfortunately, the original melodies of the *Zemirot* are lost and those we sing today are replacements with local tunes which go back no more than 300 years.

Short songs

Biblical

מַה טֹּבוּ אֹהָלֶיךָ יַעֲקֹב,
מִשְׁכְּנֹתֶיךָ יִשְׂרָאֵל.

Mah tovu *oha-leh-kha Ya-a-kov,*
mish-k'no-tekha Yisrael.

While the prophet Bilaam with the famous talking ass initially intended to curse Israel, when he actually saw them he was inspired to bless them in the poem that became the daily prayer: "How beautiful are your tents, Israel." *(Numbers 24:5)*

דּוֹדִי לִי וַאֲנִי לוֹ
הָרוֹעֶה בַּשּׁוֹשַׁנִּים.

Dodi li *va-a-ni lo*
ha-ro-eh ba-sho-shanim.

Solomon's love songs include this declaration:
"I am yours and you are mine." *(Song of Songs 2:16)*

לֹא יִשָּׂא גוֹי אֶל גּוֹי חֶרֶב
לֹא יִלְמְדוּ עוֹד מִלְחָמָה.

Lo yisa goy el goy kheh-rev
Lo yil-m'du od mil-khama.

Shabbat tranquility is a foretaste of the messianic world envisioned by Isaiah: "No nation shall lift up sword against another nation nor learn war anymore" *(Isaiah 2:4)*. (That quote decorates the United Nations building in New York City).

כָּל הַנְּשָׁמָה
תְּהַלֵּל יָהּ, הַלְלוּיָהּ.

Kol ha-neshama
T'Hallel Yah! Hallel-u-jah!

"Let every breath and every breathing being sing: Hallelujah!" *(Psalm 150:6)*

יִשְׂמְחוּ הַשָּׁמַיִם
וְתָגֵל הָאָרֶץ,
יִרְעַם הַיָּם וּמְלֹאוֹ.

Yi-s'm'khu ha-sha-mayim
v'tageil ha-aretz,
yir-am ha-yam u-m'lo-oh.

In *Kabbalat Shabbat* we sing this song: "Let heaven and earth rejoice, the ocean and all its contents." *(Psalm 96:11)*

Rabbinic and Hassidic

וְנֹאמַר לְפָנָיו
שִׁירָה חֲדָשָׁה,
הַלְלוּיָהּ.

V'nomar l'fanav
shira khadasha,
Hallel-u-jah!

In the Haggadah we thank God for our liberation from slavery with these words: "Let's recite before God, a new song: Hallelujah! — Praise God!" *(Based on Psalm 96)*

עֹשֶׂה שָׁלוֹם בִּמְרוֹמָיו
הוּא יַעֲשֶׂה שָׁלוֹם עָלֵינוּ
וְעַל כָּל יִשְׂרָאֵל
וְאִמְרוּ אָמֵן.

Oseh shalom beem-romav,
hu ya-aseh shalom aleinu,
V'al kol Yisrael
v'imru Amen.

May the Divine maker of peace in heavens make peace upon us and all Israel. *(Rabbinic Siddur)*

עַל שְׁלוֹשָׁה דְבָרִים
הָעוֹלָם עוֹמֵד:
עַל הַתּוֹרָה
וְעַל הָעֲבוֹדָה
וְעַל גְּמִילוּת חֲסָדִים.

Al sh'losha d'varim,
ha-olam omeid:
Al ha-Torah
v'al ha-avodah
v'al g'milut khassadim.

"On three things the world stands: on Torah, on worship and on acts of loving kindness." *(Pirkei Avot 1:2)*

כָּל הָעוֹלָם כֻּלּוֹ
גֶּשֶׁר צַר מְאֹד
וְהָעִקָּר לֹא לְפַחֵד כְּלָל.

Kol ha-olam kulo,
gesher tzar m'od:
V'ha-ikar lo l'fa-kheid k'lal.

Rebbe Nachman's song urges Jews to overcome despair: "The whole world is like a very narrow bridge and it is essential to cross it without succumbing to fear at all." (It was sung in particular by his followers in the Warsaw Ghetto and in Israel during the surprise-attack, the Yom Kippur War in 1973.)

אָז איך וועל זינגען:	**Az ikh vel zingen:**
לכה דודי,	l'kha doydi,
זאָלסטו זינגען:	zolstu zingen:
טשירי־בירי־בים.	chiri biri bim.
אָז איך וועל זינגען:	Az ikh vel zingen:
לקראת כלה,	lik'ras kaleh,
זאָלסטו זינגען:	zolstu zingen:
טשירי־בירי־באָם.	chiri biri bom
לכה דודי,	L'kha doydi:
טשירי־בירי־בים.	chiri biri bim.
לקראת כלה,	Likras kaleh:
טשירי־בירי־באָם.	chiri biri bom.
לכה דודי, לקראת כלה,	L'kha doydi likras kalo!
טשירי־בירי־בירי־בירי־באָם.	chiri biri biri biri bom.
טשירי־בים טשירי־באָם, (2x)	Chiri-bim, chiri-bom, (2x)
טשירי־באָם טשירי־בים,	chiri-bom, chiri-bim,
טשירי־בים־באָם־בים־באָם־	chiri-bim-bom-bim-bom-
בירי־באָם.	biri-bom.
איַיַ, טשירי־בירי־בירי־ (3x)	Ay, chiri-biri-biri- (3x)
בים־באָם־באָם	bim-bom-bom
טשירי־בירי־בירי־	Chiri-biri-biri-
בירי־בירי־באָם.	biri-biri-bom.

This Hassidic Yiddish song describes the rebbe leading his hassidic followers in a melody *(niggun)* for greeting the Shabbat bride: "When I sing 'l'kha doydi' then you sing, 'chiri-biri-bim,'" and so forth. Second verse, same as the first, except substitute "Yerushalayim" and "Eer ha-koy-desh."

Contemporary Israeli and American

עַם יִשְׂרָאֵל חָי.	Am Yisrael khai
עוֹד אָבִינוּ חָי.	Od avinu khai.

Reb Shlomo Carlebach's song became popular for its use in the American movement for liberating Soviet Jewry in the 1960's. It declares faithfully: "The Jewish people, our father, is still alive and well." This answers Joseph's question: "Is our father still alive?" *(Genesis 45:3)*. The wealthy secure immigrant in Egypt wanted to know that his elderly father Yisrael was still alive back in the old country even after the famine and after his long enforced separation from his father. American Jews of Russian origin echoed Joseph's experience of reawakened concern after a long estrangement from what were then called the Jews of Silence.

הָבָה נָשִׁירָה	**Hava nashira**
שִׁיר הַלְלוּיָהּ.	Shir hallelujah.

Let's sing a song of Hallelujah.

דָּוִד מֶלֶךְ יִשְׂרָאֵל	**David melekh Yisrael**
חַי וְקַיָּם.	Khai v'kayam.

David, king of Israel, still lives!

בַּשָּׁנָה הַבָּאָה	**Ba-shana ha-ba-a**
נֵשֵׁב עַל הַמִּרְפֶּסֶת	nei-sheiv al ha-mirpeset
וְנִסְפֹּר צִפֳּרִים נוֹדְדוֹת.	v'nispor tziporim nod'dot.
יְלָדִים בְּחֻפְשָׁה	Y'ladim b'khufsha
יְשַׂחֲקוּ תּוֹפֶסֶת	y'sakhaku tofeset
בֵּין הַבַּיִת לְבֵין הַשָּׂדוֹת.	bein ha-bayit l'vein ha-sadot.
עוֹד תִּרְאֶה עוֹד תִּרְאֶה	Od tir-eh od tir-eh
כַּמָּה טוֹב יִהְיֶה	kama tov yih'yeh
בַּשָּׁנָה בַּשָּׁנָה הַבָּאָה.	ba-shana ba-shana ha-ba-a.

Next year we will sit on the porch and count migrating birds. On vacation children will play tag between the house and the fields. You will see how good next year will be. *(Ehud Manor, ©1969, ACUM)*

Guidelines

getting started

> There are halls in the heavens above that open only to the sound of song.
>
> — Zohar

What matters is not what you sing or how much or how well, but that you open your mouth and sing — by yourself or with others. As soon as we begin to sing at the table, a transformation occurs: our breathing changes, we move together from a more intellectual mode to a more emotional one, from an individual experience to a communal one, conversation turns into harmonizing around the table. Whereas before only our head, arms, and mouth acted (eating and drinking and speaking), now our whole body becomes involved in movement and sounding out the rhythm of the songs.

But how do we get started?

Music breeds music. Play Jewish music before Shabbat in the car or the house. If it's your custom to use electricity on Shabbat, play some as background music during Shabbat meals. Sing along, hum, tap the table to the rhythm. For those who use musical instruments on Shabbat, play an instrument or invite someone to play the piano. If Hebrew is a special challenge, start by choosing one of the short songs transliterated in any of the standard Shabbat table song books *(see a few examples on pages 93-94).* Many are familiar tunes from the *siddur,* or beloved Israeli tunes and camp songs). Or try an American Jewish melody such as those written by Debbie Friedman. Or simply hum a *niggun* — a wordless melody — while meditating deeply on how you feel this Shabbat.

It is a greater challenge to learn the long medieval poems traditionally called Shabbat *zemirot.* These are often written as acrostics with multiple allusions to Biblical and Rabbinic terms which even many of the people who sing them weekly do not understand. *(See above, pages 101-105, traditional* Zemirot, *fully annotated).* The melody for these long poems has varied between generations and locations of Jewish communal life. If you do not know a tune, pick a melody that you know and love and apply it to the traditional words of the *zemirot.* Some families use Beethoven's Ninth Symphony or Sloop John B. or Rogers & Hammerstein's "The Sound of Music." After all, many so-called Jewish tunes are actually ones borrowed and adapted from popular music of other historical periods!

So that everyone can sing together you will need sufficient copies of a small songbook for your family — one per person and some for guests. Try the movement books — NCSY (Orthodox youth movement), Reform, Reconstructionist, Conservative, or Harvard, NYU, or Yale Hillel. Each has transliteration and some background on a song's origin.

Musical tales

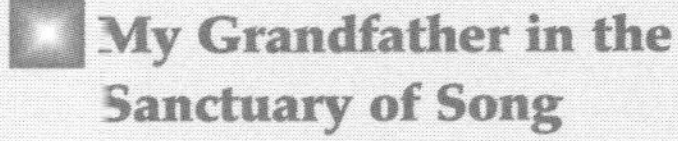

My Grandfather in the Sanctuary of Song

And how alive he was, my grandfather, alive and magnificent. Yes, I know, most grandchildren adore their grandfathers. But mine was truly special. If that makes you smile, so be it, for it is with a smile that I recall him. He allowed me — obliged me — to love life, to assume it as a Jew, to celebrate it for the Jewish people. A devout follower of the Rabbi of Wizhnitz, he was the embodiment of Hasidic creative force and fervor . . . Visiting him was a festival for the heart and mind . . . .

He was a marvelous singer, with a warm, melodious voice that could conjure worlds near and far. He knew the songs of the Wizhnitz court, those sung on the eve of Shabbat and those murmured at dusk the next day, at the hour of its departure. He knew the romantic, mystical songs the Rebbe of Kalev sang in Hungarian, and the nostalgic tunes of Romanian shepherds, slow and thundering *doinas* that were calls to glorious dreams and the love of broken hearts. When he stopped to catch his breath, I would beg him for more, and with an ever more gleeful smile he would recall a new song attributed to this or that *tzaddik.* Once he stopped in the middle of a *niggun.* Eyes closed, he seemed asleep. Afraid of waking him, I didn't budge. But he wasn't sleeping. "I'm dreaming," he said. "I've never sung so much. Thanks to you, I think I can rise to *Haikhal HaNeggina,* the celestial sanctuary where words become song." "Grandpa," I ask him [imagining him after his death in the Holocaust], "what is the Sanctuary of Song like?" And he answers: "The Sanctuary blazes and illuminates; its flame warms the most frigid hearts."

— Elie Wiesel

Guidelines

parent-child corner

Repetition: The Spice of Life

For younger children create a repertoire of your family Shabbat tunes. Begin with those taught in Jewish nursery schools. Buy — and play often — CDs of children's Jewish holiday music. Repetition is in fact the "spice" of a young child's life. Bring musical instruments (like a Miriam's drum) to the table, or simply bang away with spoons on not-too-expensive glasses filled with different levels of water. The Tribe of Levi was the "philharmonic" of the ancient Temple in Jerusalem, and they performed the Psalms using all sorts of instruments.

For much more information about Shabbat songs for children and adults, see the *Educator's Guide* to *A Day Apart*.

Advice from a Summer Camp: You Can't Go Wrong with Folk Singing at the Table

For many of us, folksongs played a significant role in our lives when we were young. Elementary schools often had children's choirs perform them at school assemblies. In camps and youth movements, singing was a cause for camaraderie. Banging on the table, friendly inter-table musical competition, harmonies and rounds, made singing lots of fun. In the 1950s, American folk rock revived the folksong tradition, which had atrophied as people moved away from its original rural settings. Musicians created the rock concert and used folksong styles for protest and in celebration of youth culture. Israeli folk songs (including Naomi Shemer's many works from *Jerusalem of Gold* to *Al Kol Eleh*) have also given birth to a sophisticated yet accessible and singable tradition. The enormous influence of Shlomo Carlebach stimulated a revival of spiritual, Hasidic singing. Debbie Friedman, among many other American artists, has combined English and Hebrew in song-prayers.

You cannot "go wrong" with Shabbat singing. You can learn its art, to be sure, develop a taste for it — but the singing of *zemirot* around the table is neither a complex mitzvah nor a ritual performance. The words — often layered in Biblical and mystical allusions — should not be a stumbling block. As the Hasidim taught us, the *niggun*, the wordless melody, may be the best song that we can offer to God. Singing from the heart around the table, at home among family and friends, whatever their Hebrew or musical talents or lack thereof, gives God pleasure and God's creatures as well.

"When the people of Israel eat and drink, bless and praise the Holy One, God hears their voice and is pleased." (*Midrash Song of Songs; see Talmud Megillah 12b*)

Will the Spiritually Deaf Ever Learn to Sing and Dance?

The Baal Shem Tov taught about the physical and spiritual power of music:

"A musician was playing on a very beautiful instrument, and the music so enraptured the people that they were driven to dance ecstatically. Then a deaf man who knew nothing of music passed by, and seeing the enthusiastic dancing of the people he decided they must be insane. Had he been wise he would have sensed their joy and rapture and joined their dancing."

Morroccan Klezmer band, 1924

Reflections כַּוָּנוֹת

soul singing: three all-important relationships

Reb Nachman of Bratslav used to explain that repentance/*teshuvah* represents three types of "turning": turning in to one's self, turning out to others, and turning "up" to God. Singing *Zemirot* involves all three types of relationship. Imagine them as concentric circles: the smallest inner circle represents one's self; the second circle represents one's relationship with other people; the third, outermost circle represents one's relationship with God.

Song of the Self

"'Where is the song before it is sung?' Where indeed?

'Nowhere!' One creates the song by singing it, by composing it.

So too, we create life as we live it, step by step."

— Alexander Herren

Human beings spend most of the time defining and shaping our existence. For six days of the week we craft our lives. On Shabbat, we sit back, reflect and celebrate. As we sing *Zemirot* — expressing joy, love, and appreciation, while pounding on the table and belting out melodies from our hearts — we embrace our lives. This level of singing reflects a person's relationship to his or her own life/*bein adam l'atzmo.*

Debbie Friedman leads singing atop a mountain in Aspen, Colorado. Photo by Zion Ozeri, reprinted by permission.

Song with and for Others

Shabbat is contemplative and interpersonal; at its core are both individual joy and communal connection. Profound moments of relationship/*kesher* to other people come in moments of song. One voice begins, and others join until there is a chorus of voices singing — sometimes in unison and often in harmony — so that each person feels that somehow the ears of Heaven must be listening. There is also a remarkable sense of trust — as well as intimacy — established among a circle of singers. This expansion of experience with our neighbors and friends reflects the second tier of relationship/*bein adam l'khavero.*

Song to the Divine

The poet Yehuda Halevi used the metaphor of song to describe one's most intimate relationship to God:

"Source of my life, I bless you while I live; My Song, I sing to You while yet I breathe."

Contemporary religious thinker Rabbi Abraham Joshua Heschel used to say that song not only expresses our feelings for the Divine but actually brings spiritual power into our earthly lives:

"Song, and particularly liturgical song, is . . . a way of bringing down the spirit from heaven to earth."

Song is a form of communication in the relationship between human and divine/*bein adam laMakom.* Melody can be a means of drawing closer to God . . . or of drawing God closer to us.

The Beggars' Dance

Every Friday afternoon the Hasidic rebbe, Reb Michoel Vorker, used to wander the streets of the old Jewish quarter in Jerusalem collecting guests for his Shabbat table from the most unfortunate Jews, especially the beggars wrapped in rags and frequenting trashbins. On Shabbat evening each one was served a portion of precious gefilte fish, hot soup and meat. After the meal Reb Michoel and his guests sang Shabbat songs and then rose to dance together in joy around the table.

"He used to say: When I arrive at the Heavenly tribunal, they may hesitate over whether to open the gates of the Garden of Eden to the likes of me. Then I will gather all of my beggars — all those who used to dine at my Shabbat table — and we will dance and sing before the Heavenly gates just as we danced every Friday evening. Then no one will dare to close the gates in our face."

Rabbi Abraham Isaac Kook's Songs of the Soul

There is one who sings **the song of his soul**, discovering in it everything — utter spiritual fulfillment.

Then there is one who sings **the song of his people**. Emerging from the private circle of his soul — not expansive enough, not yet tranquil — he strives for fierce heights, clinging to the entire community of Israel in tender love. Together with her, he sings her song, feels her anguish, delights in her hopes. He conceives profound insights into her past and her future, deftly probing the inwardness of her spirit with the wisdom of love.

Then there is one whose soul expands until it extends beyond the border of Israel, singing **the song of humanity**. In the glory of the entire human race, in the glory of the human form, his spirit spreads, aspiring to the goal of humankind, envisioning its consummation. From this spring of life, he draws all his deepest reflections, his searching, striving, and vision.

Then there is one who expands even further until he unites with all existence, **with all creatures**, with all worlds, singing a song with them all.

Then there is one who ascends with all these songs in unison — the song of the soul, the song of the nation, the song of humanity, the song of the cosmos — resounding together, blending in harmony, circulating the sap of life, the sound of holy joy.

This full comprehensiveness rises to become the song of holiness, the song of God, the song of Israel, in its full strength and beauty, in its full authenticity and greatness. The name *Isra-EL (Yashir-El)* stands for the Song of God. It is a simple song, a twofold song, a threefold song and a fourfold song. It is the Song of Songs of Solomon (Shlomo) whose name means Shalom — peace or wholeness. It is the song of the Sovereign in whom is wholeness.

David's Harp by Rembrandt
David was the first recorded music therapist. "David would take his harp and play it. Then King Saul would find relief and feel good, for the bad mood would depart . . ." *(I Samuel 16: 17-23).*

Songs/ Zemirot

Michel Kichka ©04
שבת שלום
פסח
Zemirot Shabbat
Zemirot Shabbat
ברכת המזון
שבת שלום
Torah
יין
כשר

Birkat HaMazon

בִּרְכַּת הַמָּזוֹן

gratitude for nourishment: blessings before and after eating

Birkat HaMazon is a supremely important act. To be able to eat and drink is as extraordinary, as miraculous, as crossing the Red Sea. We do not recognize the miracle because, for the moment, we live in a world of plenty and because our memory is so short. Yet those in less fortunate lands understand that to satisfy one's hunger is a miracle of miracles . . . The route that bread travels — from the earth where it grows to our mouth where it is eaten — can be as perilous as crossing the Red Sea.

— Emmanuel Levinas
(French Jewish philosopher of ethics and Holocaust survivor)

Judaism encourages us to enjoy God's creation and appreciate that it is "very good" (*Genesis 1:31*). Then we are asked to translate God's blessing into human blessing — blessings received into blessings given. Breathing in, or *in-spiration*, is God's gift of life; breathing out we reciprocate with a prayer of thanks, turning an ordinary flow of air into a song of praise. Teacher and philosopher Abraham Joshua Heschel insists that we complete the giving and receiving cycle this way:

"In receiving a pleasure, we must return a prayer; in attaining a success, we radiate compassion. We have the right to consume because we have the power to celebrate." (*Abraham Joshua Heschel, Who is Man?*)

The food somehow tastes better when we appreciate it and the after-taste of our satisfaction grows when "we sing about our supper." We can understand the integration of the food into our system, our digestive process, as a part of our personal integration into the Divine processes of Creation. Our pleasure in eating carefully prepared dishes gives pleasure to our human hosts and our Divine Benefactor. Giving and receiving pleasure merge.

Life is not always a struggle for survival of the fittest. It is not necessarily a competition in which one can only gain at another's expense. *Birkat Hamazon* highlights the exchange of "gift and gratitude" (inspiration and praise) as a life-giving process initiated by God. "Thank you, I enjoyed that very much" is more than a polite expression; it is a perspective on life.

Collage Shabbat tivities Michel ichka, raeli litical rtoonist, 04. *(Why the little gel so gry? See ge 42, elcoming igelic spectors.)*

In this chapter . . .

Birkhot Nehenin/Blessings Before Enjoying God's World 116

Birkat HaMazon
- Full Traditional Rabbinic Blessings After a Meal 118

Kavanot/Reflections 129

Guidelines
- Getting Started............. 130
- Parent-Child Corner........... 130
- From Tradition: Arranging the Table after Dinner.................. 131

Tales of Gratitude and Ingratitude................ 132

(For various medium-length versions of the Blessing after Eating, see Reform, Reconstructionist or Conservative prayer books).

Birchot HaNehenin *Blessings upon enjoying God's world*

The Earth belongs to Adonai; and all that fills it, the world and all who dwell there.

— *Psalms 24:1*

Food drawings by Tanya Zion

Kind of Food		Examples	Blessing Before
Bread made from 5 grains: wheat, barley, oats, spelt, rye		Bread	**HaMotzi**
5 grains or rice when cooked or baked with so many added ingredients as to become a cake, kugel or cracker rather than a bread		Grain-based dishes: crackers, cookies, pasta, kugel	**M'zonot**
Roots, leaves, fruit of trees that live for only one year or of trees close to the ground		Most vegetables, bananas, watermelon (unless their form changs from the natural state like pumpkin pie or tomato soup)	**Ha-Adama**
Fruit of trees that bear fruit for many years		Most fruits/ Fruits of Seven Species of Land of Israel (olive, date, fig, pomegranate)	**Ha-Etz**
Miscellaneous		Most drinks, animal products, vegetables and fruits transformed by cooking	**Sheh-ha-Kol**
Fruit of the vine		Wine and grape juice	**Ha-Gafen**

Blessing AFTER fruits, vegetables, rice, and miscellaneous foods not from grains
(and not from the 7 species of the Land of Israel):

שׁ כָּל חָי. בָּרוּךְ חֵי הָעוֹלָמִים.

Ba-rukh ata Adonai, Elo-hei-nu me-lekh ha-olam, borei n'fashot rab

Blessed are You, Adonai our God, Ruler of the Universe, who creates many creatur

The Rabbis taught that "no one is allowed to enjoy something from this world without reciting a blessing/bracha" (Talmud Berachot 35a). When we behold the beauty of the world or its utility for humans, then we bless the Creator: "How lovely this bread is, bless God who made it." (Talmud Berachot 40b). That is our way of asking permission before taking food from our host's — our Divine benefactor's — table.

	Blessing After
בָּרוּךְ אַתָּה יְיָ אֱלֹהֵינוּ מֶלֶךְ הָעוֹלָם, הַמּוֹצִיא לֶחֶם מִן הָאָרֶץ. **Ba-rukh ata Adonai, Elo-hei-nu me-lekh ha-olam, ha-motzi lekhem min ha-aretz.** Blessed are You, Adonai our God, Ruler of the Universe, who brings forth bread from the earth.	**Birkat HaMazon** (covers all foods when eaten with bread)
בָּרוּךְ אַתָּה יְיָ אֱלֹהֵינוּ מֶלֶךְ הָעוֹלָם, בּוֹרֵא מִינֵי מְזוֹנוֹת. **Ba-rukh ata Adonai, Elo-hei-nu me-lekh ha-olam, borei mi-nei m'zonot.** Blessed are You, Adonai our God, Ruler of the Universe, who creates species of nourishment.	**Bracha Mei-ein Shalosh** (not in this book — see any prayerbook)
בָּרוּךְ אַתָּה יְיָ אֱלֹהֵינוּ מֶלֶךְ הָעוֹלָם, בּוֹרֵא פְּרִי הָאֲדָמָה. **Ba-rukh ata Adonai, Elo-hei-nu me-lekh ha-olam, borei p'ri ha-adama.** Blessed are You, Adonai our God, Ruler of the Universe, who creates the fruit of the earth.	**Borei N'fashot Rabot** (see bottom of this page)
בָּרוּךְ אַתָּה יְיָ אֱלֹהֵינוּ מֶלֶךְ הָעוֹלָם, בּוֹרֵא פְּרִי הָעֵץ. **Ba-rukh ata Adonai, Elo-hei-nu me-lekh ha-olam, borei p'ri ha-eitz.** Blessed are You, Adonai our God, Ruler of the Universe, who creates the fruit of the tree.	**Borei N'fashot Rabot/ Bracha Mei-ein Shalosh**
בָּרוּךְ אַתָּה יְיָ אֱלֹהֵינוּ מֶלֶךְ הָעוֹלָם, שֶׁהַכֹּל נִהְיָה בִּדְבָרוֹ. **Ba-rukh ata Adonai, Elo-hei-nu me-lekh ha-olam, sheh-ha-kol ni-h'yah bi-d'varo.** Blessed are You, Adonai our God, Ruler of the Universe, through whose word everything came to be.	**Borei N'fashot Rabot**
בָּרוּךְ אַתָּה יְיָ אֱלֹהֵינוּ מֶלֶךְ הָעוֹלָם, בּוֹרֵא פְּרִי הַגָּפֶן. **Ba-rukh ata Adonai, Elo-hei-nu me-lekh ha-olam, borei p'ri ha-gafen.** Blessed are You, Adonai our God, Ruler of the Universe, who creates the fruit of the vine.	**Bracha Mei-ein Shalosh**

בָּרוּךְ אַתָּה יְיָ אֱלֹהֵינוּ מֶלֶךְ הָעוֹלָם, בּוֹרֵא נְפָשׁוֹת רַבּוֹת וְחֶסְרוֹנָן, עַל כָּל מַה שֶּׁבָּרָא לְהַחֲיוֹת בָּהֶ

'khes-ronan, al kol mah sheh-bara l'ha-khayot ba-hem nefesh kol khai. Ba-rukh khei ha-olamim.

nd their needs. For all that You have created to sustain every living creature, we praise You, the One whose life is eternal.

Birkat HaMazon בִּרְכַּת הַמָּזוֹן

Blessing God, the Source of nourishment, after eating bread or a complete meal

A self-made man is as unlikely as a self-laid egg.

— Mark Twain

The world was not made by man . . . What we own, we owe . . . Indebtedness is given with our very being. It experiences life as receiving, not only as taking. Its content is gratitude for a gift received.

— Abraham Joshua Heschel, *Who is Man?*

A Shabbat Family Dinner in Poland (1940)

This photograph appeared in the official Nazi propaganda publication, *Der Stuermer,* in May 1940, with the caption: "Family Sabbath celebration. The Jews keep their hats on during the ceremony. Pay attention to the Talmudic grimaces." Repinted by per mission of *Der Stuermer* Archive, Nurnberg, photo courtesy of USHMM Photo Archive.

Introduction

The full traditional structure of *Birkat HaMazon* makes it an extensive prayer not only about food but about basic Jewish hopes: a return to the promised land, political sovereignty, and messianic ideas of world peace and plenty.

Its basic structure is:

1 Psalm — *Shir HaMaalot*

(Optional, sung on Shabbat and Festivals and sometimes at life cycle celebrations on weekdays)

2 Zimun — The Invitation to Join in Birkat HaMazon

(When three or more Jewish adults are present)

3 First Blessing — HaZan et HaKol

"Blessing the One who feeds all"

4 Second Blessing — Al HaAretz v'al HaMazon

"Blessing the Land and its Food"

5 Third Blessing — Bonei Yerushalayim

"Blessing the One who will rebuild Jerusalem"

6 Fourth Blessing — Hatov v'HaMeitiv

"Blessing God who gives us so much good"

Blessing the Hosts; the Shabbat (or the Festival); the State of Israel, the Jewish people, etc.

7 Concluding Hope — Oseh Shalom Bimromav

Praying for World Peace

1. **SING** the Psalm *Shir HaMaalot* for Shabbat and Festivals.

2. **INVITE** everyone to join in the blessing for the food using the formula: *Khaveirai, Nevarekh* "My Friends, Let us bless God," if there are at least three people of post- Bar-/Bat-Mitzvah age)

3. **RECITE** the *Birkat HaMazon* (according to your custom — an abbreviated or full version).

1 *Psalm 126 – Shir ha-ma-alot –* שִׁיר הַמַּעֲלוֹת

Shir ha-ma-a-lot.	**שִׁיר הַמַּעֲלוֹת**	**A Song of Ascents.**
B'shuv Adonai	בְּשׁוּב יְיָ	When Adonai restores
et shi-vat Tzion,	אֶת שִׁיבַת צִיּוֹן	the fortunes of Zion —
ha-yinu k'khol-mim.	הָיִינוּ כְּחֹלְמִים.	we see it as in a dream —
Az y'ma-lei s'khok pi-nu	אָז יִמָּלֵא שְׂחוֹק פִּינוּ	our mouths shall be filled with laughter,
u'l-sho-nei-nu ri-na.	וּלְשׁוֹנֵנוּ רִנָּה.	our tongues, with songs of joy.
Az yo-m'ru va-goyim	אָז יֹאמְרוּ בַגּוֹיִם	Then shall they say among the nations,
hig-dil Adonai la-asot im eleh.	הִגְדִּיל יְיָ לַעֲשׂוֹת עִם אֵלֶּה.	"Adonai has done great things for them!"
Hig-dil Adonai la-asot imanu	הִגְדִּיל יְיָ לַעֲשׂוֹת עִמָּנוּ	Adonai will do great things for us
ha-yinu s'mei-khim.	הָיִינוּ שְׂמֵחִים.	and we shall rejoice.
Shuva Adonai, et sh'vi-teinu	שׁוּבָה יְיָ אֶת שְׁבִיתֵנוּ	Restore our fortunes, Adonai,
ka-afikim ba-negev.	כַּאֲפִיקִים בַּנֶּגֶב.	like watercourses in the Negev.
Ha-zor-im b'di-ma,	הַזֹּרְעִים בְּדִמְעָה	They who sow in tears
b'ri-na yik-tzoru.	בְּרִנָּה יִקְצֹרוּ.	shall reap with songs of joy.
Ha-lokh yei-lekh u-va-kho	הָלוֹךְ יֵלֵךְ וּבָכֹה	Though he goes along weeping,
no-sei me-shekh hazara,	נֹשֵׂא מֶשֶׁךְ הַזָּרַע	carrying the seed-bag,
Bo yavo v'ri-na,	בֹּא יָבֹא בְרִנָּה	he shall come back with songs of joy,
no-sei alu-mo-tav.	נֹשֵׂא אֲלֻמֹּתָיו.	carrying his sheaves. (Psalm 126)

they who sow in
tears... הזרעים בדמעה

2 *Zimun — Invitation to join the blessing —* זִמּוּן

		Leader (raises the cup and begins):
Kha-vei-rai n'va-rekh.	**חֲבֵרַי נְבָרֵךְ!**	My friends, let us bless God for the meal.
		All:
Y'hi sheim Adonai m'vo-rakh	יְהִי שֵׁם יְיָ מְבֹרָךְ	"May Adonai's name be blessed
mei-ata v'ad olam.	מֵעַתָּה וְעַד עוֹלָם.	from now and forever." *(Psalm 113:2)*
		Leader (repeats):
Y'hi sheim Adonai m'vo-rakh	יְהִי שֵׁם יְיָ מְבֹרָךְ	"May Adonai's name be blessed
mei-ata v'ad olam.	מֵעַתָּה וְעַד עוֹלָם.	from now and forever."
		Leader (adds words in parenthesis when there is a minyan):
Bi-r'shoot, kha-vei-rai,	בִּרְשׁוּת חֲבֵרַי,	With your permission, my friends,
n'va-rekh (Eloheinu)	נְבָרֵךְ (אֱלֹהֵינוּ)	let us bless (our God)
sheh-akhal-nu mi-shelo.	שֶׁאָכַלְנוּ מִשֶּׁלּוֹ.	whose food we have eaten.
		All:
Ba-rukh (Eloheinu)	בָּרוּךְ (אֱלֹהֵינוּ)	Blessed be (our God)
sheh-akhal-nu mi-shelo,	שֶׁאָכַלְנוּ מִשֶּׁלּוֹ	whose food we have eaten
uv'tu-vo kha-yinu.	וּבְטוּבוֹ חָיִינוּ.	and through whose goodness we live.
		Leader (repeats):
Ba-rukh (Eloheinu)	בָּרוּךְ (אֱלֹהֵינוּ)	Blessed be (our God)
sheh-akhal-nu mi-shelo,	שֶׁאָכַלְנוּ מִשֶּׁלּוֹ	whose food we have eaten
uv'tu-vo kha-yinu.	וּבְטוּבוֹ חָיִינוּ.	and through whose goodness we live.
		All:
Ba-rukh hu	בָּרוּךְ הוּא	Blessed be God,
u-varukh sh'mo.	וּבָרוּךְ שְׁמוֹ.	Blessed be the Divine Name.

---

* The Talmud specifies that when a minyan of ten adults is present, God's presence dwells among us, so we add the word *Eloheinu* — "our God." On weddings, circumcisions, there is a more elaborate *Zimum* invitation to *Birkat HaMazon.*

3 *First blessing — Who nourishes all —* הַזָּן אֶת הַכֹּל

Ba-rukh ata Adonai	בָּרוּךְ אַתָּה יְיָ	Blessed are You, Adonai
Elo-hei-nu me-lekh ha-olam,	אֱלֹהֵינוּ מֶלֶךְ הָעוֹלָם	our God, Ruler of the universe,
ha-zan et ha-olam	הַזָּן אֶת הָעוֹלָם	who nourishes the world
ku-lo b'tuvo,	כֻּלּוֹ בְּטוּבוֹ,	in your goodness —
b'khen, b'khesed,	בְּחֵן, בְּחֶסֶד	with grace and kindness,
u-v'ra-kha-mim	וּבְרַחֲמִים,	and with mercy.
Hu no-ten le-khem	הוּא נוֹתֵן לֶחֶם	God gives bread
l'khol ba-sar,	לְכָל בָּשָׂר,	to all living flesh
ki l'olam khas-do.	כִּי לְעוֹלָם חַסְדּוֹ.	for your kindness lasts for ever.
Uv-tu-vo ha-gadol,	וּבְטוּבוֹ הַגָּדוֹל	Thanks to your great goodness
tamid lo khasar lanu,	תָּמִיד לֹא חָסַר לָנוּ,	we have never lacked,
v'al yekh-sar lanu	וְאַל יֶחְסַר לָנוּ	nor shall we lack
ma-zon, l'olam va-ed,	מָזוֹן לְעוֹלָם וָעֶד,	for food forever,
ba-avur sh'mo ha-gadol.	בַּעֲבוּר שְׁמוֹ הַגָּדוֹל.	because of your great name.
Ki hu Eil zan	כִּי הוּא אֵל זָן	For You are God who nourishes,
um-far-neis la-kol	וּמְפַרְנֵס לַכֹּל,	who provides for all,
u-mei-tiv la-kol,	וּמֵטִיב לַכֹּל	who is good to all,
u-mei-khin ma-zon	וּמֵכִין מָזוֹן	who prepares food
l'khol bri-yo-tav	לְכֹל בְּרִיּוֹתָיו	for all your creatures
asher ba-ra.	אֲשֶׁר בָּרָא.	that You created.
Ba-rukh ata Adonai,	בָּרוּךְ אַתָּה יְיָ	Blessed are You, Adonai,
ha-zan et ha-kol.	הַזָּן אֶת הַכֹּל.	who nourishes all.

...will reap with joy!
...ברינה יקצורו!

4 *Second blessing — the land and its food —* עַל הָאָרֶץ וְעַל הַמָּזוֹן

נוֹדֶה לְּךָ יְיָ אֱלֹהֵינוּ	We thank You, Adonai our God,
עַל שֶׁהִנְחַלְתָּ לַאֲבוֹתֵינוּ (וּלְאִמּוֹתֵינוּ)	for granting our ancestors an inheritance,
אֶרֶץ חֶמְדָּה טוֹבָה וּרְחָבָה	a land — desirable, good and broad
וְעַל שֶׁהוֹצֵאתָנוּ יְיָ אֱלֹהֵינוּ מֵאֶרֶץ מִצְרַיִם,	and for taking us, Adonai our God, out of the land of Egypt,
וּפְדִיתָנוּ מִבֵּית עֲבָדִים,	redeeming us from a house of slavery.
וְעַל בְּרִיתְךָ	We thank You for your covenant [CIRCUMCISION]
שֶׁחָתַמְתָּ בִּבְשָׂרֵנוּ,	which You inscribed on our flesh,
וְעַל תּוֹרָתְךָ שֶׁלִּמַּדְתָּנוּ,	for teaching us your Torah,
וְעַל חֻקֶּיךָ שֶׁהוֹדַעְתָּנוּ,	for communicating to us your laws,.
וְעַל חַיִּים חֵן וָחֶסֶד שֶׁחוֹנַנְתָּנוּ,	and for the life, grace, and kindness You endowed in us.
וְעַל אֲכִילַת מָזוֹן	Thank You for the food we eat,
שָׁאַתָּה זָן וּמְפַרְנֵס אוֹתָנוּ תָּמִיד,	for nourishing us, providing for us always —
בְּכָל יוֹם וּבְכָל עֵת וּבְכָל שָׁעָה.	every day, every season, every hour.

on Hannukah

עַל הַנִּסִּים	[Thank You God,] for the miracles,
וְעַל הַפֻּרְקָן וְעַל הַגְּבוּרוֹת	for the liberation from the foreign yoke and for the rescues,
וְעַל הַתְּשׁוּעוֹת וְעַל הַמִּלְחָמוֹת	for the heroism and for the military victories
שֶׁעָשִׂיתָ לַאֲבוֹתֵינוּ (וּלְאִמּוֹתֵינוּ)	that You did for our ancestors
בַּיָּמִים הָהֵם בַּזְּמַן הַזֶּה.	in those days at this season [and in our own era].

בִּימֵי מַתִּתְיָהוּ בֶּן יוֹחָנָן כֹּהֵן גָּדוֹל	In the days of Mattathias, son of Yochanan [High Priest],
חַשְׁמוֹנַאי וּבָנָיו	the Hasmonean, and his children,
כְּשֶׁעָמְדָה מַלְכוּת יָוָן הָרְשָׁעָה	the evil Greek kingdom [of Antiochus IV of Greater Syria]
עַל עַמְּךָ יִשְׂרָאֵל	set out to make the Jewish people
לְהַשְׁכִּיחָם תּוֹרָתֶךָ וּלְהַעֲבִירָם מֵחֻקֵּי רְצוֹנֶךָ,	forget your Torah and violate your laws.

continued on next page ⇛

וְאַתָּה בְּרַחֲמֶיךָ הָרַבִּים	You acted with great mercy
עָמַדְתָּ לָהֶם בְּעֵת צָרָתָם,	and stood up for Israel in its time of trouble.
רַבְתָּ אֶת רִיבָם, דַּנְתָּ אֶת דִּינָם,	You argued their case, You vindicated them,
נָקַמְתָּ אֶת נִקְמָתָם,	and You avenged their wrongs.
מָסַרְתָּ גִּבּוֹרִים בְּיַד חַלָּשִׁים,	You handed over the strong into the hands of the weak,
וְרַבִּים בְּיַד מְעַטִּים, וּטְמֵאִים בְּיַד טְהוֹרִים,	the many to the few, the corrupt to the pure,
וּרְשָׁעִים בְּיַד צַדִּיקִים,	the guilty to the innocent,
וְזֵדִים בְּיַד עוֹסְקֵי תוֹרָתֶךָ,	the arrogant to those loyal to the Torah.
וּלְךָ עָשִׂיתָ שֵׁם גָּדוֹל וְקָדוֹשׁ בְּעוֹלָמֶךָ,	Thereby You made a great and holy name for Yourself
וּלְעַמְּךָ יִשְׂרָאֵל עָשִׂיתָ תְּשׁוּעָה גְדוֹלָה וּפֻרְקָן כְּהַיּוֹם הַזֶּה.	and You brought great redemption and liberation to your people.
וְאַחַר כֵּן בָּאוּ בָנֶיךָ לִדְבִיר בֵּיתֶךָ,	Then your children reentered the Holy of Holies,
וּפִנּוּ אֶת הֵיכָלֶךָ, וְטִהֲרוּ אֶת מִקְדָּשֶׁךָ	purified your Sanctuary
וְהִדְלִיקוּ נֵרוֹת בְּחַצְרוֹת קָדְשֶׁךָ	and lit the lights in your Temple courtyard.
וְקָבְעוּ שְׁמוֹנַת יְמֵי חֲנֻכָּה אֵלּוּ,	They enacted these eight days of Hanukkah,
לְהוֹדוֹת וּלְהַלֵּל לְשִׁמְךָ הַגָּדוֹל.	dedicated to thanking You and to praising your great name.

	וְעַל הַכֹּל	And for everything,
	יְיָ אֱלֹהֵינוּ אֲנַחְנוּ מוֹדִים לָךְ	Adonai our God, we thank You
	וּמְבָרְכִים אוֹתָךְ,	and bless You:
	יִתְבָּרַךְ שִׁמְךָ בְּפִי כָּל חַי	your name will be blessed in the speech of all living things
	תָּמִיד לְעוֹלָם וָעֶד,	constantly and forever.
Ka-ka-tuv	**כַּכָּתוּב:**	The Torah says:
v'akhal-ta,	וְאָכַלְתָּ	"And you shall eat,
v'sa-vata u-vei-rakh-ta,	וְשָׂבָעְתָּ וּבֵרַכְתָּ	and be satisfied, and bless
et Adonai Elo-he-kha,	אֶת יְיָ אֱלֹהֶיךָ	Adonai your God
al ha-aretz ha-tova	עַל הָאָרֶץ הַטֹּבָה	for the good land
asher natan lakh.	אֲשֶׁר נָתַן לָךְ.	God gave you." (Deuteronomy 8:10)
Ba-rukh ata Adonai	בָּרוּךְ אַתָּה יְיָ	Blessed are You, Adonai
al ha-aretz	עַל הָאָרֶץ	for the homeland
v'al ha-mazon.	וְעַל הַמָּזוֹן.	and for the produce.

5 Third blessing — Builder of Jerusalem — בּוֹנֵה יְרוּשָׁלָיִם

רַחֵם נָא יְיָ אֱלֹהֵינוּ עַל יִשְׂרָאֵל עַמֶּךָ,
וְעַל יְרוּשָׁלַיִם עִירֶךָ
וְעַל צִיּוֹן מִשְׁכַּן כְּבוֹדֶךָ
וְעַל מַלְכוּת בֵּית דָּוִד מְשִׁיחֶךָ,
וְעַל הַבַּיִת הַגָּדוֹל וְהַקָּדוֹשׁ שֶׁנִּקְרָא שִׁמְךָ עָלָיו.
אֱלֹהֵינוּ אָבִינוּ, רְעֵנוּ זוּנֵנוּ פַּרְנְסֵנוּ וְכַלְכְּלֵנוּ,
וְהַרְוִיחֵנוּ וְהַרְוַח לָנוּ,
יְיָ אֱלֹהֵינוּ, מְהֵרָה מִכָּל צָרוֹתֵינוּ,
וְנָא אַל תַּצְרִיכֵנוּ, יְיָ אֱלֹהֵינוּ, לֹא לִידֵי מַתְּנַת בָּשָׂר וָדָב,
וְלֹא לִידֵי הַלְוָאָתָם,
כִּי אִם לְיָדְךָ הַמְּלֵאָה, הַפְּתוּחָה, הַגְּדוּשָׁה וְהָרְחָבָה,
שֶׁלֹּא נֵבוֹשׁ וְלֹא נִכָּלֵם לְעוֹלָם וָעֶד.

Be merciful, please, Adonai our God, with Israel your nation
and with Jerusalem your capital,
and with Zion, where your presence dwells,
and with the dynasty of David, your messiah,
and with the magnificent, sacred home bearing your name.
Our God, our parent, shepherd us, nourish us,
provide our livelihood and welfare,
relieve us quickly, Adonai our God from all troubles.
Prevent us please, Adonai our God, from needing the favor
or handout of mortal beings,
instead of your full and overflowing hand, opened wide,
so that we should never feel shamed nor debased.

on Shabbat:

רְצֵה וְהַחֲלִיצֵנוּ
יְיָ אֱלֹהֵינוּ בְּמִצְוֹתֶיךָ
וּבְמִצְוַת יוֹם הַשְּׁבִיעִי
הַשַּׁבָּת הַגָּדוֹל וְהַקָּדוֹשׁ הַזֶּה,
כִּי יוֹם זֶה גָּדוֹל וְקָדוֹשׁ הוּא לְפָנֶיךָ
לִשְׁבָּת בּוֹ וְלָנוּחַ בּוֹ בְּאַהֲבָה כְּמִצְוַת רְצוֹנֶךָ
וּבִרְצוֹנְךָ הָנִיחַ לָנוּ יְיָ אֱלֹהֵינוּ,
שֶׁלֹּא תְהֵא צָרָה וְיָגוֹן וַאֲנָחָה בְּיוֹם מְנוּחָתֵנוּ,
וְהַרְאֵנוּ יְיָ אֱלֹהֵינוּ בְּנֶחָמַת צִיּוֹן עִירֶךָ,
וּבְבִנְיַן יְרוּשָׁלַיִם עִיר קָדְשֶׁךָ,
כִּי אַתָּה הוּא בַּעַל הַיְשׁוּעוֹת וּבַעַל הַנֶּחָמוֹת.

Let it be your wish to grant us relief,
Adonai our God, through your commandments —
for the commandment of the seventh day,
this great and sacred Shabbat.
For it is a great and sacred day to be in your presence, an occasion
for taking pause and resting with love, as your will commands.
If it is your will, Adonai our God, relieve us,
on our day of rest, from trouble, grief, and dejection;
and show us, Adonai our God, how You console your city Zion,
and how You rebuild Jerusalem your sacred capital,
for You bring redemption and comfort.

continued on next page ⇛

added on Rosh Hodesh, Yom Tov, Hol Hamoed, and Rosh Hashanah

אֱלֹהֵינוּ וֵאלֹהֵי אֲבוֹתֵינוּ (וְאִמּוֹתֵינוּ),	Our God and the God of our ancestors,
יַעֲלֶה וְיָבֹא וְיַגִּיעַ, וְיֵרָאֶה	may these thoughts ascend, enter, arrive and be seen;
וְיֵרָצֶה וְיִשָּׁמַע, וְיִפָּקֵד וְיִזָּכֵר:	may they be desirable, heard, recorded and remembered.
זִכְרוֹנֵנוּ וּפִקְדוֹנֵנוּ,	May you remember us and our records,
וְזִכְרוֹן אֲבוֹתֵינוּ (וְאִמּוֹתֵינוּ),	our ancestors,
וְזִכְרוֹן מָשִׁיחַ בֶּן דָּוִד עַבְדֶּךָ,	the messiah descendant of David, your servant,
וְזִכְרוֹן יְרוּשָׁלַיִם עִיר קָדְשֶׁךָ	Jerusalem, your sacred capital,
וְזִכְרוֹן כָּל עַמְּךָ בֵּית יִשְׂרָאֵל;	your entire people, the House of Israel.
לְפָנֶיךָ לִפְלֵיטָה, לְטוֹבָה,	Recall them for rescue and for goodness,
לְחֵן וּלְחֶסֶד וּלְרַחֲמִים,	for grace, kindness and mercy,
לְחַיִּים וּלְשָׁלוֹם בְּיוֹם	for life and peace, on this holiday of:
ON ROSH HODESH רֹאשׁ הַחֹדֶשׁ הַזֶּה.	Rosh Hodesh
ON PESACH חַג הַמַּצּוֹת הַזֶּה.	Pesach, holiday of matzot,
ON SHAVUOT חַג הַשָּׁבֻעוֹת הַזֶּה.	Shavuot
ON SUCCOT חַג הַסֻּכּוֹת הַזֶּה.	Sukkot
ON SHEMINI ATZERET/SIMCHAT TORAH הַשְּׁמִינִי חַג הָעֲצֶרֶת הַזֶּה.	Shimini Atzeret and Simchat Torah, the Eighth Day Conclusion [of Sukkot]
ON ROSH HASHANA הַזִּכָּרוֹן הַזֶּה.	Rosh Hashana
זָכְרֵנוּ יְיָ אֱלֹהֵינוּ בּוֹ לְטוֹבָה	Remember us for good, Adonai our God;
וּפָקְדֵנוּ בוֹ לִבְרָכָה,	record us for blessing;
וְהוֹשִׁיעֵנוּ בוֹ לְחַיִּים (טוֹבִים),	and redeem us for (a good) life.
וּבִדְבַר יְשׁוּעָה וְרַחֲמִים:	With a proclamation of redemption and mercy,
חוּס וְחָנֵּנוּ, וְרַחֵם עָלֵינוּ וְהוֹשִׁיעֵנוּ;	protect us, grant us grace and compassion and save us,
כִּי אֵלֶיךָ עֵינֵינוּ,	for we turn our eyes to You,
כִּי אֵל מֶלֶךְ חַנּוּן וְרַחוּם אָתָּה.	for You are our God, our Sovereign, merciful and gracious.

U-v'nei	**וּבְנֵה**	And rebuild
Yerushalayim	יְרוּשָׁלַיִם	Jerusalem
ir hakodesh	עִיר הַקֹּדֶשׁ	as the sacred capital —
bi-m'heira v'yameinu.	בִּמְהֵרָה בְיָמֵינוּ.	quickly, in our age.
Ba-rukh ata Adonai,	בָּרוּךְ אַתָּה יְיָ,	Blessed are You, Adonai,
Boneh v'rakha-mav,	בּוֹנֵה בְרַחֲמָיו	who in your mercy are rebuilding
Yerushalayim, Amen.	יְרוּשָׁלָיִם. אָמֵן.	Jerusalem, Amen.

Jerusalem Holiday Stamps (1968) by B. Ben Dov. Courtesy of the Israeli Philatelic Society.

6 *Fourth blessing — Good to all —* הַטּוֹב וְהַמֵּטִיב

בָּרוּךְ אַתָּה יְיָ אֱלֹהֵינוּ מֶלֶךְ הָעוֹלָם	Blessed are You Adonai our God, Ruler of the Universe
הָאֵל אָבִינוּ מַלְכֵּנוּ אַדִּירֵנוּ	the God — our parent, our ruler, our champion,
בּוֹרְאֵנוּ גּוֹאֲלֵנוּ יוֹצְרֵנוּ	our creator, our redeemer, our designer
קְדוֹשֵׁנוּ קְדוֹשׁ יַעֲקֹב,	our Holy One, sacred to Jacob,
רוֹעֵנוּ רוֹעֵה יִשְׂרָאֵל,	our shepherd, shepherd of Israel.
הַמֶּלֶךְ הַטּוֹב וְהַמֵּטִיב לַכֹּל,	Our generous ruler shares goodness with all.
שֶׁבְּכָל יוֹם וָיוֹם הוּא הֵטִיב,	Daily God is good
הוּא מֵטִיב, הוּא יֵיטִיב לָנוּ,	and will be good to us.
הוּא גְמָלָנוּ, הוּא גוֹמְלֵנוּ, הוּא יִגְמְלֵנוּ לָעַד,	God rewarded us, rewards us, and will continue to reward us forever.
לְחֵן וּלְחֶסֶד וּלְרַחֲמִים,	You share grace, kindness and mercy,
וּלְרֶוַח, הַצָּלָה וְהַצְלָחָה,	relief, rescue, and success,
בְּרָכָה וִישׁוּעָה, נֶחָמָה, פַּרְנָסָה וְכַלְכָּלָה,	blessing and redemption, comfort, income, and support,
וְרַחֲמִים וְחַיִּים וְשָׁלוֹם וְכָל טוֹב,	love, life, and peace — all that is good.
וּמִכָּל טוּב לְעוֹלָם אַל יְחַסְּרֵנוּ.	May we never lack any of the good things — forever more.
הָרַחֲמָן הוּא יִמְלוֹךְ עָלֵינוּ לְעוֹלָם וָעֶד.	May the Merciful One reign over us forever.
הָרַחֲמָן הוּא יִתְבָּרַךְ בַּשָּׁמַיִם וּבָאָרֶץ.	May the Merciful One be blessed in Heaven and on Earth.
הָרַחֲמָן הוּא יִשְׁתַּבַּח לְדוֹר דּוֹרִים,	May the Merciful One be praised by all generations to come,
וְיִתְפָּאַר בָּנוּ לָעַד וּלְנֵצַח נְצָחִים,	adored by us forever and ever,
וְיִתְהַדַּר בָּנוּ לָעַד וּלְעוֹלְמֵי עוֹלָמִים.	and glorified by us from now until eternity.
הָרַחֲמָן הוּא יְפַרְנְסֵנוּ בְּכָבוֹד.	May the Merciful One grant us an honorable living.
הָרַחֲמָן הוּא יִשְׁבּוֹר עֻלֵּנוּ מֵעַל צַוָּארֵנוּ	May the Merciful One break the yoke (of oppression) from our neck
וְהוּא יוֹלִיכֵנוּ קוֹמְמִיּוּת לְאַרְצֵנוּ.	and lead us upright into our land.
הָרַחֲמָן הוּא יִשְׁלַח לָנוּ בְּרָכָה מְרֻבָּה	May the Merciful One send ample blessing
בַּבַּיִת הַזֶּה וְעַל שֻׁלְחָן זֶה	into this house, and upon this table
שֶׁאָכַלְנוּ עָלָיו.	at which we have eaten.
הָרַחֲמָן הוּא יִשְׁלַח לָנוּ	May the Merciful One send us
אֶת אֵלִיָּהוּ הַנָּבִיא זָכוּר לַטּוֹב,	Elijah the prophet,
וִיבַשֶּׂר לָנוּ בְּשׂוֹרוֹת טוֹבוֹת	who will bring us good tidings
יְשׁוּעוֹת וְנֶחָמוֹת.	of consolation and comfort.

Harakhaman, hu yi-sh'lakh la-nu, et Eli-yahu hanavi, zakhur la-tov, vee-vaser lanu, b'sorot tovot, y'shu-ot v'nekhamot.

הָרַחֲמָן הוּא יְבָרֵךְ אֶת כָּל הַמְּסֻבִּין כַּאן
אוֹתָנוּ וְאֶת כָּל אֲשֶׁר לָנוּ
כְּמוֹ שֶׁנִּתְבָּרְכוּ אֲבוֹתֵינוּ אַבְרָהָם יִצְחָק וְיַעֲקֹב
(וּכְמוֹ שֶׁנִּתְבָּרְכוּ אִמּוֹתֵינוּ שָׂרָה רִבְקָה רָחֵל וְלֵאָה)
בַּכֹּל מִכֹּל כֹּל.
כֵּן יְבָרֵךְ אוֹתָנוּ כֻּלָּנוּ יַחַד בִּבְרָכָה שְׁלֵמָה וְנֹאמַר אָמֵן.

The Merciful One should bless all who are gathered here
us and all that is ours
just as you blessed our ancestors Abraham, Isaac and Jacob
(and as you blessed our ancestors Sara, Rivka, Rachel and Leah)
in everything, from everything, and with everything.
So should you bless us together with a complete blessing, Amen.

בַּמָּרוֹם יְלַמְּדוּ עֲלֵיהֶם וְעָלֵינוּ
זְכוּת שֶׁתְּהֵא לְמִשְׁמֶרֶת שָׁלוֹם
וְנִשָּׂא בְרָכָה מֵאֵת יְיָ
וּצְדָקָה מֵאֱלֹהֵי יִשְׁעֵנוּ.
וְנִמְצָא חֵן וְשֵׂכֶל טוֹב
בְּעֵינֵי אֱלֹהִים וְאָדָם.

May there be invoked on high, for them and for us,
a merit that will earn us the protection of peace,
and we shall receive a blessing from Adonai
and a just reward from the God of our redemption.
May we find grace and good favor
in the eyes of God and human beings.

on Shabbat:

הָרַחֲמָן, הוּא יַנְחִילֵנוּ יוֹם שֶׁכֻּלּוֹ שַׁבָּת
וּמְנוּחָה לְחַיֵּי הָעוֹלָמִים.

May the Merciful One grant us a day of complete Shabbat [the messianic era],
and eternal rest [for the world to come].

on Rosh Hodesh

הָרַחֲמָן, הוּא יְחַדֵּשׁ עָלֵינוּ
אֶת הַחֹדֶשׁ הַזֶּה לְטוֹבָה וְלִבְרָכָה.

on Rosh Hodesh

May the Merciful One renew for us
a new month for good and for blessing.

on Festivals

הָרַחֲמָן, הוּא יַנְחִילֵנוּ יוֹם שֶׁכֻּלּוֹ טוֹב.

on Festivals

May the Merciful One grant us a Yom Tov, a day of complete goodness.

on Rosh HaShanah

הָרַחֲמָן, הוּא יְחַדֵּשׁ עָלֵינוּ
אֶת הַשָּׁנָה הַזֹּאת לְטוֹבָה וְלִבְרָכָה.

on Rosh HaShanah

May the Merciful One renew for us
a new year for good and for blessing.

on Sukkot

הָרַחֲמָן, הוּא יָקִים לָנוּ אֶת סֻכַּת דָּוִד הַנּוֹפֶלֶת.

on Sukkot

May the Merciful One restore King David's "Sukkah," his faltering dynasty.

הָרַחֲמָן הוּא יְבָרֵךְ אֶת מְדִינַת יִשְׂרָאֵל.

May the Merciful One bless the State of Israel.

הָרַחֲמָן הוּא יַשְׁכִּין שָׁלוֹם
בֵּין בְּנֵי יַעֲקֹב וּבְנֵי יִשְׁמָעֵאל.

May the Merciful One grant peace
between the children of Jacob and the children of Ishmael.

הָרַחֲמָן הוּא יְזַכֵּנוּ לִימוֹת הַמָּשִׁיחַ
וּלְחַיֵּי הָעוֹלָם הַבָּא.

May the Merciful One admit us to the era of the Messiah
and to life in the World to Come.

7 *Concluding hope — Making world peace —* עֹשֶׂה שָׁלוֹם

Mi-g'dol y'shu-ot malko,
v'oseh khesed li-m'shi-kho,
l'David u-l'zar'o ad olam.
Oseh shalom bi-m'romav,
hu ya-aseh shalom,
aleinu v'al kol yisrael
v'imru Amen.

מִגְדּוֹל יְשׁוּעוֹת מַלְכּוֹ	"God is a tower of strength,
וְעֹשֶׂה חֶסֶד לִמְשִׁיחוֹ	and does kindness for God's anointed one,
לְדָוִד וּלְזַרְעוֹ עַד עוֹלָם.	for David and his descendants forever." *(II Samuel 22:51)*
עֹשֶׂה שָׁלוֹם בִּמְרוֹמָיו	God who creates peace in the heavenly heights,
הוּא יַעֲשֶׂה שָׁלוֹם	may you grant peace
עָלֵינוּ וְעַל כָּל יִשְׂרָאֵל	for us and for all Israel,
וְאִמְרוּ אָמֵן.	and let us say Amen.

יְראוּ אֶת יְיָ קְדוֹשָׁיו	"Revere Adonai, God's holy ones,
כִּי אֵין מַחְסוֹר לִירֵאָיו.	for those who revere God know no want.
כְּפִירִים רָשׁוּ וְרָעֵבוּ	Young lions may growl and go hungry,
וְדוֹרְשֵׁי יְיָ	but those who seek Adonai
לֹא יַחְסְרוּ כָל טוֹב.	lack nothing good." *(Psalm 34:10-11)*
הוֹדוּ לַייָ כִּי טוֹב	"Thank Adonai, for God is good,
כִּי לְעוֹלָם חַסְדּוֹ.	for God's kindness endures forever." *(Psalm 118:1)*
פּוֹתֵחַ אֶת יָדֶךָ	"Opening your hand
וּמַשְׂבִּיעַ	You satisfy
לְכָל חַי רָצוֹן.	the desire of every living being." *(Psalm 145:16)*
בָּרוּךְ הַגֶּבֶר	"Blessed are those
אֲשֶׁר יִבְטַח בַּייָ	who trust in Adonai;
וְהָיָה יְיָ מִבְטַחוֹ.	Adonai is their source of reliance." *(Jeremiah 17:7)*
נַעַר הָיִיתִי	"I have been young
גַּם זָקַנְתִּי	and now I am old,
וְלֹא רָאִיתִי	but never have I seen
צַדִּיק נֶעֱזָב	the innocent abandoned,
וְזַרְעוֹ מְבַקֶּשׁ לָחֶם.	their children wanting bread." *(Psalm 37:25)*
יְיָ עֹז לְעַמּוֹ יִתֵּן	"Adonai will give strength to our people,
יְיָ יְבָרֵךְ	Adonai will bless
אֶת עַמּוֹ בַשָּׁלוֹם.	our people with peace." *(Psalm 29:11)*

Oseh Shalom
The Paint Box

I had a paint box,
Each color glowing with delight;
I had a paint-box with colors
Warm and cool and bright.
I had no red for wounds and blood,
I had no black for an orphaned child.
I had no white for the face of the dead.
I had no yellow for burning sands.
I had orange for joy and life.
I had green for buds and blooms.
I had blue for clear bright skies.
I had pink for dreams and rest.
I sat down
and painted
Peace.

— *Shurak Tall, Age 13*

Adonai oz l'amo yi-tein
Adonai y'va-reikh
Et amo va-Shalom.

Reflections כַּוָּנוֹת

a silent prayer

For an End to Famine, by A. Calderon, Israeli stamp, 1963

לֹא רָאִיתִי צַדִּיק נֶעֱזָב — "I have never seen the innocent abandoned"

How do we recite words of prayer that we don't believe? What happens when our reality contradicts our theology? This issue arises for many people in relation to one of the last verses of *Birkat HaMazon* — "I have been a child and now I am old, and I have never seen a righteous person abandoned or his descendants begging for bread." (Psalm 37: 25)

Lawrence Hoffman, the great scholar of liturgy, explains his own research into this problematic verse:

"For good reason Jews throughout history have had trouble saying this line. Some prayerbooks [including the one attributed to Rabbi Elijah HaGaon of Vilna, 18th century] . . . include it in tiny type alone to remind worshippers that even though it is passed down as tradition, they may skip it — or at least, if they do say it, they should do so silently rather than embarrassingly out loud. I confess that for years, the only way I could read it was to supply my own punctuation. Since classical Hebrew texts come unpunctuated, and supplying them with printed periods and commas is a modern innovation . . . I decided to read it as, "I have been young, and have grown older, and have I not seen? There are righteous people abandoned by God, with their children seeking bread."

It turns out, however, that there is also a traditional understanding of our troublesome line, perfectly in keeping with the utopian claim that God feeds everyone, and with the recognition that the blessing over bread refers to the ultimate messianic future rather than to our own world and time. The entire meal liturgy is eschatological and . . . should be said as an extended statement of what we hope for, not what we already see in existence. (*The Way into Jewish Prayer*)

Noam Nadav, The Israeli Yuppie and the Homeless.

Guidelines
getting started

How can I introduce Birkat HaMazon into my Shabbat dinner ritual?

No one opposes saying "thank you" as a matter of faith or principle. Doing so is a matter of good manners. Yet getting everyone at the table to chant the full *Birkat HaMazon* can be difficult because of its length, its language and its complexity. Its many paragraphs not only thank God for food, but also pray for restoration of the land of Israel, the rebuilding of Jerusalem and the coming of the messianic age. The expansive *Birkat HaMazon* is really a mini-service instituted by the Rabbis.

One may choose to do an abbreviated version, to recite a paragraph of thanks in English or to set the blessings to upbeat melodies. These melodies make the recitation more enjoyable and fast-paced. Many Jews sing the longer versions only at formal occasions or with friends well-versed in its words and tunes. Remember: while it is traditional to recite at least part of *Birkat HaMazon* in Hebrew, it is equally valid to use English to fulfill the mitzvah of expressing our gratitude to God.

"Who is rich? One who is happy with his lot." (Pirkei Avot) Shabbat in a Coal Cellar in New York City in 1880. Reprinted by permission of the Beit Hatefutsot Archive, Tel Aviv.

Guidelines
parent-child corner

Often our children — older and younger — leave the table in the midst of a meal: to sleep, to play, to study. Sometimes they ask permission; sometimes there is a telephone call and then a television show, and they can disappear without ceremony — even from a carefully orchestrated Shabbat family meal.

We know some families that have instituted a rule that no one can leave the table without thanking the hosts, both human and divine. These families established a household norm that everyone acknowledges those who graciously shared with us the blessing of food. The expression of gratitude varies according to the personality of the family. Some parents ask their children to be specific about what they most enjoyed from the meal. Others just insist upon a general expression of appreciation.

Many families try to make *Birkat HaMazon* as joyful as possible, especially on Shabbat. They use popular tunes for various parts of Birkat HaMazon that they have learned by heart at camp or at religious school.

— Noam Zion

Making a Pledge to Tzedakah at Every Meal

Ideally we should do something to advance the cause of feeding the world at every meal. However, inviting the poor to our table is not common today because of geographic and social segregation between the homeless and those with the resources to maintain households. The Rabbi and co-author of the *Jewish Catalogue*, Michael Strassfeld finds a solution in the kabbalist Elijah de Vidas:

> "In a place where poor people are not to be found, what can a person do? . . . You should estimate the cost of what the meal for a poor person would have been, and put that amount a side for Tzedakah before you eat." *(Reshit Hochmah)*

It is often possible in large grocery stores to buy food coupons for the needy when you shop for Shabbat. In my family my 13-year-old son saves our grocery receipts, totals them monthly and everyone donates 5% to the poor at the end of the month. I hope he will understand what Francis Bacon wrote:

> "If a man be gracious to strangers, it shows that he is a citizen of the world, and his heart is no island, cut off from other islands, but a continent that joins them." *(Francis Bacon, 1561-1626, English philosopher, jurist and scientist)*

— Noam Zion

A One-Line Blessing?

Some children in Jewish summer camp favor the succinct and colorful blessing: "Rub-a-dub-dub, thanks for the grub! Yea, God!" Fortunately, there are less flippant, but still abbreviated, traditional versions of *Birkat HaMazon*.

As a child, my father taught me the one line, seven word, *Brikh Rakhamana* blessing *(see below)*, which has served me well when I have been too lazy or rushed to say a fuller *Birkat HaMazon*. Quoted in the Talmud in its everyday language, Aramaic:

בְּרִיךְ רַחֲמָנָא מַלְכָּא דְעָלְמָא מָרֵיהּ דְּהַאי פִּתָּא. אָמֵן.

Brikh Rakhamana Malka D'Alma Mara d'hai Pitah. Amen.

Blessed are You the Merciful One, the Ruler, the Master of the World, for this bread (literally, pita). Amen.

Notice that this (like the Kaddish) is composed not in Hebrew but in Aramaic — the most widely spoken language of the Middle East for a thousand years until the Arab Conquest in the seventh century.

— Noam Zion

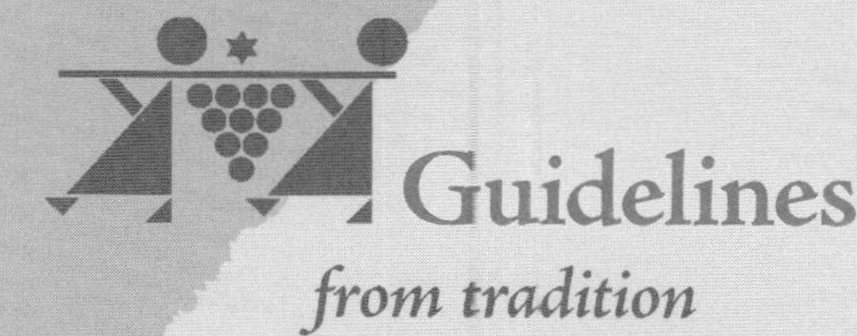

Guidelines *from tradition*

Arranging the Table after Dinner in Preparation for *Birkat HaMazon*

In order to make a more dignified setting for blessing God, some people clear the table before reciting *Birkat HaMazon*. The Rabbis established etiquette for those objects at the table during *Birkat HaMazon*. Here is the checklist:

On the Table

What? Wine, some of the Hallah, and salt — these three foods make the table a symbol of abundance.

Why? Mystically speaking, "it is a general rule that no heavenly blessings descend on an empty table." In addition, if bread is left on the table during *Birkat HaMazon*, and if hungry people arrive late, there will still be something for them to eat, and they will not feel excluded or forgotten even though we ate without them.

Not on the Table

What? Knives.

Why? Knives symbolize war and death, so the Rabbis preferred not to have them around at moments of blessing.

The custom of covering the knife during Birkat HaMazon derives from the mitzvah "not to use iron (cutting implements) in making the altar." *(Deuteronomy 27:5)*. Rabbi Shimon ben Elazar explains: "The altar was created to lengthen a human being's years by bringing atonement and forgiveness, while iron was created to shorten human life. It is inappropriate for the 'shortener' of life to be raised over the 'lengthener' of life."

In fact, the name of the first blacksmith (who created sharp metal implements) in the Torah is 'Tuval-Cain,' reminding us of his ancestor, Cain — the first murderer in history *(Genesis 4: 22)*. *(For more detailed halachic guidelines for* Birkat HaMazon, *see the companion educator's guide).*

Tales of gratitude and ingratitude

For every breath of life one takes, one should offer praise to the Holy One.

— MIDRASH, GENESIS RABBAH 14:9

Guilty of Stealing a Meal

A nineteenth-century story tells of two Eastern European rabbis who were traveling together. They both ate a meal at an inn owned by a pious widow. While eating, one rabbi engaged in a long, detailed conversation with the rather talkative woman; the other sat quietly and, when not eating, turned his attention to a holy text he was studying.

When they rose to leave, the widow refused to let the rabbis pay for the meal. Outside, the more convivial of the two turned to his friend, commenting, "It seems to me that you are guilty of stealing a meal from that woman."

His friend looked up in astonishment. "She herself told us that we didn't have to pay."

"She didn't want us to pay money," the first rabbi answered. "But the payment she wanted was that we listen and talk to her. This you didn't do."

Guests, not just hosts, have ethical obligations. For example, Jewish tradition teaches that during the *Birkat Hamazon* (the blessings after the meal), guests are to invoke a special blessing for the family that has to be considerate and polite, and to bring pleasure to the person who is hosting them. Guests should express gratitude for what they are served and make efforts to be sociable (and not sit at the table quiet and withdrawn). As every parent knows, guests can bring great joy to their hosts by finding things in their children to complement, too. Most of all, engage your hosts. If they need to speak, lend them your ear.

Jewish law demands additional, perhaps surprising sensitivity, on the part of guests. If they have been treated with truly generous hospitality, they should not praise their hosts lavishly to many other people; such praise might cause others to come to the host family to exploit their generosity.

— JOSEPH TELUSHKIN, THE BOOK OF JEWISH VALUES

An Appreciative Guest and a Muffin

A man who spent much time with Rabbi Shlomo Carlebach, used to speak of his ability to compliment and express gratitude . . . even for a muffin.

On one occasion he sat with Reb Shlomo in a dingy restaurant, presided over by a sour-looking proprietress and waitress. The woman was unusually homely, and unpleasant as well. He was happy when she put down their breakfast order and returned to the counter. But after taking one bite of the muffin she had brought him, Reb Shlomo summoned her back. "My most beautiful friend," he said to her gently, "are you by any chance the person who baked this muffin?"

"Yeah, I am, what about it?"

"I just want you to know that this is the most delicious muffin I have ever tasted in my life."

The woman gave a hint of a smile, thanked him, and started to walk away.

"And I also want you to know," Reb Shlomo continued, "that I have eaten muffins all over the world, but none came close to this one."

Again, the woman thanked him, but Reb Shlomo still was not finished. "And *mamesh* (truly), I have to thank you because I was so hungry, and you did me the greatest favor in the world by so expertly baking this muffin, which is surely a taste of the World-to-Come."

By now the woman was smiling broadly: "Well, gee, thanks a lot. It's very nice of you to say so. Most people never comment when the food is good; you only hear from them when they have a complaint."

Reb Shlomo went on to ask the woman about the special ingredients she used in preparing the muffin, and listened attentively. He was specific with his compliments as well, commenting on the muffin's airy texture, its buttery and fragrant quality. Carlebach's friend recalls that he was watching Reb Shlomo's paean to a muffin with a mixture of amazement and amusement, until he gazed at the woman. "I was taken aback. The homely woman was no more. A few minutes with Shlomo had done the trick. She was transformed. She had become beautiful."

— JOSEPH TELUSHKIN, THE BOOK OF JEWISH VALUES

You should eat, and
be satisfied. Then
you should bless
Adonai, your God.

— *Deuteronomy 8:10*

It is gratefulness which
makes the soul
great.

— *Abraham Joshua Heschel, Man's Quest for God*

If a Jew breaks his leg,
he thanks God that
he did not break
both legs.
If he breaks both legs,
he thanks God he
did not break his
neck.

— *Anonymous Jewish comedian*

Cholent — Shabbat stew — was prepared in Poland in a communal oven to and from which Jews carried the crockpot (1930-1939). USHMM, Washington, D.C.

In the world to come, each of us will give an accounting for every time our eyes beheld a delight but we did not partake of it.

— *Talmud Yerushalmi, Kiddushin* 4:12

New Russian Jewish Immigrant to Israel, Lod, 1997.
Photo © Zion Ozeri.

Oneg Shabbat
a day of delights

עֹנֶג שַׁבָּת

"Call Shabbat a Delight!" (ISAIAH 58:13) means a delight for both body and soul, a delight for celestial and earthly realms.

— TALMUD YERUSHALMI, KIDDUSHIN 4:12

What a radical message Isaiah the prophet taught 2500 years ago!

God's holiest day is designed to be a day of pleasure, a different delight — *Oneg*. Shabbat is a return to the Garden of Eden — whose name means literally a "garden of delights" — and at the same time it is a foretaste of the world to come. Isaiah's prophecy is read on Yom Kippur morning and it preaches that God rejects fast days of mere self-affliction and prefers feast days in which we share all we have with the poor.

Sanctity *does* involve distancing ourselves from the mundane, our everyday business, but it *does not* entail an ascetic denial of physical pleasures and human joy.

Holy R&R — A Menu for Shabbat: Life as Leisure

Shabbat offers opportunities not just for prayer, ritual and study, but also for unstructured relaxation. The goal of this time is not just to rest the body, but also to elevate the soul.

How shall we fill the "free time" of Shabbat? Some suggestions in the spirit of Shabbat:

- ▲ **Shabbat Torah Study — *Talmud Torah***
- ▲ **Visiting the Ill and Comforting the Mourners — *Bikkur Holim and Nikhum Avelim***
- ▲ **Reading — Novels and Newspapers**
- ▲ **Revisiting Creation: Walks in Nature — *Zecher L'Maasei Breshit***
- ▲ **Rest and Relaxation — "Sleep on Shabbat is an *Oneg*"**
- ▲ **Play and games**
- ▲ **DO NOTHING! The Art of Hanging Around**
- ▲ **Meditation: Deep Breathing — *Nishama and Nishima* — (*Soul and Breathing*)**
- ▲ **Music**
- ▲ **Dispel Depression Anyway you Can: The Hassidic Battle against the *Mara Shekhora* (depression)**
- ▲ **Reminiscing with Family and Friends: Judaism, A Religion of Memory/*Zikaron***

The pleasures of Shabbat food

What does Oneg Shabbat include?

First it involves "eating and drinking."

"It is a mitzvah to enjoy oneself on Shabbat. Just as there is pleasure in food, so there is enjoyment in the bodily pleasures." (*Sefer Yerem*)

"It is a duty to eat three meals on Shabbat [in contradistinction to the usual two meals in the ancient world] . . . The Rabbis used to prepare the richest foods and finest wines that one can afford. The more one spends for the Shabbat and for the preparation of tasty and numerous dishes, the more one is to be commended. If, however, one cannot afford this, it is sufficient to make Shabbat a delight by preparing a simple vegetable dish. For one is not obligated to humiliate oneself by begging from others just in order to provide a large quantity of food for Shabbat. The Rabbis used to say: 'Better make your Shabbat [meals] like those of the weekday, than to depend on the charity of others.'" (*Maimonides, Laws of Shabbat 30:7,9, Mishne Torah*)

To enjoy the food we need heat and light which are provided by lighting a candle before Shabbat and by preparing a fire (or today a hot plate or oven on low heat) before sunset. On Israeli-made ovens the setting for "warm" is officially labeled "Shabbat." The 9th-century Karaite sect — which understood the Torah to require that all fires be extinguished on Shabbat — required one to sit in the dark and eat cold food to "honor" the sanctity of the day. But the Rabbis required that food be warm and candles be lit in advance of the sunset.

A well-stocked hearth includes "cholent" — a slow-cooking dish buried in the fireplace or today prepared in a crockpot. The light of the candles provides not only for *Shalom Bayit* — greater sociability and tranquillity around the table at a candle lit dinner — but also an aesthetic of eating. As the Rabbis put it colloquially:

"It is not the same experience to eat food one can see and to consume food one cannot see." (*Talmud Yoma 74b*)

"Satisfaction in eating depends on the visual presentation . . . Therefore, the Rabbis required the lighting of a candle on Shabbat, so we might take full pleasure in our drinking and eating." (*Midrash Lekach Tov, Va-Yakhel 35:3*)

Shabbat kugel. Alphonse Levy (France, 19th century)

Neverthless:

Some authorities admit that, if eating will harm someone, and it is more of a pleasure not to eat, then one should not eat on Shabbat. (*Shulchan Aruch 288:2*)

Oneg of course also involves physical and emotional pleasures like love-making and simply sleeping.

- The letters of the word ShaBaT may stand for **Sh**eina **B**'Shabbat **T**aanug — "Sleeping on Shabbat is a pleasure." (*Yalkut Shimoni, Va-et-chanan*)
- Rabbi Yitzkhak Naphkha says: *Oneg* is a good bed with lovely bedding and linens.
- Rabbi Yirmiya says: *Oneg* is going to the bathhouse.
- Rabbi Yochanan says: *Oneg* is washing one's hands and feet in warm water. (*Talmud Shabbat 25*)

Mourning is proscribed on Shabbat.

It is forbidden to fast or to cry out to God in prayerful requests for mercy. (*Maimonides, Laws of Shabbat 30:12, Mishne Torah*)

However, individual expressions of emotonal satisfaction may overrule even that common sense idea. When Rabbi Akiba was challlenged by his students:

"Why are you shedding tears on Shabbat?" he responded: "That is my prerogative for it is my *Oneg* on Shabbat to indulge my sadness." (*Shibolei HaLeket*)

Pick Your Oneg Shabbat Pleasure Card

Hillel lived by the principle that "to do good to yourself is a form of piety" (PROVERBS 11:17), for you are created in the image of God, so he went off to take a dip in the Roman baths — an elaborate ancient sauna. As we saw above, Rabbi Akiba said, I enjoy having a good cry on Shabbat. Pleasures are a matter of personal preference, but they are enhanced when shared. **Survey your friends and family for their top three choices of pleaures that can be realized on Shabbat without exorbitant expense or effort.** Then prepare nicely designed Oneg Shabbat Cards that may be drawn, like Monopoly cards, while sitting at the Shabbat table. If the family or friends are willing to help make Oneg cards come true, then throw dice to determine whose choice will be given priorty. Some pleasures may need to be postponed to later Shabbatot, so parents and friends should be prepared to make and keep promises. Most important one should be willing to seize the moment and to enjoy their Oneg today on this Shabbat, if possible. "If not now, when?" asked Hillel.

Oneg Cards:

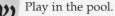

- ש Read me a story. (Being read to aloud can be a pleasure for adults as well as children, for short readings at the table or longer ones on the couch or in bed. Perhaps pick a Jewish ghost story before Halloween or a Jewish love story before Valentine's Day. *See Howard Schwartz's wonderful anthologies of Jewish tales.*)
- ש Play a group game (like Monopoly or Scrabble or Clue).
- ש Play cards or assemble a big puzzle.
- ש Sing a song (and perhaps accompany it with instrumentation in the style of a jam session. Rounds are lots of fun).
- ש Watch a movie together (if appropriate for your household's Shabbat).
- ש Act out a Biblical story (use puppets and the *Sedra Scenes* scripts by Stan Beiner)
- ש Hold a quiz with prizes (try out Jewish Trivia or Jeopardy).
- ש Build a Lego castle.
- ש Serve an edible treat (like an ice cream sundae in the shape of Mount Sinai).
- ש Take a nap (and have others agree to play quietly or take the little children for a walk).
- ש Play in the pool.
- ש Put on a talent show.
- ש Share family memories or describe an exotic vacation (take out the albums, if you wish).
- ש Dance around the table or in the living room.
- ש Offer someone a massage.
- ש Visit friends at their home, or invite them to yours for dessert.
- ש Go for a walk in nature; play ball or Frisbee outside (recreation is re-creation).

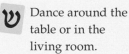

Tu B'Shevat stamp, A. Calderon (1975)

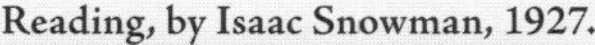

Reading, by Isaac Snowman, 1927.

Oneg/ Pleasures

The delights of Shabbat table talk

Shabbat is a day for informal conversation, personal sharing and dreaming. Make your Shabbat table a place to share these thoughts, hopes, and questions. (One Midrash expresses our need for this kind of human connection when it explains the verse "There are many days of trouble, but one day belongs to him" *(Psalm 139:16)*: "This verse means that "one day" — that is, Shabbat — will be reserved for "him" — the Jewish people, Israel.)

Rest and relaxation on the seventh day — after a long work week — gives us a day when a person works to make peace with all members of the household.

Often a person goes out to work and faces difficulties for six days, then on the seventh one may forget all the pain suffered. That is human nature, as the idiom goes, "One good day wipes out the memory of a bad one, but a bad one makes a person forget the good day." *(Midrash Tana d'bei Elijah 1)*

Shabbat table conversations should however steer clear of gossip and slander (because you never know who is listening, as the tradition teaches us):

"Someone sits in the gardens, while friends are listening to her voice. Let me hear your voice, says the beloved." *(Song of Songs 8:13)*

Rabbi Akha interpreted this verse as follows:

"Even though the Jewish people are working six days a week, on Shabbat they get up early and go to the synagogue to recite *Shma* (listen!), to pray, to read Torah and the prophets.

"Then God says: A little louder, please, so that your "friends" — the angels — can hear you. But make sure not to hate one another, not to be jealous of one another, to compete with one another, and to embarrass one another [on Shabbat]. Otherwise the angels will report back to me and say: Master of the Universe! Not only aren't the Jewish people busy studying the Torah You gave them, but they are torn asunder by hate, jealousy, strife and competition.

"Therefore I suggest you just continue to observe the Torah in peace." *(Midrash Song of Songs 8)*

Shabbat conversation may rise above weekly affairs and take a broader perspective. Shabbat is a time for **remembering the creation**. You might take out some beautiful nature books, or describe a striking aspect of nature that means a great deal to you. Going for a walk may be even better — looking can be more powerful than verbalizing. In addition to God's creativity, there is God's human partners' creativity. Ask others to describe what they have created during the week, or take out art books which showcase the best of human creativity. Shabbat encompasses the creation of the past, the joy of the present, and the possibilities of the future. Let yourself dream about how things could be.

Shabbat sharing . . .

"Either companionship or death" was a watchword of the Rabbis. They recommended we strive to "acquire a friend" meaning find someone to share your food, your study, your secrets *(based on Avot d Rabbi Natan)*. Shabbat is an ideal time to devote to cultivating those friendships and sharing those personal perspectives.

A Shabbat meal is a good setting for playful as well as serious discussions that undergird sharing. Here are some suggestions for conversation-starters to begin Shabbat sharing.

- ☐ For the month of Adar, especially before picking a costume on Purim, you might ask: If you could be anyone in the world for a day, **whose life would you pick?**
- ☐ In one's **Bar/Bat Mitzvah** year, or near an anniversary of a Bar or Bat Mitzvah, ask: What is your favorite mitzvah? What mitzvah have you done this past week?

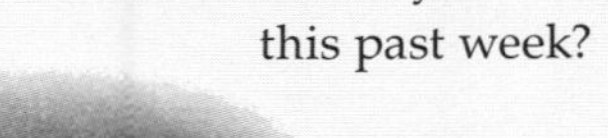

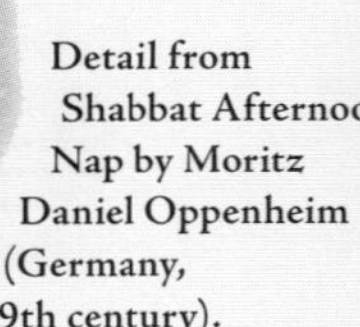

Detail from Shabbat Afternoon Nap by Moritz Daniel Oppenheim (Germany, 19th century).

. . . getting to know one another better

☐ ***Hakhnasat Orkhim***, hospitality, gives us an opportunity to meet people. ***Ushpizin*** is the Sukkot custom of inviting our ancestors for an imaginary visit. Whom would you invite to your Shabbat table if you could and why? Pick anyone living or dead.

☐ ***Tikkun HaMidot*** is an attempt to correct some of our character traits. What one trait would you add to your personality if you could? Why?

☐ ***Nachas*** is the pleasure you get from family and friends who have done something wonderful. What has given you *Nachas* recently? When and to whom have you given it?

☐ ***Gemilut Hassadim*** are the acts of kindness — not financial contributions but rather volunteering, doing favors, and helping out. What little acts of kindness were done for you recently?

☐ ***Tokhei-kha*** is rebuke — that is, the uncomfortable obligation to tell others how they might improve. The hard part is finding an artful and effective way to communicate that advice. When and how did you give this kind of advice recently? Was the mitzvah a success for you and the other person?

☐ "Eat and be satisfied and then bless God." *(Deuteronomy 8)* Name your **favorite food** and describe how you feel when eating it.

☐ **"Love your neighbor as yourself."** *(Leviticus 19:18)* How do your family and friends show love for one another?

☐ **"To work the earth and to tend it"** *(Genesis 2:15)*. Those were God's words about the purpose of human life. What do you think our purpose is on earth?

☐ ***Tikkun Olam*** — repairing the world. Abraham was not afraid to stand up to God and demand that justice be done. Pick one cause for which you think you should stand up and fight.

☐ King Solomon was asked in a dream, "What would be your **one wish from God** — wealth, long life, or wisdom?" How would *you* answer this question? Would your list include other options?

☐ It is a mitzvah to **bless the world for its beauty**. Pick one truly beautiful thing — natural or human-made — that you have seen or want to see and to acknowledge.

☐ Name a place where you would want to spend a **Shabbat vacation**. Would it be a mountaintop or a beach? Or in the city of Jerusalem? What would that Shabbat be like?

☐ Name your **hero**. What makes that person heroic?

☐ If you could **star in a movie**, or write your own — what would it be? If the movie were a Torah story, what narrative would you choose to act in? Which one might you want to direct? Why?

☐ **"For you were strangers in the land of Egypt"** *(Leviticus 19:34)*. As a result, it is a mitzvah to try to understand the heart of the stranger. Describe a moment where you saw prejudice against outsiders. What role (victim, bystander, other) did you play and what did you learn?

☐ Mordechai **refused to bow down** to Haman. Have you ever refused to render honor to someone who did not deserve it?

☐ Who was your **best teacher** and what did they teach you and how did they teach you it?

☐ "A ewe follows a ewe" said the Rabbis about mothers and daughters. **What traits have you adopted** willingly or not from either of your parents?

☐ **"Who is truly wise?" "Who is truly rich?"** Those are questions the Rabbis discussed 2000 years ago. What is your definition of wealth? What does it mean to be wise, in today's times? Why?

☐ Name your **favorite book or painting or musical composition**. Explain your choice.

☐ **"You shall tell your child"** *(Exodus 13:8)* is the mitzvah on Pesach. What is the best story or memory your parents have shared with you?

☐ "Every Jew is obligated to feel as if they personally went out from Egypt." *(Haggadah)* At what **historical event** would you have liked to be an eyewitness?

Onah and Oneg: a sacred time for lovemaking

> We must learn love as a profession.
>
> Those who love must act as if they had a great work to accomplish.
>
> — Rainer Maria Rilke (German poet, 20th century)

Introduction

Shabbat is a dimension of time that allows us to live in a different mode. Process and free play *(sha'ashuim)* — not effectiveness and goal-orientation — characterize this holy time. The most intense difference is felt in the realm of personal intimacy with friends, with the Divine aspect of receptivity — the Shekhina, and with one's spouse. The terms "husband" (derived from husbanding or cultivating the land as in Adam from *Adama*, human from humus) and "wife" (from weaver of cloth) are put aside as too functional and one rediscovers the early days in the Garden of Eden when humans named themselves "man and wo-man," *ish* and *isha*, which express their fundamental oneness and harmony without regard to procreative or production goals. Shabbat as a revival of the Garden of Eden is also a return to the honeymoon of one's relationship described in the wedding's *Sheva Brachot* blessings as *reim ahuvim* — "like the beloved companions or friends in the Garden of Eden."

A Couple's Prayer

Teach us reverence, God, for the sacred joining of our bodies and souls.
Remind us to be present in every touch, to be attentive to every response.
Prevent us from acting without feeling.
Remind us, God, to open our hearts and to shut out all distractions.

Grace us with your light, God.
Let our love-making lead us to joy, blessings and peace. Amen.

— Naomi Levy

Making Peace before Making Love

The great medieval Polish legal authority, Rabbi Yoel Sirkis explains the special recommendation that "a Torah scholar should take care to fulfill the mitzvah of his conjugal duties to his spouse on the evening of Shabbat." (Talmud Ketubot 62b)

"The husband needs to be cautious even before nightfall to enhance his affection and love for his partner. Obviously he needs to avoid verbal battles on the afternoon before Shabbat. If there is contention between them before Shabbat, then he should appease her. That is the 'care' necessary to perform *Onah* — one's conjugal obligations — which is prior to the act itself. It means actively pursuing love and fraternity between them all of Shabbat eve, so they will not detract from the mitzvah of *Oneg Shabbat*." (Bach on the Tur O.H. 280)

As the Zohar says:

"In contrast to one who often has intercourse during the week when the atmosphere is one of contention and separation, on Shabbat one should only make love out of an atmosphere of peace and tranquillity . . . Shabbat provides the peacefulness that affects the marital partners." (Tikkunei HaZohar – Tikkun 21, 57a)

While the graceful art of intercourse is not only for Shabbat, the liberation from time pressures, the reduction of product-oriented household management which is so central an aspect of married life and the addition of extra soul, an extra energized spiritual dimension, may create an environment in which loving friends can rediscover their relationship. Obviously this kind of intimacy is not restricted to the physical and it applies in different ways to all one's relationships.

Shabbat as a Reliving of the Honeymoon

As a person rejoices all the days of the wedding feast,
So does one rejoice on Shabbat.
As the groom does no work on the day he is wed,
So he does none on Shabbat.

— *A Nakawa*

One must have memories of many nights of love, none of which was like the others.

— *Ben Shahn*

The Sabbath evening table is a dramatic celebration and exaltation of human love. This is a hidden truth, all too often unrecognized . . . The Sabbath is a reliving of the honeymmon. For what is a honeymoon but the declaration that the world and its pressures must give way to the two of us and our love! We proclaim that our occupations and varied pursuits — crucial, stature-nourishing, time-consuming as they are — must yet be in balance and made to enhance and nurture the ultimate satisfaction of our hearts: "Male and female, God created them and blessed them and called their name — Adam — 'Human.'" *(Genesis 1:27)*

The Hebrew idiom speaks not of honeymoon but of *Sheevat Y'mei Mishteh* — Seven Days of the Wedding Feast . . . We could playfully merge the two terms and call it a "**honeyweek**." Then we might say that Shabbat enables us to recapture the wonder, vision, and avowals of that honeyweek weekly!

— *Alan S. Green*

Marc Chagall, Lovers on the Promenade, 1917, copyright © ADAGP Paris 2004

Oneg/ Pleasures

Alternative Expanded Kiddush Rabbah:

If you refrain from going out to do business on Shabbat,
from taking care of your affairs on my holy day,
and if you dedicate Shabbat to *oneg*, physical pleasure,
treating it with the honor due to God,
refraining from procuring objects you desire
and talking business;
then God will take pleasure in you.
God will place you on the heights of the earth
and feed you from your father Jacob's inheritance,
as God has spoken. *(Isaiah 58:13-14)*

אִם תָּשִׁיב מִשַּׁבָּת רַגְלֶךָ
עֲשׂוֹת חֲפָצֶךָ בְּיוֹם קָדְשִׁי,
וְקָרָאתָ לַשַּׁבָּת עֹנֶג
לִקְדוֹשׁ יְיָ מְכֻבָּד,
וְכִבַּדְתּוֹ מֵעֲשׂוֹת דְּרָכֶיךָ
מִמְּצוֹא חֶפְצְךָ וְדַבֵּר דָּבָר.
אָז תִּתְעַנַּג עַל יְיָ,
וְהִרְכַּבְתִּיךָ עַל בָּמֳתֵי אָרֶץ,
וְהַאֲכַלְתִּיךָ נַחֲלַת יַעֲקֹב אָבִיךָ,
כִּי פִּי יְיָ דִּבֵּר.

The children of Israel should guard the Shabbat,
observing it for generations as an eternal covenant.
It is an eternal sign between Me and the children of Israel
that God made the sky
and the earth in six days
and on the seventh day God stopped and was refreshed.
(Exodus 31:16-17)

וְשָׁמְרוּ בְנֵי יִשְׂרָאֵל אֶת הַשַּׁבָּת
לַעֲשׂוֹת אֶת הַשַּׁבָּת לְדֹרֹתָם בְּרִית עוֹלָם.
בֵּינִי וּבֵין בְּנֵי יִשְׂרָאֵל אוֹת הִיא לְעוֹלָם,
כִּי שֵׁשֶׁת יָמִים עָשָׂה יְיָ
אֶת הַשָּׁמַיִם וְאֶת הָאָרֶץ,
וּבַיּוֹם הַשְּׁבִיעִי שָׁבַת וַיִּנָּפַשׁ.

Remember Shabbat to sanctify it.
Six days you shall work doing all your skilled labor.
However the seventh day belongs to Adonai your God,
do no skilled labor,
neither you nor your son, your daughter,
your male and female servant, your work animals
or even the stranger resident in your gates.
For in six days God made the heavens
and the earth and all that is in them.
Then God rested and thus
God blessed the day of Shabbat and made it holy.
(Exodus 20:8-11)

זָכוֹר אֶת יוֹם הַשַּׁבָּת לְקַדְּשׁוֹ.
שֵׁשֶׁת יָמִים תַּעֲבֹד וְעָשִׂיתָ כָּל מְלַאכְתֶּךָ.
וְיוֹם הַשְּׁבִיעִי שַׁבָּת לַייָ אֱלֹהֶיךָ,
לֹא תַעֲשֶׂה כָל מְלָאכָה,
אַתָּה וּבִנְךָ וּבִתֶּךָ
עַבְדְּךָ וַאֲמָתְךָ וּבְהֶמְתֶּךָ,
וְגֵרְךָ אֲשֶׁר בִּשְׁעָרֶיךָ.
כִּי שֵׁשֶׁת יָמִים עָשָׂה יְיָ אֶת הַשָּׁמַיִם
וְאֶת הָאָרֶץ, אֶת הַיָּם וְאֶת כָּל אֲשֶׁר בָּם,
וַיָּנַח בַּיּוֹם הַשְּׁבִיעִי.
עַל כֵּן בֵּרַךְ יְיָ אֶת יוֹם הַשַּׁבָּת וַיְקַדְּשֵׁהוּ.

With your permission . . .

סַבְרִי . . .

BLESSED ARE YOU, ADONAI, RULER OF THE UNIVERSE,
CREATOR OF THE FRUIT OF THE VINE.

בָּרוּךְ אַתָּה יְיָ אֱלֹהֵינוּ מֶלֶךְ הָעוֹלָם,
בּוֹרֵא פְּרִי הַגָּפֶן.

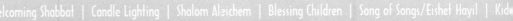

Shabbat morning

Kiddush Rabbah and the second Shabbat meal

קִדּוּשׁ רַבָּא

Introduction to Kiddush Rabbah

Kiddush Rabbah, literally, the "Great Kiddush," is ironically the shortest and least significant Kiddush on Shabbat. Even wine is not obligatory. Often hard liquor is used; Lubavitch Hassidim prefer vodka. This minor Kiddush may be recited without eating bread and having a full meal; a smaller snack will suffice (Jews from Eastern Europe would often drink schapps and eat kugel, herring and chopped liver with crackers).

Decanter for wine for Kiddush. Inscribed with Exodus 23:16-17 and its owner's name. (18th-19th century, possibly Syrian. *Jewish Museum, London.*)

Thus God blessed the day of Shabbat and made it holy.	**עַל כֵּן בֵּרַךְ יְיָ אֶת יוֹם הַשַּׁבָּת וַיְקַדְּשֵׁהוּ.**	Al kein beirakh Adonai et yom HaShabbat va-y'kad'shei-hu (Exodus 20: 11)
For wine or grape juice:		
BLESSED ARE YOU, ADONAI . . . Creator of the fruit of the vine.	**בָּרוּךְ אַתָּה יְיָ אֱלֹהֵינוּ מֶלֶךְ הָעוֹלָם, בּוֹרֵא פְּרִי הַגָּפֶן.**	Ba-rukh ata Adonai, Elo-hei-nu me-lekh ha-olam, borei pri hagafen.
OR — for liquor:		
BLESSED ARE YOU, ADONAI . . . Creator of everything by the power of your word.	**בָּרוּךְ** אַתָּה יְיָ אֱלֹהֵינוּ מֶלֶךְ הָעוֹלָם, שֶׁהַכֹּל נִהְיָה בִּדְבָרוֹ.	Ba-rukh ata Adonai, Elo-hei-nu me-lekh ha-olam, she-hakol ni-h'yah beed'varo.
For washing hands before eating bread:		
BLESSED ARE YOU, ADONAI . . . who commanded us to wash our hands.	**בָּרוּךְ** אַתָּה יְיָ אֱלֹהֵינוּ מֶלֶךְ הָעוֹלָם, אֲשֶׁר קִדְּשָׁנוּ בְּמִצְוֹתָיו וְצִוָּנוּ, עַל נְטִילַת יָדָיִם.	Ba-rukh ata Adonai, Elo-hei-nu me-lekh ha-olam, asher ki-d'shanu b'mitz-votav v'tzi-vanu al netillat yadaim.
For Hallah:		
BLESSED ARE YOU, ADONAI . . . who brings forth bread from the earth.	**בָּרוּךְ** אַתָּה יְיָ אֱלֹהֵינוּ מֶלֶךְ הָעוֹלָם, הַמּוֹצִיא לֶחֶם מִן הָאָרֶץ.	Ba-rukh ata Adonai, Elo-hei-nu me-lekh ha-olam, ha-motzi lekhem min ha-aretz.
OR — For cakes, cookies:		
BLESSED ARE YOU, ADONAI . . . Creator of all sorts of baked goods.	**בָּרוּךְ** אַתָּה יְיָ אֱלֹהֵינוּ מֶלֶךְ הָעוֹלָם, בּוֹרֵא מִינֵי מְזוֹנוֹת.	Ba-rukh ata Adonai, Elo-hei-nu me-lekh ha-olam, Borei minei m'zo-note.

Introduction: Longing and Expectation in the Third Meal

The Talmud is explicit about the need to arrange three meals on Shabbat (Talmud Shabbat 118-119) — including one in the late afternoon, *Seudah Shlishit*, the "third meal." The first is Friday night dinner and the second is Shabbat lunch. (Breakfast is not counted since on Shabbat morning it includes no bread but merely some cake.) Historically, Shabbat's three meals signified a special day of leisure, since people usually ate only two meals on a weekday.

During the late Middle Ages, the atmosphere of the third meal developed into a mood of longing for redemption. This is a difficult transition period as we prepare to say farewell to Shabbat's heightened spirituality and foretaste of the World-to-Come (Talmud Berachot 57b), and to reenter the world of *Galut*/Exile which the Kabbalists considered to be a world of harsh judgment and restricted spiritual powers. It is a time we anticipate the painful separation from Shabbat; we begin our grieving for the imminent departure of our "extra soul" and for the loss of intimacy with the Divine presence.

Yet this is also a time to expect the Messiah who, according to one tradition (Talmud Eruvin 43b), will not arrive on Shabbat, but rather immediately after Shabbat due to the merit of our having observed Shabbat (Talmud Shabbat 118b). The Kabbalists called the third meal *ra'vah d'ra'avin*, which might be translated as "the time of desire, good will, and Divine favor."

Initial Letters of the Ten Sefirot, where the first Sefira, כתר or the Divine Crown, is the outer layer. (Moses Cordovero, Pardes Rimonim, Cracow, 1592)

"The Lord is My Shepherd" — Psalm 23

The famous Psalm about relaxing under God's protection like sheep under the watchful eye of a shepherd at an oasis in the desert is often sung at Shabbat day Kiddush as well as at the Third Meal. The imagery is appropriate for the young David — traditionally understood as the author of this song — since he was a young shepherd who felt God's support when fighting against the wild animals that attacked his flock (I Samuel 17:34).

מִזְמוֹר לְדָוִד

A Psalm of David:	**מִזְמוֹר לְדָוִד**
The Lord is my Shepherd, I shall not want.	**יְיָ רֹעִי לֹא אֶחְסָר.**
God makes me to lie down in green pastures;	בִּנְאוֹת דֶּשֶׁא יַרְבִּיצֵנִי
and leads me beside the still waters.	עַל מֵי מְנֻחוֹת יְנַהֲלֵנִי.
God restores my soul;	נַפְשִׁי יְשׁוֹבֵב יַנְחֵנִי
and leads me in the paths of righteousness for God's name.	בְמַעְגְּלֵי צֶדֶק לְמַעַן שְׁמוֹ.
Even though I walk through the valley of the shadow of death,	גַּם כִּי אֵלֵךְ בְּגֵיא צַלְמָוֶת
I will fear no evil, for You are with me;	לֹא אִירָא רָע כִּי אַתָּה עִמָּדִי
your rod and your staff comfort me.	שִׁבְטְךָ וּמִשְׁעַנְתֶּךָ הֵמָּה יְנַחֲמֻנִי.
You prepare a table before me in the presence of my enemies;	תַּעֲרֹךְ לְפָנַי שֻׁלְחָן נֶגֶד צֹרְרָי
You anoint my head with oil; my cup runs over.	דִּשַּׁנְתָּ בַשֶּׁמֶן רֹאשִׁי כּוֹסִי רְוָיָה.
Surely goodness and mercy shall follow me	אַךְ טוֹב וָחֶסֶד יִרְדְּפוּנִי
all the days of my life;	כָּל יְמֵי חַיָּי
and I will dwell in the house of the Lord forever.	וְשַׁבְתִּי בְּבֵית יְיָ לְאֹרֶךְ יָמִים.

סְעוּדָה שְׁלִישִׁית

Shabbat afternoon

and the third Shabbat meal, Seudah Shlishit

1. NIGGUN — sing a melody without words.
2. NETILAT YADA-YIM — hand-washing; see page 81.
3. MOTZI — blessing over bread; see page 81.
4. SPECIAL SONGS for the waning moments of Shabbat include *Yedid Nefesh* and *Mizmor L'David* (Psalm 23).

The mood of a passionate lover is required for singing Yedid Nefesh. As the author wrote: "The way of anyone moved by deep desire is to sing. So since our love for our Creator is wonderful beyond human love, one who loves God with a full heart should sing before the Blessed One . . . with the inspiration of the Holy Spirit (Ruakh HaKodesh)." The first letter of each stanza spells out God's name "Y-H-V-H."

Yedid Nefesh/My Soul Mate

BY ELAZAR AZIKRI (1533-1600, SAFED)

Soul mate, loving, compassionate Parent (ISAIAH 5:1)
Draw me closer to do your will
Let your loyal servant run to You
as swiftly as a gazelle,
and bow before your Majesty.
Your loving companionship is sweeter
than honey or any other taste.

Majestic and beautiful, Light of the World
My soul is lovesick, yearning for You (SONG OF SONGS 2:4)
"I beg of You, God, heal her." (NUMBERS 12:13, MOSHE'S DESPERATE PLEA TO GOD TO SAVE HIS SISTER MIRIAM FROM LEPROSY)
Please show her the pleasure of your light.
Then she will recover strength and be healed.
She will serve You loyally forever.[1]

Ancient God (OF ABRAHAM), arouse your loving compassion.
Have mercy on the child of your friend (ISAIAH 41:8),
beloved Abraham.
For how I have longed to glimpse your glorious power
(AS JACOB YEARNED TO RETURN HOME TO ERETZ YISRAEL FROM HIS LONG EXILE – GENESIS 31:30).
I beg of You, my God, my heart's desire,
Please hurry! Do not hide yourself.[2]

Reveal Yourself, my Dear One, spread over me
your Sukkah of Shalom. (BASED ON THE EVENING PRAYER FOR PROTECTION, HASHKIVEINU)
May the entire world be illumined by your Presence (AS THE SUN BRIGHTENS UP THE EARTH EACH MORNING – SHAKHARIT PRAYERBOOK).
Then we will delight and rejoice in You (AS THE BRIDE AND GROOM CELEBRATE ONE ANOTHER AT A WEDDING – SONG OF SONGS 1:4).
Hurry, Beloved One, for the time is here,
Show me your gracious love as You did long ago.

יְדִיד נֶפֶשׁ

יְדִיד נֶפֶשׁ, אָב הָרַחֲמָן
מְשׁוֹךְ עַבְדְּךָ אֶל רְצוֹנָךְ.
יָרוּץ עַבְדְּךָ כְּמוֹ אַיָּל
יִשְׁתַּחֲוֶה אֶל מוּל הֲדָרָךְ.
יֶעֱרַב לוֹ יְדִידוּתָךְ
מִנֹּפֶת צוּף וְכָל טָעַם.

הָדוּר, נָאֶה, זִיו הָעוֹלָם,
נַפְשִׁי חוֹלַת אַהֲבָתָךְ.
אָנָּא אֵל נָא, רְפָא נָא לָהּ
בְּהַרְאוֹת לָהּ נֹעַם זִיוָךְ.
אָז תִּתְחַזֵּק וְתִתְרַפֵּא,
וְהָיְתָה לָךְ שִׁפְחַת עוֹלָם.

וָתִיק, יֶהֱמוּ רַחֲמֶיךָ
וְחוּס נָא עַל בֵּן אוֹהֲבָךְ.
כִּי זֶה כַּמֶּה נִכְסֹף נִכְסַף
לִרְאוֹת בְּתִפְאֶרֶת עֻזָּךְ.
אָנָּא, אֵלִי, מַחְמַד לִבִּי,
חוּשָׁה נָא, וְאַל תִּתְעַלָּם.

הִגָּלֶה נָא וּפְרוֹשׂ, חָבִיב, עָלַי
אֶת סֻכַּת שְׁלוֹמָךְ.
תָּאִיר אֶרֶץ מִכְּבוֹדָךְ
נָגִילָה וְנִשְׂמְחָה בָּךְ.
מַהֵר, אָהוּב, כִּי בָא מוֹעֵד
וְחָנֵּנִי כִּימֵי עוֹלָם.

---

1. The Hebrew has sometimes been corrupted to *Simchat olam* — "a joy for ever." However the original, according to a manuscript found in the handwriting of the author reads, *Shifkhat olam* — "a female servant forever" or as we translated it, "serve you loyally forever."
2. Note: the Hebrew original is not *eleh hamda libi / v'khusa na v'al na titaleim.*

Reflections כַּוָּנוֹת

on the three meals of Shabbat

Yaacov Greenvurcel, detail from Moderrn Kiddush Cups, www.greenvurcel.co.il

The Manna Model

Three Shabbat laws are learned from the experience the Jews in the desert had with the manna *(Exodus 16:22-27)*.

THREE MEALS

"Moshe said: 'Eat **today**, for **today** is Shabbat, dedicated to Adonai, and **today** you will find that no manna has fallen in the field." The Rabbis interpreted that each "today" hints at one of the three Shabbat meals. *(Talmud Shabbat 117b)*

STAY HOME

"'Look, God has given you Shabbat, therefore God gave you on the sixth day a two day portion of bread, so you may sit in your place and do not leave your place of residence on the seventh day.' So the people observed Shabbat on the seventh day" *(Exodus 16: 29-30)*. In the Torah, "sitting in one's place" transforms Shabbat into **a celebration of home life** by making the need to go out into the field unnecessary. The Rabbis expanded this notion by restricting travel outside the city. The maximum distance one may travel on Shabbat outside one's town is 2,000 steps. *(Tehum Shabbat in Talmud Eruvin 51a)*

TWO LOAVES

The third law we learn from the manna is the necessity of two loaves of bread. Since a double portion of manna fell on the sixth day, we place two Hallahs upon the Shabbat table.

What Good Pastries Shall I Serve with Kiddush?

Ideally every time Kiddush is said it should be part of a full meal which is the way to honor this important occasion. ("There is no Kiddush except where there is a [sit-down] dinner [with bread]" *Talmud Pesachim 101a*). If one drinks the wine but has no food with it, then it is not admissible as Kiddush. But by the days of the Babylonian Geonim *(9th-12th century)*, Kiddush could be accompanied by a partial meal. The custom was to eat pastry since the point is to honor Shabbat by making it a "delight." *(Rashbam on Talmud Pesachim 101a, Mishna Berura 263:21,25)*

V'Shamru / Keeping Shabbat as a Sign of the Covenant with God

(Exodus 31:16-17)

"Keeping Shabbat" involves maintaining a symbol — a token of the ongoing covenantal relationship between Israel and God. The Rabbis connected this covenant to two other rituals involving similar tokens. The first is the *brit milah,* which is also the symbol of *brit olam*/"the eternal covenant." The circumcision of a child on his 8th day takes precedence over Shabbat and is performed on time. The second sign is *tefillin,* which need not be worn on Shabbat. Why? The rabbis considered Shabbat itself an adequate symbol of Israel's relationship with the Divine *(Talmud Eruvin 96a)*.

Many Hassidim preface their meal by dedicating it with the words: *Likhvod Shabbat Kodesh* — "In honor of the Holy Shabbat."

"A Niggun for Shabbat"

For *Shalosh Seudot* [the third meal] in Wizsnitz or in Sighet we sat at the Wizsnitzer rebbe's table. It was dark. The beautiful part of the *Shalosh Seudot* was the darkness, when you saw only shadows, shadows that suddenly began to sing.

I remember the song we used to sing. It was on Shabbat, of course, the most sacred day of the week; and the most sacred hour of Shabbat was *Shalosh Seudot.* All the books I could write and all the words I could use are nothing but pale reflections, if not pale substitutes, for those songs that I shall never forget and that somehow still vibrate in me.

During *Shalosh Seudot* we used to sit in the darkness — in the semidarkness — and of course we could not distinguish one from the other, poor from rich, the erudite from the *am ha'aretzim* [common folk] . . . At one point the rebbe would begin singing in Yiddish:

"Ven ich volt hehaht kaech, volt ich in de gahssen gelohfn, un ich volt geshrien haeakh, 'Shabbes, haeliker Shabbes'" — "If I had the strength, I would run in the streets shouting and screaming with all my might, 'Shabbes, holy Shabbes.'"

Legend had it that, as long as the rebbe would sing, Shabbat would stay. I adored that song. I used to sing it not only on Shabbat. When I sang it, I made my own Shabbat.

— Elie Wiesel

Rabbi Elazar Azikri (1533-1600, Safed): The Mystical Diarist of *Yedid Nefesh* and his Holy Contracts

Scholarship can sometimes cast light on the hidden thoughts of a poet. The discovery of the diaries of Rabbi Elazar Azkiri, author of the famous song, *Yedid Nefesh*, offers such a window into his soul. In his diary, Rabbi Elazar Azikri traces his four decade-long struggle for moral perfection with his fellow human beings and for spiritual concentration on "the beloved of his soul"/ *Yedid Nefesh* — God. Beginning the diaries immediately after the tragic death of his two sons in 1564, the author sought communion with God using unusual techniques. Besides studying Torah and mysticism, Azikri spent one third of each day standing in absolutely silent meditation. He also entered into a binding legal contract, a *shtar,* with the Master of the Universe, dated 1575, attested by two witnesses. The witnesses who "signed" are Heaven and Earth, as in Moshe's poem *Haazinu* (DEUTERONOMY 32). The stipulations were read out loud four times a day, at sunrise and sunset and at noon and midnight. They include:

- ☐ loving people and not prejudging them
- ☐ contemplating God at all times and refraining from worldly activities
- ☐ praying with enthusiasm
- ☐ giving Tzedakah every night before going to sleep
- ☐ crying regularly except on Shabbat and holidays
- ☐ visiting the graves of righteous spiritual masters

Rabbi Elazar Azikri combined inter-personal and spiritual mitzvot because he believed that God's name is inscribed in the face of each human creature. He identified the four letters of God's unique name — ***Y**ud **H**eh **V**av **H**eh*, with which he begins each of the verses of *Yedid Nefesh* — in the facial structures of his fellow Jews. The ear is like ***Y**ud*; one cheek is like ***H**eh*; the nose is like ***V**av*; and the other cheek is again like ***H**eh*. The idea is that whenever we encounter a fellow Jew, we are looking in the face of God and must do so with reverence — including lowering our eyes as we would in confronting a majestic ruler.

In 1575, Rabbi Azikri created a new legal document called a *Brit Hadasha*/"New Covenant," perhaps in the spirit of Jeremiah's new covenant (which is translated by the Christians with the term New Testament):

> "A time is coming — declares God — when I will make a new brit/covenant with the House of Israel . . . and I will put my Torah inside of them and write it on their hearts." *(JEREMIAH 31:30-32)*

That contract bound together a Holy Havurah of three rabbis in Tsfat and listed ten conditions including:

- ☐ maintaining the unity of the three mystics (who would also share all of their property equally)
- ☐ honoring of both our heavenly and earthly parents
- ☐ suffering insults in silence while honoring all creatures and despising and ridiculing none
- ☐ studying with spiritual intensity the MiSHNA (the Rabbinic code of Oral Law) for that gives wings to the NiSHaMA / Soul, which shares the identical letters
- ☐ accepting the yoke of God's kingdom in our hearts constantly — without distraction

This Holy Havurah expressed their personal love for God by speaking to God regularly in private and "by singing before God to arouse their love — more wonderful than the love for women" *(AS KING DAVID SAID OF HIS LOVE FOR THE FALLEN JONATHAN IN II SAMUEL 1: 26)*. In Rabbi Elazar Azikri's book *Sefer HaHareaim* (1601), he published the songs of beloved friendship with God that he had shared with his friends in the Havurah. The most famous is *Yedid Nefesh*. We now sing this on Shabbat when we too withdraw somewhat from worldly activity and, as newlyweds on a honeymoon, create space for spiritual love with the Divine that exists in ourselves, in our friends and in the world.

Rabbi Elazar Azikri, like his teacher Rabbi Moshe Cordovero and his colleague Rabbi Haim Vital, recommended **a spiritual week-in-review** for the *Haverim*/members of the havurah. They would meet in the synagogue before Shabbat and discuss with one another how they had behaved during the previous week and then they would proceed to greet the Shabbat Queen.

Fourth Meal: *Melaveh Malka*

Just as we escort Shabbat in with a festive Friday night meal, some of the Rabbis of the Talmud *(SHABBAT 119B)* accompanied the departing Queen *(Melaveh Malka)* with another meal after the conclusion of Shabbat *(SHULCHAN ARUCH O.H. 300)*.

The Fourth Meal is also dedicated to King David, since David is the messianic *Shekhina* figure, the Queen. A legend reports that David was told in advance that he would die on Shabbat so whenever he lived through another Shabbat he celebrated a festive meal to begin another week of life.

Distinguishing

Light from Dark
Holy from Everyday,
***Kodesh* from *Hol*.**

1. **GAZE** at the sky — **SEARCH** for three stars, to make sure that it is really dark.
2. **POUR** a cup of wine (or beer, cider, grape juice or even milk). **FILL** it to the brim.
3. **LIGHT** a candle with several wicks (or hold two burning candles together). After a day of prohibited labor, the kindling of fire celebrates our capacity to create anew during this week.
4. **RECITE** seven Biblical verses about Divine protection (optional).
5. **BLESS** the wine and gaze into the cup to catch a reflection of your own smiling face (but don't yet drink it).

Havdalah. *Photo by Karl Gabor.*

Havdalah הַבְדָּלָה

separating the holy and the ordinary

6. **BLESS** and **SMELL** the spices to energize our souls, now having lost the Shabbat spirit.
7. **BLESS** and **ENJOY** the light of the flame by cupping your hand and observing the play of shadow and light on your fingers.
8. **BLESS** the separations between light and dark, holy and everyday.
9. **DRINK** the wine (at least most of the cup).

   Some people **EXTINGUISH** the candle by pouring wine over it.

   Some people **DAB** drops of wine in their pockets (hoping for material blessings) and on their eyes (for enlightenment).
10. **SING** a song about Elijah the prophet, *Eliyahu ha-Navi*, expressing a hope for redemption whose good tidings Elijah bears.
11. **WISH** everyone – "A Good Week!"

THE PREFACE: *[Optional]*

Seven Biblical Sources on Divine Protection

הִנֵּה, אֵל יְשׁוּעָתִי
אֶבְטַח וְלֹא אֶפְחָד,
כִּי עָזִּי וְזִמְרָת יָהּ יְיָ
וַיְהִי לִי לִישׁוּעָה.
וּשְׁאַבְתֶּם מַיִם בְּשָׂשׂוֹן
מִמַּעַיְנֵי הַיְשׁוּעָה.

1. *God is my life-saver,*
I trust in *God* and have no fear,
for God, who is my strength and my song,
has always been there to save me. *(Isaiah 12:2-3) (Exodus 15:20)*
Draw water joyfully
from the wells of [God's] saving power. *(Isaiah 12:2-3)*

לַיְיָ הַיְשׁוּעָה
עַל עַמְּךָ בִרְכָתֶךָ סֶּלָה.

2. For saving power belongs to Adonai,
your blessing is on your people. *(Psalm 3:9)*

יְיָ צְבָאוֹת עִמָּנוּ
מִשְׂגָּב לָנוּ אֱלֹהֵי יַעֲקֹב סֶלָה.

3. Adonai, master of all heavenly forces is with us,
the God of Jacob is our support. *(Psalm 46:12)*

יְיָ צְבָאוֹת
אַשְׁרֵי אָדָם בֹּטֵחַ בָּךְ.

4. Master of all heavenly forces,
whoever trusts in You is happy. *(Psalm 84: 13)*

יְיָ הוֹשִׁיעָה
הַמֶּלֶךְ יַעֲנֵנוּ
בְיוֹם קָרְאֵנוּ.

5. Adonai save us!
May the Supreme Ruler answer us
whenever we call out [God's name]! *(Psalm 20:10)*

Gaze at the flame while this verse is recited twice – first by the onlookers and then repeated by the Havdalah leader as we wish for a week of joy.

לַיְּהוּדִים הָיְתָה אוֹרָה
וְשִׂמְחָה וְשָׂשׂוֹן וִיקָר,
כֵּן תִּהְיֶה לָּנוּ.

6. Just as there was once light
and joy for the Jews, gladness and honor –
so too may there be for us! *(Esther 8:16)*

Raise the cup in the right hand and say:

כּוֹס יְשׁוּעוֹת אֶשָּׂא,
וּבְשֵׁם יְיָ אֶקְרָא.

7. I will raise the cup of saving power
and call out in the name of Adonai. *(Psalm 116:13)*

The Holy One lends human beings an extra soul on the eve of the Sabbath, and withdraws it at the close of the Sabbath.

— *Talmud Betza, 16a*

As the Holy darkness descends upon me, I offer this prayer to You, My God. May the peace and the holiness which I feel this night remain with me always. May my fears give way to faith and may my pain soon give way to laughter. And may the lessons of the darkness fill my days with awe so that I may learn to experience You, my God, all the days and nights of my life. Amen.

— *Naomi Levy*

A Bouquet of Spices by Katriel.
(The Gross Family Collection, Tel Aviv.)

The four blessings of Havdalah

WINE

Blessed are You Adonai,	בָּרוּךְ אַתָּה יְיָ	Ba-rukh ata Adonai,
Ruler of the universe,	אֱלֹהֵינוּ מֶלֶךְ הָעוֹלָם,	E oheinu melekh ha-Olam,
who creates **the fruit of the vine.**	בּוֹרֵא **פְּרִי הַגָּפֶן.**	Borei p'ri HaGafen.

Do not drink the wine yet. Hold a mixture of spices, and — before smelling them — recite:

SPICES

Blessed are You Adonai,	בָּרוּךְ אַתָּה יְיָ	Ba-rukh ata Adonai,
Ruler of the Universe,	אֱלֹהֵינוּ מֶלֶךְ הָעוֹלָם,	E oheinu me-lekh ha-Olam,
who creates various **kinds of spices.**	בּוֹרֵא **מִינֵי בְשָׂמִים.**	Borei minei B'samim.

Smell the spices. Then, before enjoying the benefit of the light of the Havdalah candle, recite:

FLAME

Blessed are You Adonai,	בָּרוּךְ אַתָּה יְיָ	Ba-rukh ata Adonai,
Ruler of the Universe,	אֱלֹהֵינוּ מֶלֶךְ הָעוֹלָם,	Eloheinu me-lekh ha-Olam,
who creates **the flames of light.**	בּוֹרֵא **מְאוֹרֵי הָאֵשׁ.**	Borei m'orei Ha-Esh.

Take the cup in your right hand again and bless God for making many distinctions:

SEPARATING

Blessed are You Adonai,	בָּרוּךְ אַתָּה יְיָ	Ba-rukh ata Adonai,
Ruler of the Universe, who distinguishes	אֱלֹהֵינוּ מֶלֶךְ הָעוֹלָם,	Eloheinu me-lekh ha-Olam,
between the Holy and the Ordinary *(Leviticus 10:10)*,	הַמַּבְדִּיל בֵּין קֹדֶשׁ לְחוֹל,	Hamavdil bayn kodesh l'khol.
between Light and Darkness *(Genesis 1:4)*,	**בֵּין אוֹר לְחֹשֶׁךְ,**	Bayn or l'khoshekh,
between Israel and other nations *(Leviticus 20:26)*,	בֵּין יִשְׂרָאֵל לָעַמִּים,	Bayn Yisrael l'amim,
between the Seventh day and the Six days of work *(Genesis 2:3)*.	בֵּין יוֹם הַשְּׁבִיעִי	Bayn yom ha-sh'vi-i
Blessed are You Adonai,	לְשֵׁשֶׁת יְמֵי הַמַּעֲשֶׂה.	L'sheishet y'mei ha-ma'aseh.
Ruler of the Universe,	בָּרוּךְ אַתָּה יְיָ	Ba-rukh ata Adonai
who distinguishes between the Holy and the Ordinary.	**הַמַּבְדִּיל בֵּין קֹדֶשׁ לְחוֹל.**	Hamavdil bayn kodesh l'khol.

Now drink (at least 2/3 of the cup) and extinguish the flame in the wine that remains or that spilled over.

GOOD WISHES

With kisses, handshakes, and hugs we wish Shavua Tov — Have a *Good* Week!

Eliyahu in Ladino/Hebrew

Bo yir-tom ri-kh-bo	בּוֹ יִרְתּוֹם רִכְבּוֹ
na ba-sh'vi ki bo	נָא בַּשְּׁבִי כִּי בּוֹ
lo sha-khav libo	לֹא שָׁכַב לִבּוֹ
gam lo ra-ah sheina.	גַּם לֹא רָאָה שֵׁנָה
	Refrain:
Eli Eliyahu	אֵלִי אֵלִיָּהוּ
HaNavi Ha-vei Na	הַנָּבִיא הָבֵא נָא
Eli Eliyahu	אֵלִי אֵלִיָּהוּ
por nuestras cazas venga.	por nuestras cazas venga.

The Sephardic song about Elijah comes from Turkey. It describes Elijah, who never sleeps, as riding on his chariot, the fiery one which took him to Heaven. "May God bring Elijah the Prophet back, please! "

Mark Chagall, Opening the Door for Elijah (1946)

The Prayer for Elijah

by The Maharal of Prague (16th century — associated with the legend of the Golem, the Jewish precursor of Frankenstein)

HaRakhaman! May the Merciful One send Elijah the Prophet to announce good news about redemption and comfort — just as You promised:

Here, I will send you Elijah the Prophet before the Lord's great and awesome day. **He will reconcile the hearts of parents to their children and children to their parents . . . .** *(Malachi 3:24)*

ELIJAH was the colorful, itinerant and idiosyncratic prophet from Gilad, northern Israel (8th century BCE). He fearlessly spoke out for justice when King Ahab and his malevolent, idol-worshipping wife Jezebel framed and executed a man who refused to sell his vineyard to the king. Elijah compassionately provided for a starving widow a jug of oil that replenished itself miraculously and later revived her son when he stopped breathing. At the end of his life on earth Elijah disappeared into heaven on a fiery chariot and a whirlwind. According to legend, he reappears from time to time to help the poor. The Biblical prophets predict his return in the messianic end of days — when he will reconcile parents and children. As the Seder ends, we open the door in the hopes that Elijah will arrive with good news — an imminently to-be-perfected world. At the conclusion of Shabbat, a foretaste of the world-to-come, we pray that Elijah will bring peace and redemption.

Songs of Elijah the prophet . . .

Eliyahu NaNavi

Elijah the prophet,	**אֵלִיָּהוּ הַנָּבִיא,**	Eliyahu ha-navi
Elijah the Tishbi,	אֵלִיָּהוּ הַתִּשְׁבִּי,	Eliyahu ha-Tish-bi
Elijah from Gilad.	אֵלִיָּהוּ הַגִּלְעָדִי.	Eliyahu ha-Giladi
May he soon	בִּמְהֵרָה בְיָמֵנוּ,	bim-hei-ra b'ya-mei-nu
come to us	יָבוֹא אֵלֵינוּ	yavo ei-leinu
along with the Messiah, son of David.	עִם מָשִׁיחַ בֶּן דָּוִד.	im ma-shi-akh ben David.

"MIRIAM the Prophetess," by Arthur Waskow and Leila Gal Berner (1989) celebrates Miriam's role in the long journey to redemption — past and future — and her connection to water. Miriam's name includes the word for water, and at the Nile she watched over baby brother Moshe. At the Red Sea Miriam led the people in song and in the desert she provided a legendary portable well. At Havdalah we resume our difficult weekly journey to the next Shabbat — with Miriam as our companion. In Havdalah the imagery of drawing water symbolizes redemption.

Miriam the prophetess

Miriam HaNevi'ah

Miriam the prophetess,	**מִרְיָם הַנְּבִיאָה,**	Miriam Ha-Nevi'ah
strength and song are in her hands.	עֹז וְזִמְרָה בְּיָדָהּ.	Oz v'zimrah b'yadah
Miriam will dance with us	מִרְיָם תִּרְקוֹד אִתָּנוּ	Miriam tirkod itanu
to strengthen the world's song.	לְהַגְדִּיל זִמְרַת עוֹלָם.	l'hag-dil zim-rat olam.
Miriam will dance with us	מִרְיָם תִּרְקוֹד אִתָּנוּ	Miriam tirkod itanu
to heal the world.	לְתַקֵּן אֶת הָעוֹלָם.	l'takein et ha-olam.
Soon, in our time,	בִּמְהֵרָה בְיָמֵנוּ,	Bim-heirah v'yameinu,
she will bring us	הִיא תְּבִיאֵנוּ	Hee t'vi-einu.
to the waters of redemption.	אֶל מֵי הַיְשׁוּעָה.	El mey ha-yeshuah.

"HA-MAVDIL" is a popular medieval poem for Havdalah by Yitzchak ibn Ghayyat (11th century, Spain). It asks God to forgive our sins and to multiply both our funds and our descendants.

Between holy and ordinary

Ha-mav-dil

May the One who makes a distinction	**הַמַּבְדִּיל**	Ha-mav-dil
between holy and ordinary	**בֵּין קֹדֶשׁ לְחוֹל**	bein kodesh l'khol
forgive our sins.	חַטֹּאתֵינוּ הוּא יִמְחֹל.	kha-to-tei-nu hu yim-khol.
Let our offspring and our wealth	זַרְעֵנוּ וְכַסְפֵּנוּ	Zar-ei-nu v'khas-pei-nu
increase like grains of sand at the sea	יַרְבֶּה כַּחוֹל	yar-beh kha-khol
and like the stars of the night.	וְכַכּוֹכָבִים בַּלָּיְלָה.	v'kha-ko-kha-vim ba-lai-lah.

Introduction: A Ritual of Opposites

Havdalah, which literally means differentiation, is a ritual of opposites. Havdalah marks a paradoxical border at which lighting a candle — forbidden only moments before — becomes a mitzvah. In Havdalah, sadness intermingles with hope; in sadness we bid farewell to Shabbat, whose presence is extinguished with the candle at the end of the ritual. Yet the ceremony ends with hope, when we sing *"Eliyahu HaNavi,"* a song welcoming the prophet Elijah whose coming will herald the beginning of a messianic age and universal redemption.

The ritual of Havdalah, marking the conclusion of Shabbat, functions as a book-end to Kiddush, the *bracha* that marks the beginning of Shabbat. Kiddush sanctifies and distinguishes Shabbat from the preceding days of the week; Havdalah recalls the sanctity of Shabbat and differentiates it from the days of the week that follow. Both ceremonies take place over a full glass of wine, a symbol of sanctity.

Why is it that we treat Havdalah as a ritual of sanctification when it in fact marks our return to "unholy" time?

One answer to this question lies in the concept of *yerida l'tzorekh aliya* — "descending for the purpose of ascending." Although it may seem that entering the coming week involves removing ourselves from the holy time of Shabbat, the new week promises us opportunities to raise ourselves from the mundane to new levels of spirituality. During the week, we have a unique opportunity to perform mitzvot with all the vigor and the insight that we gain from each Shabbat experience, though we leave it behind at Havdalah. Then, after a week of developing our relationship to God in more profound ways, each successive Shabbat can be an experience of even greater sanctity than its predecessor.

The light of the Havdalah candle resembles the light of Shabbat candles lit only 25 hours before. Thus the opening moments of the new week already contain a taste of the Shabbat-to-come. Like the wine overflowing from our cup in the Havdalah ceremony, the spirituality of the previous twenty-five hours spills into the week to come. Like the spices of the Havdalah ceremony, this Shabbat infuses all of our acts until Shabbat comes again. Through the Havdalah ceremony, we extend the influence of Shabbat. And while we longingly depart from Shabbat, this unique weekly experience, we also look forward, expectantly, to a future time when the whole week will be Shabbat.

— Sarah Lightman (adapted)

Etrog with cloves. *Photo by Dorit Carmel; etrog prepared by Rabbi Marvin Richardson.*

Havdalah at the Solomon Schechter Day School, Rhode Island, 1996. *Photo by Janice Newman.* (Beit Hatefutsot Archive, Tel Aviv.)

Guidelines
getting started

How do I perform Havdalah in my home?

Havdalah is a full sensory experience: we taste the wine; smell the fragrant spices; see the dancing flame; hear the words of blessing; and feel the ritual objects and often the embrace of others.

After experiencing a dramatic Havdalah ceremony at camp or a retreat, many people reenact it at home. Spices, candles, wine and the onset of darkness are ideal ingredients for a homemade sense of spiritual significance.

Create a Havdalah set and keep it in a special place. Choose sweet spices and put them in a decorative container. Use a Havdalah candle or hold any two lit candles together. A fire-resistant placemat or a bowl filled with water can serve as a base.

Set the mood with a wordless niggun or melody like *Eliyahu HaNavi* — whether sung or played from a CD. Ask someone — perhaps a child — to turn out all the lights. Give the candle, wine, and the spices to various people to hold.

The actual blessings may be edited down to four short lines: wine, spices, fire and the last line — *HaMavdil bein Kodesh L'khol.* To intensify the transitional moment, some people add to the sensory stimulation and fun by passing out sparklers, or igniting a plate of vodka with the Havdalah candle. During the ceremony people sway and interlock arms like the wicks of the candle, and at its conclusion, they sometimes dance.

Guidelines
from tradition

What, When, and Who?

What? Havdalah marks ceremonially the end of the sacred hours of Shabbat. This distinction is made in words as part of the *Motzaei Shabbat Maariv,* the Saturday evening *Amidah* prayer, during the prayer requesting that God give us the intelligence/*khonen hadaat* to make distinctions. The Rabbis also established a home ceremony with symbolic objects — fire, wine and spices — each with its own blessing plus the fourth blessing separating *kodesh vakhol*/the sacred from the secular.

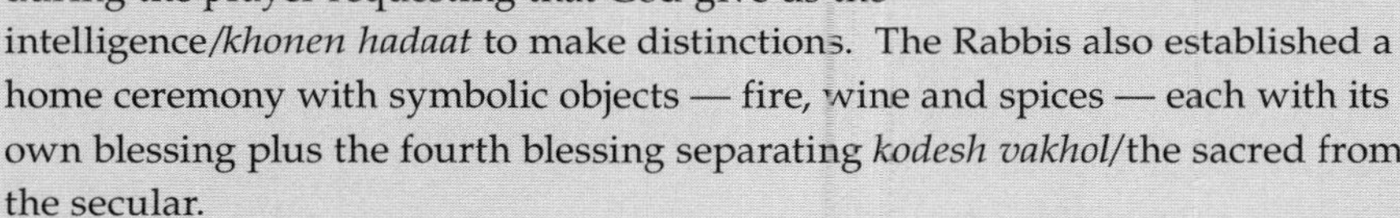

Extra verses often recited before the *brachot* are not obligatory and vary from one tradition to the next.

When? Havdalah is performed once three stars can be sighted on a clear night. In order not to appear to be rushing Shabbat "out the door" as if it were a burden rather than an honored guest, some people wait until they can see at least three small stars in the same area of the sky and not just the larger stars — actually planets — that can often be seen before it is really dark. After sunset, until Havdalah is recited, one should not eat or do any work without first reciting the blessing — *HaMavdil bein kodesh l'khol.* If Havdalah over a cup was not said on *Motzaei Shabbat,* then it can still be recited up until Tuesday afternoon — though without a candle or spices (TALMUD PESACHIM 106A).

Who? Many women now take a fully egalitarian role in all rituals. Even some Orthodox scholars hold that a woman may recite the blessings for men as well.

Why is it preferable to use a multi-wick candle?

Although not obligatory, it is desirable to use multiple wicks (or at least combine two single wick candles) to make the Havdalah flame.

There are at least two reasons for this: first, the renewal of creative activity is symbolized by creating a large torch-like flame produced by a multi-wick candle. Second, the blessing *Meorei HaEish* — "who lights flames" — is plural, "for each flame is a synthesis of many-colored flames — white, red and green."

Why extinguish the candle in the wine spilled from the cup?

This fulfills the rabbinic dictum: "Any house where wine flows generously like water is a place of blessing" (TALMUD ERUVIN 61A).

Customs Explained

Fingers and Flames

Why is it customary to cup one's fingers near the flame?

There are several rationales for this fascinating custom — halakhic, aggadic (Rabbinic law and stories), mystical, and contemporary:

HALAKHA: Using the Hand

According to Jewish law, after reciting a blessing, it is an obligation to "fulfill" that blessing immediately.

Therefore, in Havdalah, one must make use of the light of the fire (and drink the wine and smell the spices). Utilizing the candlelight, some people examine their fingernails while others look at the palms of their hands.

AGGADAH: Closed and Open

A Rabbinic story takes us back to Adam:

"Initially one closes up the palms as a sign, that on Shabbat our hands were forbidden to engage in creative labor, and then one opens the palms to declare that from now on labor is permitted." (MEIR OF ROTHENBERG)

"This recalls the rabbinic story that Adam opened his hands and drew them near the flame that he had first created on *Motzaei Shabbat* and blessed the fire. Then he withdrew his palms and acknowledged that the difference between a holy day and a secular one is the prohibition of making fire." (PIRKEI D'RABBI ELIEZER 20)

KABBALAH: Manifestations of God

Some Kabbalists put a different spin on things. Elliot Ginsburg notes:

"Non-Kabbalist sources emphasize looking at one's open hands as a sign that use of the hands to work is now permitted. However, Kabbalists generally restrict the gesture to one's right hand, to the backside of one's folded fingers. While the open hand represented God's hidden face, the outside and backside represent God's external representatives — the four angels for the four fingers — who now at the end of Shabbat, at the changing of the guards, reassert their authority."

KABBALAH: Darkness versus Light

Another Kabbalistic commentator explains the custom of examining fingernails, bending the fingers and bringing them close to the source of light, in terms of externality, the dark Other Side/*Sitra Akhra*, the *kelipot*/broken vessels:

"These evil forces gain strength as Shabbat and the *neshama y'teira*/extra soul depart since we are no longer protected by the power of the sacred. Therefore we must assert authority over the dark powers, to bend them to God's will as symbolized in bending the fingers, and to subordinate them to the sovereignty of the light, as symbolized by bringing our fingers to the source of the flame on Havdalah."

CONTEMPORARY: Illuminating Differences

A recent interpretation of the examination of the nails and their differentiation from the finger emphasizes the all-important distinction between life and death. Nails are composed of dead cells while the finger consists of living cells.

Another contemporary use of the light is to distinguish between the faces of those gathered around the flame. Our ability to make those fine differentiations reflects the way God made each human being unique in face as well as in personality.

Sensory Blessings

An easy way to remember the order of blessings in Havdalah is to think of them in the order of the senses in the head — from bottom to top. You can recall the acrostic YaVNeH, the city of Rabban Yochanan ben Zakkai.

After all, making distinctions is also a kind of "sense" — common sense:

Yayin = **Y** = the tongue (at the bottom of the head) is used to taste the wine over which we recite the first bracha

V'Samim = **V** = the nose smells the spices which are blessed next

Ner = **N** = the eyes see the light of the candle

Havdalah = **H** = the brain with its "common sense" at the top of the head distinguishes between Holy and secular

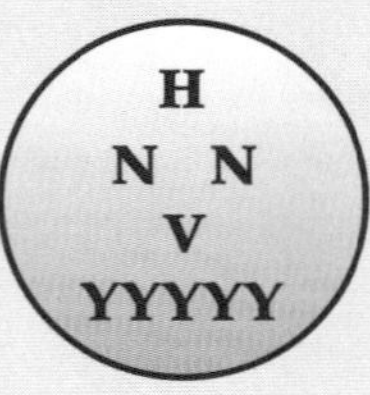

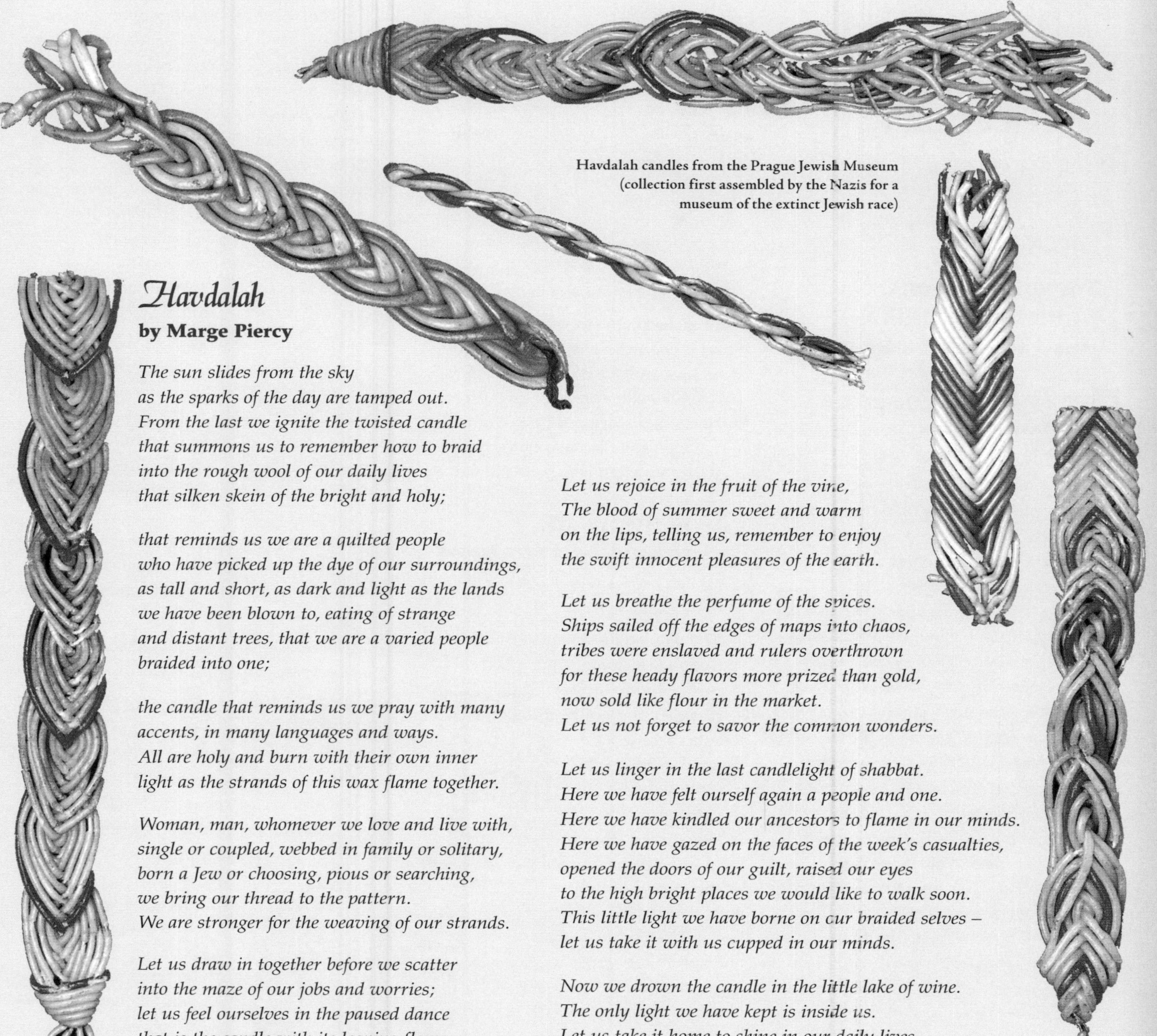

Havdalah candles from the Prague Jewish Museum
(collection first assembled by the Nazis for a
museum of the extinct Jewish race)

Havdalah

by Marge Piercy

The sun slides from the sky
as the sparks of the day are tamped out.
From the last we ignite the twisted candle
that summons us to remember how to braid
into the rough wool of our daily lives
that silken skein of the bright and holy;

that reminds us we are a quilted people
who have picked up the dye of our surroundings,
as tall and short, as dark and light as the lands
we have been blown to, eating of strange
and distant trees, that we are a varied people
braided into one;

the candle that reminds us we pray with many
accents, in many languages and ways.
All are holy and burn with their own inner
light as the strands of this wax flame together.

Woman, man, whomever we love and live with,
single or coupled, webbed in family or solitary,
born a Jew or choosing, pious or searching,
we bring our thread to the pattern.
We are stronger for the weaving of our strands.

Let us draw in together before we scatter
into the maze of our jobs and worries;
let us feel ourselves in the paused dance
that is the candle with its leaping flame:
let us too pause before shabbat lets us go.

Let us rejoice in the fruit of the vine,
The blood of summer sweet and warm
on the lips, telling us, remember to enjoy
the swift innocent pleasures of the earth.

Let us breathe the perfume of the spices.
Ships sailed off the edges of maps into chaos,
tribes were enslaved and rulers overthrown
for these heady flavors more prized than gold,
now sold like flour in the market.
Let us not forget to savor the common wonders.

Let us linger in the last candlelight of shabbat.
Here we have felt ourself again a people and one.
Here we have kindled our ancestors to flame in our minds.
Here we have gazed on the faces of the week's casualties,
opened the doors of our guilt, raised our eyes
to the high bright places we would like to walk soon.
This little light we have borne on our braided selves –
let us take it with us cupped in our minds.

Now we drown the candle in the little lake of wine.
The only light we have kept is inside us.
Let us take it home to shine in our daily lives.

FROM THE ART OF BLESSING THE DAY

Reflections כַּוָּנוֹת

on the art of saying farewell and making distinctions

Farewell, my love —

Two Introductions to Havdalah: for the Head and for the Heart

FOR THE HEAD: On the Art of Making Distinctions

Havdalah marks the close of Shabbat. With its three powerful symbols — wine, spices and fire — the ceremony helps us to make the sudden transition from a holy day in eternity to six very temporal weekdays. All present stand like an honor guard sending off a very important dignitary: the Shabbat Queen. On the one hand, we are sorry to lose the special quality of sacred rest, which she represents. Yet on the other hand, we are happy to inaugurate another six days of human creativity following in the footsteps of our Divine Creator. In those first six days of Creation God introduces many distinctions *(VaYavdeil)* into the chaos, beginning with the separation between light and darkness. That is the first distinction that we as humans acknowledge as the new work week begins on *Motzaei Shabbat.* We also celebrate the distinction between holy *(Kodesh)* — that which has already been consecrated by being singled out — and secular *(Hol)* — that which is not yet sanctified but still in process of formation. Not only time but people too are consecrated to higher purposes. The calling of the Jewish people as a separate nation is a sacred task acknowledged here.

Like the Divine Mind, the human mind is endowed with a unique ability to make distinctions *(Chonein HaDaat).* Havdalah — the cognitive exercise of distinction, discernment, discrimination — is a manifestation and outcome of *Daat* — wisdom, awareness, perception, insight.

FOR THE HEART: Living with Necessary Losses

Havdalah carries with it a sense of loss, or even of abandonment.

The *Shekhina* — the maternal presence of God — which had enwrapped us, departs with the sunset. *Shalom Bayit* — domestic tranquility and family togetherness — becomes secondary to the rush of activity as people move back into the flow of the week. The *neshama y'teira* — the extra soul that we enjoy on Shabbat — with its extra powers of sanctity and spirituality, takes its leave. Very quickly, it seems, Shabbat is gone and we find ourselves thrust into the world of everyday.

Scholar Aviva Zornberg understands the separation/*havdalah* process in analogy to the pain and struggle of an infant born out of her mother's body. Thus a midrash (Genesis Rabbah 5:3) pictures the lower waters weeping when they are separated by God from the upper waters. Zornberg "suggests there is something poignant in the creative process when things once united are separated." Emotional ambivalence about separation/*havdalah*, even though it is Divinely mandated, is reflected in the farewell ceremony from Shabbat.

Of course, the work week can be an opportunity to add to the Divine creation. Thus the Havdalah blessing refers to "the six days of Creation." The flame we light is also a symbol of the power to harness energy for human productivity. According to the Midrash, God taught the first man at the end of Shabbat to chase away fear and darkness by igniting his own flame. Clearly, our own sense of loneliness and the fear of the darkness reflect deep human experience.

Judith Viorst, in her book *Necessary Losses,* notes as well:

"All of our loss experiences hark back to Original Loss, the loss of that ultimate mother-child connection . . . We begin life with loss. We are cast from the womb . . . Our mother interposes herself between us and the world, protecting us from overwhelming anxiety. We shall have no greater need than this need for our mother . . . Separation anxiety [means that] the need for human connection is fundamental. We are wired for love from the start.

Medieval towers as spice boxes

The Losing, Leaving, Letting Go of Paradise

"It's hard to become a separate self, to separate both literally and emotionally, to be able to outwardly stand alone and to inwardly feel ourselves to be distinct. We acknowledge a paradise and a paradise lost. We acknowledge a time of harmony, wholeness, unbreachable safety, unconditional love, and a time when that wholeness was irretrievably rent. We acknowledge it in religion, myth and fairy tales, our conscious and unconscious fantasies . . . While we fiercely protect the boundaries of self that clearly demark the 'you' from the 'me,' we also yearn to recapture the lost paradise of that ultimate connection. That is why the first event is known to have been an expulsion, and the last is hoped to be a reconciliation and return.

"In the course of our life we leave and are left and let go of much that we love. Losing is the price we pay for living. It is also the source of much of our growth and gain . . . We have to deal with our necessary losses . . . In confronting the many losses . . . we have many opportunities for creative transformations." *(Judith Viorst, Necessary Losses)*

Looking backward, during Havdalah, we see loss; but looking forward, we see hope. Havdalah concludes with the promise: a world restored and — *yom shekulo Shabbat* — an era which is one long Shabbat.

The World of Opposites: Integrating the Shadows

Separation, in Hebrew called Havdalah, is essential to the unfolding of the spirit in the world. It was the separation of the heavens and the earth that allowed for creation.

Yet that is only the first step. The next and more spiritually powerful step is called by the Baal Shem Tov, the Hasidic Master of the Good Name, *Hamtakat HaDinim* — the **"sweetening of judgment."** In *Hamtaka*, the separation becomes a staging ground for unity consciousness; otherwise, its shadows — fragmentation and alienation — ultimately foster collapse. For the Kabbalists, all fragmentation is the opposite of God.

Fragmentation sees opposites; it focuses on the dividing principle instead of the uniting principle. In the world of division, *Pirud*, everything comes in opposites: beautiful/ugly, success/failure, freedom/slavery, intelligent/stupid, true/false. We imagine that if we could just destroy the evil properties of these pairs, redemption would be at hand. So we seek to overcome death, to destroy evil, to uproot pain, and to avoid failure at all costs. This is the world of judgment and of discrimination — *Dinim* . . . .

Of course this never works. Boundaries are also places of meetings. Wherever one property exists, so does the other. Life cannot exist without death, and there is no virtue without sin. There is no such thing as success without failure, and the idea of pleasure has no meaning without pain. In the same way that you cannot draw a concave line without a convex line, there is no good without evil. The possibility of one creates the other.

The beginning of the circle of unity is the realization that opposites are close neighbors. The words of the *Sefer Yetzira* — the mystical Book of Creation — come back to us: "The end is in the beginning and the beginning is in the end." This is the world of *Iggul*, the circle, when history has come full circle. The wave becomes water and continues its cycle. Good and evil are both from God. God is the source who, in the prophet's words, "fashions light and creates darkness, makes peace and creates evil" (Isaiah 45:7).

—Mordechai Gafni
(from The Mystery of Love)

Havdalah *by Moritz Daniel Oppenheim (Germany, 1866)*

Bread vs. Spices

The Friday night ritual parallels the closing Havdalah ceremony quite neatly: candles, wine, and bread/spices. But note two differences. The spiritual progress we have made from the beginning of Shabbat is symbolized by the two distinct candles merging into a single braided one — expressing the idea that what was once separate is now integrated and united (surprising for a ritual called Havdalah, which means separation!). Secondly, Shabbat begins with tasty bread (Hallah); to enjoy the spiritual day, we need physical sustenance. But at Havdalah, the spices replace the bread. At the end of Shabbat, we no longer worry about physical sustenance. We begin the work week with spiritual nourishment (the spices) to sustain us.

— Baruch Sienna

Home-grown garden spices. ***Photo by Ben Shatz.***

From Fire, Light

We are the generation that stands between the fires . . .
The task for us is to turn fire into light:
Light to see each other with,
Light to see the Image of God in every face.
The task for us is to live between the fires of Shabbat:
Behind us the candles that begin Shabbat,
Before us the candles that end it with Havdalah.
Within us the pause of rest, of peace, of mystery: Shabbat.

We are the generation that must live between the fires:
Between the candles of Shabbat, or the flames of Holocaust.
The flickering candle flames of Mystery,
Or the consuming flames of Mastery.

Blessed is the One Who creates from fire, light.

— Arthur Waskow, CCAR Yearbook, 1984

Havdalah,
by Herman Struck

Tales of the ever-present Elijah

In the Middle Ages, folk belief held that Elijah, the forerunner of the redemption (MALACHI 3:23), made his appearance whenever it was thought the messiah might come. On Seder night it was appropriate because the Rabbis predicted that as we were once redeemed in the month of Nisan on Seder night, so we would be redeemed at the same auspicious time of the year in the future. Shabbat, on the other hand, was a poor time for God to send Elijah, for it would be too much work to get ready for the messiah on Shabbat. Our ever-considerate God would rather delay Elijah's arrival until after Shabbat. In fact, if all of Israel would observe Shabbat diligently for two consecutive *Shabbatot*, Rabbi Shimon bar Yochai promised, we would be rewarded immediately with redemption.

— SEFER HAMANHIG

Elijah Prophesies Making a Mess at the Table

Many years ago in Bagdad there lived an honest and decent couple whose greatest sorrow was that they had no children. At the seder with no child to ask the four questions, the wife was deeply saddened, while her loving husband tried to comfort her: "Don't worry, the Holy One will not forget us. One day we will be privileged to have a child."

Then as they spoke a knocking was heard and a poor old man appeared and they invited him to join them. They honored him and shared their table. Yet when he got up to leave, rather than thanking them, he said something very strange: "I pray to God that when I next visit you at the Pesach Seder [which literally means 'order'] your table will be a mess." The couple felt that the old man's curse was no way to thank them but they quickly forgot his words and went on with life.

A month later the wife sensed a change in her body — she was pregnant. The couple was joyful beyond words when she gave birth to a child.

Two years later they sat at the Seder table with their child on their lap. In the way of children he laughed and played, he climbed on the table and spilled wine on the white tablecloth, he knocked over glasses and plates. Yet his indulgent, loving parents were still overjoyed with their firstborn, no matter what disorder he brought to their Seder.

Suddenly they heard a knock on the door and in came the ungrateful old man, their guest from two years before. Then they looked at him and at their table in disarray and they understood that what they had taken to be a curse was in fact a blessing. They hugged and kissed him and asked his forgiveness for thinking badly of him. He just smiled broadly and said: "I forgive you. May you be privileged to raise this child to perform mitzvot and good deeds." Then just as suddenly as he had appeared, the old man disappeared. Only then did the couple realize that their guest had been none other than Elijah who bears good news.

Elijah Cup, 19th century Bohemia

Learning Things the Easy Way

Why do human beings have an indentation above the mouth? A legend tells us that "when the baby was in the mother's womb, Elijah used to teach the child the whole Torah. However when the child left the womb and entered the air of the world, an angel slapped the baby across the mouth and all that was learned was forgotten" (TALMUD NIDAH 30B). Now children must relearn everything the hard way, but at times there is an "aha" experience of recognition for they once knew these truths at a primordial level.

Elijah Counts up Israel's Merits

On *Motzaei Shabbat* Elijah sits beneath the Tree of Life and writes down all the merits of the people of Israel (RABBI SHALOM OF AUSTRIA QUOTED BY THE MAHARIL). Hence it is appropriate for us to do the same — to appreciate the sanctity of our people . . . for there is no limit to the light of holiness in each and everyone of them . . . One should tremble in awe before the holiness of the supreme Divine soul in each one. So we wish for the success of every individual Jew in all their material and spiritual pursuits . . . I love my people and I desire with all the warmth in my heart . . . that all their wonderful hidden capacities will be realized . . . .

— RABBI ABRAHAM ISAAC KOOK

Three Friends and Three Days of Rest in a Row

Many years ago, in a small village in Eretz Yisrael there lived three friends, a Moslem, a Christian and a Jew. The Moslem kept his Shabbat on a Friday, the Christian on Sunday, and the Jew, of course, on Saturday.

On Friday, the Jew and the Christian set out for their fields. When the Jew saw that the Moslem's field was but half ploughed, he said: "Today my friend can do no work. It is his Shabbat. Tomorrow it may rain, and he may not have his field ploughed in time for the sowing. I shall plough his field a little, and thereby his work will be easier for him." In the meantime the Christian had said much the same thing to himself, so that unawares of the presence of one another, each of them ploughed the Moslem's field; one from the east, the other from the west.

Havdalah in New York, 1896, *The Century Magazine*

On the next day, when the Moslem came and found his field all ploughed he wondered, saying to himself, "Who could have ploughed my field? It must have been that God sent angels to help me."

Months passed by, and the time of reaping came. It was Sunday. The Jew and the Moslem had gone to their fields, and the Christian remained at home to keep his Shabbat. When the Jew saw that the Christian friend's corn was full and ready to cut, he said: "Today my neighbor cannot cut his grain, tomorrow a wind may come and scatter his seeds. I shall cut a little for him while I have the time." Now, strange to say, while the Jew was thinking of his Christian friend's corn, the Moslem had the same thought, so that, unseen by one another, they cut the Christian's grain, one from the south, one from the north.

Next day, the Christian went out to cut his corn, and found it all done. He was so surprised that he could not explain it. "It must be that God has sent good angels to cut my corn for me," he mused.

Reaping time passed and the season of threshing approached. It was Saturday. The Jew remembered his Shabbat day "to keep it holy." The Christian and the Moslem were at work. Looking up at the clouded sky the Moslem thought to himself, "Ah, the rain is coming, and it is the day of rest of our Jewish friend. Alas! The rain will wash his grain away." And going to his Christian neighbor he said, "Come, neighbor, let us thresh the grain for our friend, the Jew." To this the Christian gladly agreed, and after threshing the grain they bound it up and covered it with straw to protect it from the rain. When Sunday came and the Jew set out for his field, he found his grain not only well threshed, but dry under the straw. Then, lifting up his eyes to Heaven, he exclaimed, "Blessed are You, Lord, who sends your angels to help those who remember your Shabbat to keep it holy."

— The Seventh Day, UJS/Limud

A personal retelling of the first havdalah after the Garden of Eden

Light in the Darkness

by Shawn Fields-Meyer

> Text and experience are mutually enlighteniong.
>
> — Judah Goldin

A traditional Midrash in contemporary garb:

Adam Ha-Rishon, the first man, was created on the eve of the first Shabbat, before nighttime, and then fell asleep.

The next morning he awoke and again saw daylight. But as the hours went on, and night began to fall, Adam Ha-Rishon grew terrified. He did not know what darkness was, and felt himself becoming enveloped in a sea of blackness.

So he screamed. He cried out to God: "What is happening? I can't see anything! I can't move! Help me!"

He groped in the darkness, hoping for divine intervention.

When my second of three sons was two and a half years old, we began to notice some strange behavior. Day by day, as he played, and ate, and spoke; at school, in stores, at synagogue, in the back yard: nothing seemed quite right. Ezra was hard to grasp. He would not connect.

At home, his favorite thing to do was to drag a blanket outside, turn on the garden spigot so there was the sound of a trickle, and roll himself into the blanket until he was fully cocooned inside. He would lie there for long stretches of time, just listening to the sound of the water. Other times he would burrow himself in his brother Noam's crib, under huge piles of stuffed animals. One afternoon, I became panicked because I could not find him anywhere. After a long search, I finally discovered my son on a shelf in the back of a deep linen closet, in the dark, hugging the pillows.

When I told him how upset I'd been, he just walked away silently.

At school, he interacted with no one. He had no interest in friends. He seemed to look right through everyone: teachers, peers, even his own brothers. He was most animated with his menagerie of plastic dinosaurs and jungle creatures.

Ezra had an odd rigidity, unmatched by other children we knew: he would only eat white food. He insisted on wearing corduroy pants exclusively. He had an insistent, almost urgent desire for certain sensory experiences, but an extreme dislike of others. He could not stand to hold a hand, or have his head stroked, or keep his clothes on. Haircuts were torment. This made ordinary family life very difficult.

His speech was odd. He mimicked words and phrases from books, tapes and videos (Winnie the Pooh, Sesame Street). He repeated them tens of times in a row, like a broken record. You never knew if you were talking to Ezra, or to a character in a story.

But most disturbing was Ezra's almost haunting retreat from the world. And every time we tried to bring him into our orbit, we were met by either tortured screams or an empty, far-away stare. Nothing we did seemed to bring him back.

All this came to the surface one morning a month before his third birthday, at a parent-teacher conference at his nursery school. The teacher gave us example after example of Ezra's distance and withdrawal. I asked her what she was doing to help him. She shrugged, and said, "I don't know what to do. I'm telling you."

That night, I could not sleep. In the darkness and silence, I asked myself: what is wrong with this child? Finally, I sat up in bed and, in tears, wrote out a list. Under the heading **"Who and what is my son Ezra?"** I wrote down every detail I could think of what he liked, what he felt, how he did things. And I finally concluded the answer to my own question: **I don't know.**

Every parent has dreams. Fantasies of what might be. You hold a little baby in your arms, you feed him and sing to him you rock him and comfort him. And as the hours and days go by, you just dream and dream. And plan. And expect. And all of us know, that life never turns out the way you planned it.

But months of living with this beautiful, sweet, little boy; months of watching our formerly normal child slip away to some alternate reality; months of looking him in the eye and having him look the other way; this was more than unplanned. This was out of control. **This was chaos! Like Adam on that first day, we stumbled in the darkness.**

Stumbling through the darkness means not knowing where you're going. It means being filled with fear, insecurity, aloneness, limitations, uncertainty, powerlessness, and even some shame and embarrassment. My husband and I stumbled there for a long while. Really, just stood there, groping in the darkness.

In the still moments, out of the silent darkness, we began to discern something. We began to hear a word: Autism. It was a word. Just a name. A concept. But it was hearing that word, speaking it, that brought the very first spark of light into that darkness — as God spoke, "Let there be light" in the midst of the original darkness and the power of the word brought some enlightenment, though the night still remained alongside the light God created.

The word was in fact spoken by many people, but the first time I heard it with real comprehension was from the mouth of a psychiatrist who is also a rabbi. He said to us: Not only is there a name for this collection of symptoms. There is something you can **do** to help him . . . **A spark.**

We began to follow some of the many leads given to us by him and others — many others. Slowly, tentatively at first, and then with growing speed and agility we have learned to navigate the waters of what my husband Tom has described so articulately as a neurological disorder whose cause is not known, whose diagnosis is vague, whose prognosis is uncertain and whose treatment is constantly under dispute.

Sparks, sometimes even rays, of light.

Once a week Ezra visits an occupational therapist who helps him discover physical activity to regulate himself. Ten minutes of swinging before dinner can make the difference between chaos and calm. Rolling in blankets regulates his system and helps him to sleep at night. The therapist calls it a sensory diet. We built these activities into our daily lives. Sparks.

We found that what appears to be withdrawal is in fact masking an almost desperate desire for human connection. I used to refer to his retreat as Planet Ezra. But we have learned to travel to that planet, to follow his lead, his interests. To wait patiently for him on his planet, communicate with him there, and then ask him to come with us. And he does. Sparks of light.

And we have learned that we are not the only ones. Stumbling in the darkness, we felt isolated. These days, we swap concerns and success stories every week with friends in a meeting of autism parents. And we study Torah and offer support every month with a Jewish group we created of special-needs moms and dads. We have drawn a circle of love and light around us: teachers, specialists, family, and friends who love Ezra. **Sparks.**

Some months ago, I was in the car with Ezra and, no surprise, I told him what I tell him and his brothers countless times every day: "I love you," I said. "I love you, Ezra." He paused, and looked me in the eye. "I love you too, Ima." And I realized, that was the first time, in his nearly 5 years of life, that he had ever spoken those words.

My son, who once would pass through our house seeming not to notice anyone around him, now spends his mornings giggling through silly games and chasing around the playroom with his brother and best friend Noam. My son, who once constructed lonely, impenetrable worlds of plastic zebras and giraffes now invites us over to join him as he pets a poodle at the park. My son, whose love of books once meant sitting alone and flipping rapidly through pages, ignoring words . . . Last week, sitting in our kitchen that same son, who is now in kindergarten, read my husband a sentence. "I see the yellow car." . . . **Little by little, light is dispelling the darkness.**

In the autism world, most people don't talk about a cure. Rather, the task is to nurture our child, to respect his unique personality; not to change him, but to give him tools.

Back to the traditional Midrash for Havdalah:

What did God do, when God heard the Adam's cry? How did God respond to the human's terror, his utter paralysis in the enveloping darkness of the Garden of Eden? This is the God we know because we have read the rest of the Tanakh, the God who can send plagues and part the waters and cause the sun to stand still. So what does God do for the man stumbling, frightened of the black night? Does God perform a miracle? Turn day into night? Lighten up the horizon? No.

Instead, God says to the man: Feel around you. See, there are two flints by your feet. Take those flints, and rub them together until you see a spark. Eventually you will create a flame, and with that flame you will light up the darkness and stop stumbling.

God long ago created all the miracles-to-be. They are out there. Now, God points us to the tools, the ones often in our own gardens, that help us light the sparks that dispel our darkness. That is what we celebrate when we kindle the Havdalah candle at the same time of the week when **God first taught Adam to light his own fire and to begin to do his own labor of dispelling the darkness each week.**

In appreciation תּוֹדָה

AS THE INITIATOR of this complex project I would like to express my thanks to both institutions and individuals who contributed to this undertaking. The most important "institution" is my wife Marcelle who urged me to write and share this vision of Jewish family celebration. Next is the Shalom Hartman Institute, led by Rabbis David and Donniel Hartman and Yehudit Schweig, who for me and many others have created an inspiring, intellectually stimulating environment that helps Jewish learning reach thoughtful, open-minded people everywhere. Then there are Jake and Linda Kriger, longtime believers in Jewish books in service of renewed Jewish life, who made a decisive financial contribution so this could become a beautiful Shabbat book that speaks to the eye and the heart as well as the mind. In compiling this diverse book Moshe Silberschein was my first collaborator and his knowledge of liturgy gave us a solid academic foundation. Then Shawn Fields-Meyer, a superb educator deeply concerned with personal spirituality and prayer, became the partner who saw the book through its long editing process and a dynamic force who will help carry it beyond publishing to educational outreach. Arielle Parker arrived just in time to be the editorial midwife of this book. The many words we wrote and collected became visually accessible and attractive thanks to my partner in content and form, Joe Buchwald Gelles, the talented and very devoted graphic artist, consultant and fellow Jewish entrepreneur.

— *Noam Zion*

ALMOST INNUMERABLE consultants, editors and proofreaders have helped along the way including: Scott Aaron, Julie Auerbach, Rachel Bashevkin, Bill Berk, Tim Bernard, Aryeh Bernstein, Gloria Bieler, Lee Buckman, Dianne Cohler-Esses, Rachel Cowan, David Estrin, Ed Feinstein, Tom Fields-Meyer, Jonathan Freund, Mark Friedman, Laura Geller, Mollie Gilbert, Elliot Ginsburg, Mel Glatzer, Lisa Goldberg, Daniel Gordis, Lenny Gordon, Laurie Hahn, Sharon Halperin, Ephraim Hazan, Marc Hirschman, Holy Blossom focus group, Jewish Women's Archive (especially Jennifer Sartori) at www.jwa.org, Arie Katz, Jeremy Kraff, Leah Kroll, Ruth Langer, Jay Leberman, Marty Lee, Lori Lefkovitz, Alan Lettofsky, Dvora Lifshitz, Jessica Lissey, Martin Lockshin, Ziva Maisels, Tamar Malino, Yedidya Melchior, Margaret Meyer, Goldie Milgram, Marsha Mirkin, Ellen Mirowitz, Sharon Muller (USHMM Photo Archive), Eynat Nawy, Jacob Ner-David, Vanessa Ochs, Sally Oren, Becky Paley, Alan Rabishaw, Freda Reider (author of *The Hallah Book*), Marvin Richardson, Dorothy Richman, Peretz Rodman, Jaclyn Rubin, Shira Tova Rubin, Raymond Scheindlin, Lisa Schlaff, Edwin Seroussi, Sara Shahak, Simcha Shtull, Elie Spitz, Gordon Tucker, Ari Vernon, Barry Walfish, Stuart Weinblatt, Cynthia Weinger, Talya Weisbard, Carl Wolkin, Elie Wurtman, Raphael Zarum, Larry Zierler.

Contributions were very generously granted by authors and photographers: Maya Bernstein, Phyllis Cincinatus, Tully Filmus' sons Michael and Steven Filmus, Jeni Friedman (from *The Personal Theology Haiku Series* – unpublished), Mordechai Gafni *(The Mystery of Love)*, Otto Geismar's daughters Ruth Harris and Gisela Gordon, Elliot Ginsburg (*Shabbat in the Classical Kabbalah*), Blu Greenberg, Yaacov Greenvurcel, Joel Lurie Grishaver, Bill Gross, David Hartman, Israeli stamps from the Israeli Philatelic Authority, Elizabeth Kessler, Levi Lauer, Ebn David Leader, Naomi Levy (*Talking to God* pp. 44-45 and *To Begin Anew* pp. 83-84, 132-133, 206, 209), Daniel Matt (*The Essential Kabbalah* p. 99), Shira Milgrom, Elizabeth Ochs (for Shabbat Angel Cards – *Malakhei HaShabbat*, prepared for her Bat Mitzvah, 1999, and reprinted with generous permission of Vanessa, Julie and Elizabeth Ochs), Dov Noy (*Folktales*), Marc-Alain Ouaknin, Dan Reisinger, Marvin Richardson, Alice Shalvi, Benjamin Shatz, Baruch Sienna, Abram Sterne and Marcus Freed (editors of *The Seventh Day*), Joseph Telushkin (*Book of Values* pp. 19, 141, 228-229, 237-239, 434, 483-484), *UJS/Limmud Shabbat Book* with article by Sarah Lightman and Lionel Blue), David Wolpe, Raphael Zarum (*Torah La'Am*) and the UJIA.

Credits by permission of contributors and/or publishers: Bill Aron, Beit Hatefutsot Photo Archive, Tel Aviv; Leila Gal Berner; Rickie Burman (Jewish Museum, London, UK); Lawrence Bush; Marcia Falk; Debbie Friedman and Drorah Setel *(Mi Shebeirach)* from *And You Shall Be A Blessing*, © 1988, Sounds Write Productions, Inc. (ASCAP) www.debbiefriedman.com; Karl Gabor; Beth Grossman; Michel Kichka; Lawrence Kushner (*The Book of Words: Talking Spiritual Life, Living Spiritual Talk* © 1993 and *Honey from the Rock: An Introduction to Jewish Mysticism — Special Anniversary Edition* © 2000, p. 69-7, www.jewishlights.com 800-962-4544, permission granted by Jewish Lights Publishing, POB 237, Woodstock, VT 05091); Zion Ozeri; Abel Pann (Mayanot Gallery and Itiel Pann); Marge Piercy, ("Havdalah" © 1999 by Marge Piercy and Middlemarsh, Inc. from *The Art of Blessing the Day*, Alfred A. Knopf, 1999, Random House); Charles Shultz (Peanuts, United Features Syndicate); Mark Podwal; Hannah Senesh *(Walking to Caesaria)* and Ehud Manor *(L'shana Habba)* copyrights of authors and ACUM; David Sharir; Daniel Siegel; Michael Strassfeld (*A Book of Life*, Schocken, pp. 306, 503); *Temple Emanuel Siddur*, 2003, edited by Judy Greenfeld and Laura Geller, including Sabine Y. Meyer, Diann Neu, Ron Rosenblatt and Harlow Shapely p. 9, 31, 177 in draft); Aliza Urbach; Arthur Waskow; Zelda (Light a Candle); Zionist Archive (Jerusalem).

Endnotes:

We apologize to copyright holders whom we were unable to contact despite many efforts and look forward to their making contact with us. Very short selections from longer works are, according to our lawyers, permitted by the fair use clause.

Introduction

David Wolpe, "Eternity Utters A Day" from OLAM Winter 2000, The Buzz about Shabbat, edited by David Suissa; David Hartman, from "Shabbat and the Human Experience of Labor," study unit from the Shalom Hartman Institute; Mordechai Gafni, original for ADA; Joel Grishaver, from Shabbat Parent-Child Kit; Michel Kichka, "Modern Slavery" from *Halaila Hazeh Haggadah* by Mishael Zion.

Likrat Shabbat

Tekhina translated by Chava Weissler in *"The Traditional Piety of Ashkenazic Women"*; Pre-Shabbat *Boi Kallah* snack reported in Ben-Ish Hai, 19th century Iraqi scholar (*Lech L'cha*, second year); Daniel Siegel, *Gymshoes and Irises*; Tales of Giving about Salanter adapted from a retelling by Joel

Lurie Grishaver in his booklet for LABJE on Tzedakah; Tzvi Marx from "The Dynamics of Tzedakah" study unit, Shalom Hartman Institute; Wendy Mogel, *The Blessing of a Skinned Knee,* p. 170 (Penguin Compass, 2001).

Candle lighting

Blu Greenberg, *How to Run a Traditional Jewish Household*; Michael Strassfeld, *A Book of Life* (p. 306); Basha in Aliyah Center in California quoted in *Number Our Days* by Barbara Myerhoff (1978) cited in Sandee Brawarsky's *Two Jews, Three Opinions,* page 467); "Space Travel, The Arctic Circle and Candle Lighting" based on Rabbi David Golinkin, "A Responsum Regarding Space Travel," June, 2002, published in *Insight Israel* p. 103 ff, published by the Schechter Institute in Jerusalem, 2002; Phyllis Cincinatus, from Holy Blossom Temple, Toronto, original for ADA; Joseph Telushkin, *Book of Values*, p. 434, Wayne Muller, *Sabbath: Restoring the Sacred Rhythm of Rest*; Zelda, "Light a Candle" from *The Spectacular Difference: Selected Poems of Zelda,* translated by Marcia Lee Falk with her permission and that of ACUM, 2004; "A Lonely Shabbat in the Peace Corps" adapted from anecdote by Sam Horowitz, Atlantic City; Victor Frankl, *Man's Search for Meaning* pp. 62-63, psychiatrist and concentration camp survivor; Alice Shalvi, "Repentance, Responsibility, and Regeneration: Reflections on Isaiah" p. 275 in Gail Twersky Reimer and Judith A. Kates: *Beginning Anew, A Woman's Companion to the High Holy Days,* 1997, New York, Simon and Schuster; *Tkhines* translated by Chava Weissler in *"The Traditional Piety of Ashkenazic Women."*

On the halacha of candle lighting:

One may light candles before sunset without "accepting Shabbat" as long as you make this intention explicit to yourself. Thus one may light candles before sunset, make the blessings, continue last minute preparations or drive to the synagogue before sunset, and then only when at the synagogue officially "accept upon oneself" Shabbat and its restrictions. Just have that in mind as you bless them. People concerned about fire may not wish to light candles before they go out. They might light the candles at the home where they are invited. In non-traditional homes they may light the candles and then extinguish them before going out. Alternatively one may light candles long before sunset and intend to begin Shabbat and then make Kiddush and so on even several hours before the actual sunset.

The candles are lit and Shabbat is ushered in as the sun sets over the treetops at least 18 minutes before the actual sunset (in Jerusalem — 36 minutes). The 18 minutes are added both to make sure we do not violate the borders of Shabbat and to add from the holy to the mundane, *kodesh l'chol*, thus expanding our sacred time. (*Shulchan Arukh* O.H. 263:4). If the candles rest on a tray and one adds to the tray a wedding band or an expensive silver cup, then those precious items become primary and the lit candles secondary. Thus if you wish to move the ring or cup by lifting the tray and moving it, then that is not a violation of the laws of *muktza* on touching or moving objects associated with forbidden labor like burning candles.

"A Woman's Mitzvah" based on *Mishne Torah,* Shabbat 5:3; *Shulchan Arukh* OH 263:2-3; Vanessa Ochs' anecdote about her grandmother reported by e mail for publication in this book; chart of number of candles lit in different lands based on Yisrael Ta Shma, *Minhagim V'Hagim*; Daniel Sperber, *Minhagei Yisrael* 3:77, OH 263:1.

Shalom Aleichem

Lawrence Kushner, *Honey from the Rock,* p. 69-70 and "Self," *The Book of Words: Talking Spiritual Life, Living Spiritual Talk* (Jewish Lights); Mordecai Kaplan, *The Meaning of God,* 1937, p. 59-60; "Three Days of Rest" adapted from *The Seventh Day,* UJS/ Limmud Shabbat Book (p. 57); "Making Peace with My Creator" adapted from a Hassidic story cited by S. Y. Yevin and reworked by S. Y. Agnon; card of girl dressed an angel from Hayim Stayer Collection (#28592) courtesy of Beit Hatefutsot.

Birkat Banim

Sabine Y. Meyer, cited in *Temple Emanuel Siddur,* 2003; Marcia Falk from "Blessing of the Children," *The Book of Blessings: New Jewish Prayers for Daily Life, the Sabbath, and the New Moon Festival* by Marcia Falk, p. 450. Harper, 1996, Beacon Press, 1999) © 1996 by Marcia Lee Falk, by permission of the author. www.marciafalk.com. Sydney Greenberg, "A Family Prayer: To Love and To Care" by Sydney Greenberg, *Likrat Shabbat,* p. 7 compiled and translated by Rabbi Sidney Greenberg and edited by Rabbi Jonathan D. Levine, 1981, Prayer Book Press of Media Judaica, Inc; Parent-Child story of Canadian educator was told in a personal communication by Shira Ackerman-Simchovitch about "Epi," Seymour Epstein.

Eishet Hayil

Modern Day Women of Valor composed with the generous aid of the Jewish Women's Archive at www.jwa.org and permission for Emma Goldman, photograph by T. Kajiwara, from The Library of Congress — Prints and Photographs Division; Anna Sokolow, photograph courtesy of Anna Sokolow's Players' Project; Gertrude Weil, photograph courtesy of the North Carolina Division of Archives and History; Bella Abzug, photograph © by Dorothy Marder; Ray Frank, from the American Jewish Historical Society; Gertrude Elion, photograph courtesy of the Estate of Gertrude B. Elion; Bobbie Rosenfeld, image courtesy of Canada's Sports Hall of Fame; Henrietta Szold,photograph courtesy of Hadassah Archives, from Hadassah, the Women's Zionist Organization of America with the aid of Susan Woodland, Hadassah Archives; Justine Wise Polier, courtesy of the Schlesinger Library, Radcliffe Institute, Harvard University; Hannah Senesh courtesy of the Hannah Senesh Legacy Foundation and the family; Golda Meir, photograph by Dr. Theodore Cohen, Beit Hatefutsot, Photo Archive, Tel Aviv.

Israeli stamps: Mothers of Israel in the Holiday series of 1977 by A. Kalderon and M. Prague approved by generous permission of the Israeli Philatelic Authority.

Midrash on *Eishet Hayil* identifying verses with great Biblical women was prepared by Moshe Silberschein based on midrashic passages or fragments on *Eishet Hayil* found in *Yalkut Shimoni, Midrash Tehillim, Beit Midrashot bet, Midrash Hagadol, Yalkut Machiri. Midrash Tadshei* also lists nine "pious women, converts to Judaism from all the nations of the world, the most worthy of women" including Hagar, Osnat, Shifra and Pua, giving us a sum total of 32 noble women found in the Bible. Among the new names added to the honor rolls of the 22 already found in Eishet Hayil are: Devorah, Avigail, Hulda, Yehoshava and the five daughters of Tselofchad.

Some traditional Jews abbreviate the Song of Songs to four verses whose first letters spell the name of "Yaacov" who was the first Biblical character to fall in love at first sight as well as to kiss his intended even before being introduced.

Kiddush

Hassidic source based on *Degel Mahaneh Efraim*, p. 235; Guidelines: holding cup on one's open hand derives from *Zohar* (Introduction 1a), Magen Avraham 183:6.

Kiddush Choreography: (Daniel Sperber, *Minhagei Yisrael*, Volume on Shabbat, Chapter 5 on "Numerology" pp. 157ff): (1) *Talmud Pesachim 101a; Shulchan Aruch* O.H. 273:1, *Rema* and *Mishna Berura* cite Kolbo and Levush; Gaon of Vilna; (2) Rabbi Moshe Isserles, OH 271:10; Rabbi Shneor Lyadi, *Shulchan Aruch Harav* 271:19; (3) *Talmud Shabbat 119b*; (4) Rabbi Yeshayahu Horowitz, *Shnei Luchot Habrit; Zohar* 2:207b; *Tikkunei HaZohar* 24e9a.

L'Chaim — To Life! *Midrash Tanhuma, Pikudei;* Elliot Ginsburg, *Sabbath in the Classical Kabbalah* p. 135, based on *Zohar Hadash, Tikkunim 106c; Proverbs 31:6; Talmud Eruvin 65a: Midrash Tanhuma Pikudei; Shibolei HaLeket* and *Netiv Bina*, Rabbi Jakobson.

Swedish Kiddush cup commissioned by Simon Brick in memory of his wife and reprinted by permission of the photographer and the Swedish Jewish community from its delightful cookbook, *Judisk Mat I Svenskt Kok* (2002).

Laura Geller, a personal communication, rabbi of Temple Emmanuel of Beverly Hills; Erich Fromm, the *Forgotten Language*, 1979, p. 188; Rabbi J.B. Soloveitchik, *Halachic Man*, 1944, based on *Talmud Shabbat 119* (translation adapted from Lawrence Kaplan); Rav Abraham Isaac Kook, *Orot HaKodesh* 2:517 from *The Essential Kabbalah*, Daniel Matt, p. 99; *A* Kavanna/*Meditation on a Shattered World* by Michael Strassfeld, *A Book of Life*, p. 503.

Hallah

Marcel Proust's memory begins with smell. Similarly, the scholar H.L. Ginsberg suggests the Biblical term for a remembrance — *Zecher* — is similar to the word scent or fragrance *(Hosea 14: 8).*

Introduction: Wendy Mogel, *The Blessing of a Skinned Knee*, p. 181-2, 159, 162, 173; Claudia Rodin, *The Book of Jewish Food*, quoted in the inventive *The Book of Jewish Sacred Practices* edited by Vanessa Ochs and Irwin Kula, p. 23.

"Ritual Handwashing?" *Aruch haShulchan O.H. 148; 162.* (The altar is comparable to the altar based on *Aruch HaShulchan O.H. 158-159; 161-162; 167);* "The Heavenly and the Earthly" by Abraham Joshua Heschel, *Between God and Man*, p. 147; "Opening Channels" by Lawrence Kushner quoted in Dov Peretz Elkins, *Moments of Transcendence: Rosh Hashanah*, p. 134; Lawrence Hoffman, *Israel — A Spiritual Travel Guide* (Jewish Lights); Shira Milgrom's *Kol Ami Siddur* (Westchester).

"Feeding the Cats" from a speech on Dec. 28, 1971 in Yiddish quoted in *The Rav: The World of Rabbi J. B. Soloveitchik, Vol. One*, edited by Aaron Rakeffet-Rothkoff (Ktav, 2001) p. 244.

Marc-Alain Ouaknin adapted from *De Tien Geboden*, p. 209; Marc-Alain Ouaknin from his commentary on the haggadah translated by Jeffrey Green; Twin Loaves from Martin Buber, *Tales of the Hasidim* about Rabbi Naftali of Roptchitz; Afghanistani Jewish folktale adapted from collection by Dov Noy, *Folktales of Israel;* "Eve's Braids" by Moshe Silberschein weaves together *Talmud Eruvin 18a* and *Genesis Rabbah (Genesis 2:22);* The "Innovative Baker" adapted from Seder Elijah Zuta B; "Earth Prayers" by Diann Neu cited in Temple Emmauel Siddur (2003).

Zemirot

Background based on *Z'mirot: An Overview* by Neal Levin, JTSA; Rabbi Abraham Isaac Kook's "Songs of the Soul, of the Nation, of Humanity, of the Cosmos" (*Orot HaKodesh* 2:444-445 translated by Daniel Matt and adapted by Rachel Cowan in *Beginning Anew*, page 278); Elie Wiesel, *All the Rivers Run to the Sea*, Schocken, NY 1995, Alfred A. Knopf, Inc, p. 41-43; "Advice from Summer Camp" concludes by quoting *Midrash Song of Songs* (see *Talmud Megillah 12b*); Alexander Herzen. the 19th century Russian thinker (quoted in Isaiah Berlin's biography); Abraham Joshua Heschel, *God in Search of Man: A Philosophy of Judaism*, p. 249; card of singing Bundist, Hasid and Zionist from Jewish National Library (#34869), photo courtesy of Beit Hatefutsot.

Birkat HaMazon

Emmanuel Levinas, adapted from *The Nine Talmudic Readings*; Shurak Tali, unknown source; Noam Nadav by generous permission of the Shalom Hartman Institute from *Yahid vHevra*, 2003.

Guidelines from Tradition: *Zohar II* 63b; Daniel Sperber, Minhagei Yisrael 3:184, *Shulchan Aruch* O.H. 180;1-2.

Reflections: Lawrence Hoffman, *The Way into Jewish Prayer*, p. 140, Jewish Lights Publishing, 2000.

Kavanot: Making A Pledge: Elijah deVidas, *Reshit Hochma: Sh'ar HaKedusha* 15:64, quoted in Michael Strassfeld, *The Book of Life* (Schocken) p. 76.

Oneg Shabbat

Eliezer Schweid, *The Jewish Experience of Time* (Jason Aronson, 2000), p. 54; Alan S. Green, cited in *A Shabbat Reader* by Dov Peretz Elkins, p. 65, from *Sex, God and the Sabbath.*

Kiddush Rabbah

Elie Wiesel, *All Rivers Run to the Sea*, Schocken.

Havdalah

Eliyahu in Ladino from Isaac Levy, *Liturgia Judeo Espanola*, Vol I #148. "The generation that must live between the fires" by Rabbi Arthur Waskow (Copyright © 1995 by Arthur Waskow). *Miriam HaNeviah* conceived by Rabbi Leila Gal Berner and Rabbi Arthur Waskow; Hebrew text by Rabbi Leila Berner. Copyright © 1989 by Leila Berner. Reprinted by permission of the authors. Other works of Rabbi Waskow can be seen on the Shalom Center website at www.shalomcenter.org and in his book *Godswrestling – Round 2* (Jewish Lights, 1996). Sarah Lightman, *The Seventh Day*, UJS/Limmud Shabbat Book); HaMavdil's alternative text is *ushlomeinu* — our peace instead of our funds; Rav Kook, from his commentary on the Siddur *Olat Har'eeyah* p. 211; "Elijah Prophesies a Mess" is adapted from the Kurdish Muhtar Ezra as retold by Avraham Barzani and printed in *Omer*, The Hebrew Newspaper for New Immigrants.